ink & wash florals

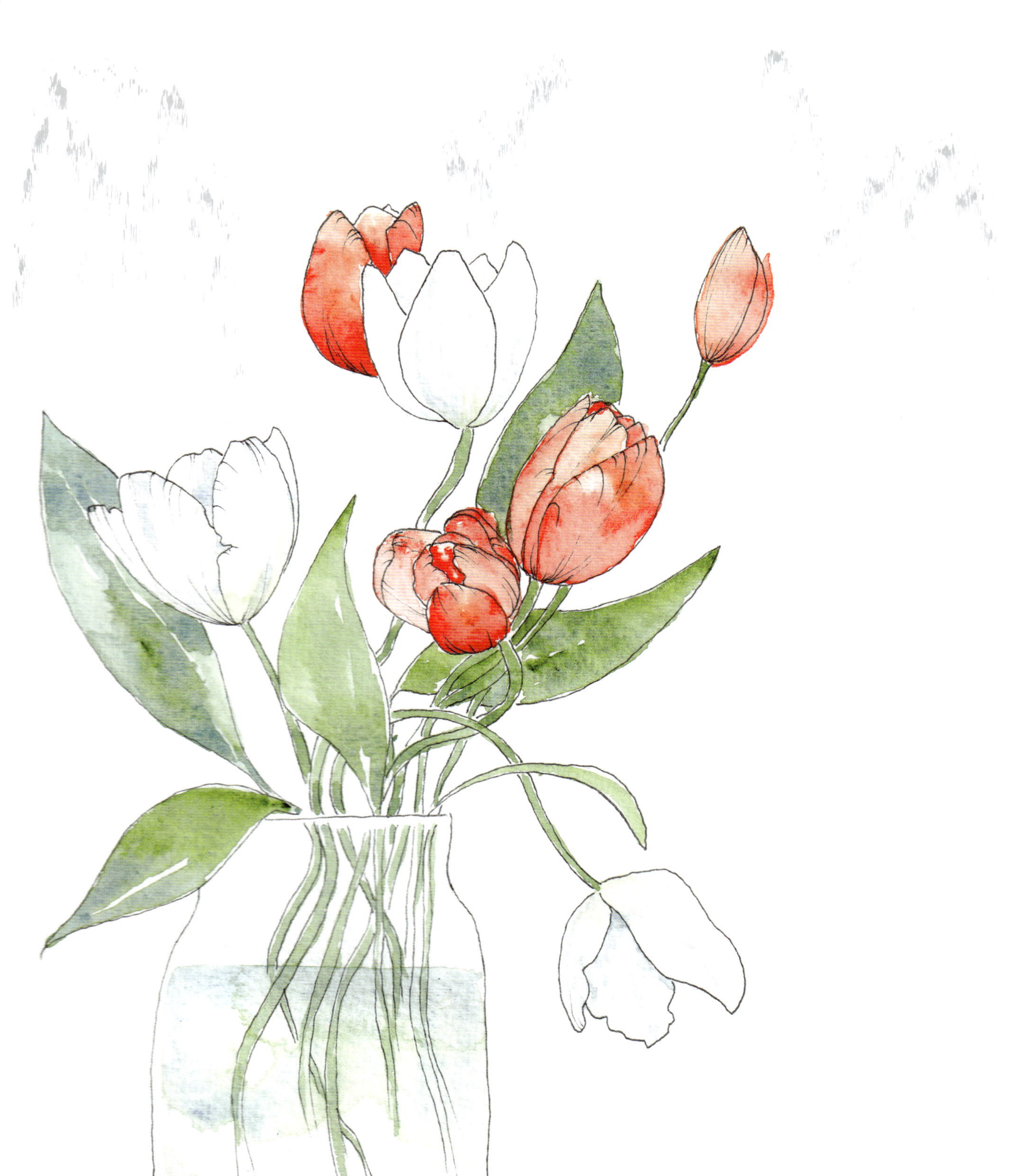

ink & wash florals

stunning botanical projects in watercolor & ink

camilla damsbo brix
artist, teacher & creator of camilla damsbo art

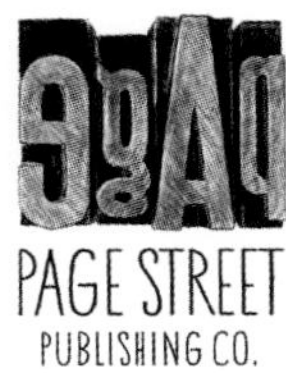

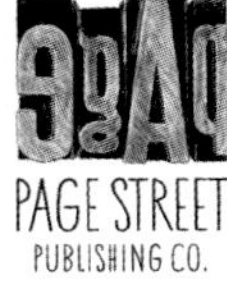

First published in 2022 by
Page Street Publishing Co.
27 Congress Street, Suite 1511
Salem, MA 01970
www.pagestreetpublishing.com

Distributed by Macmillan, sales in Canada by The Canadian Manda Group.

28 27 26 25 6 7 8

ISBN-13: 978-1-64567-699-7
ISBN-10: 1-64567-699-4

Library of Congress Control Number: 2022935166
Cover and book design by Emma Hardy for Page Street Publishing Co.
Photography by Camilla Damsbo Brix. Photo on page 139 by Line Kongsted.

Printed and bound in the United States of America

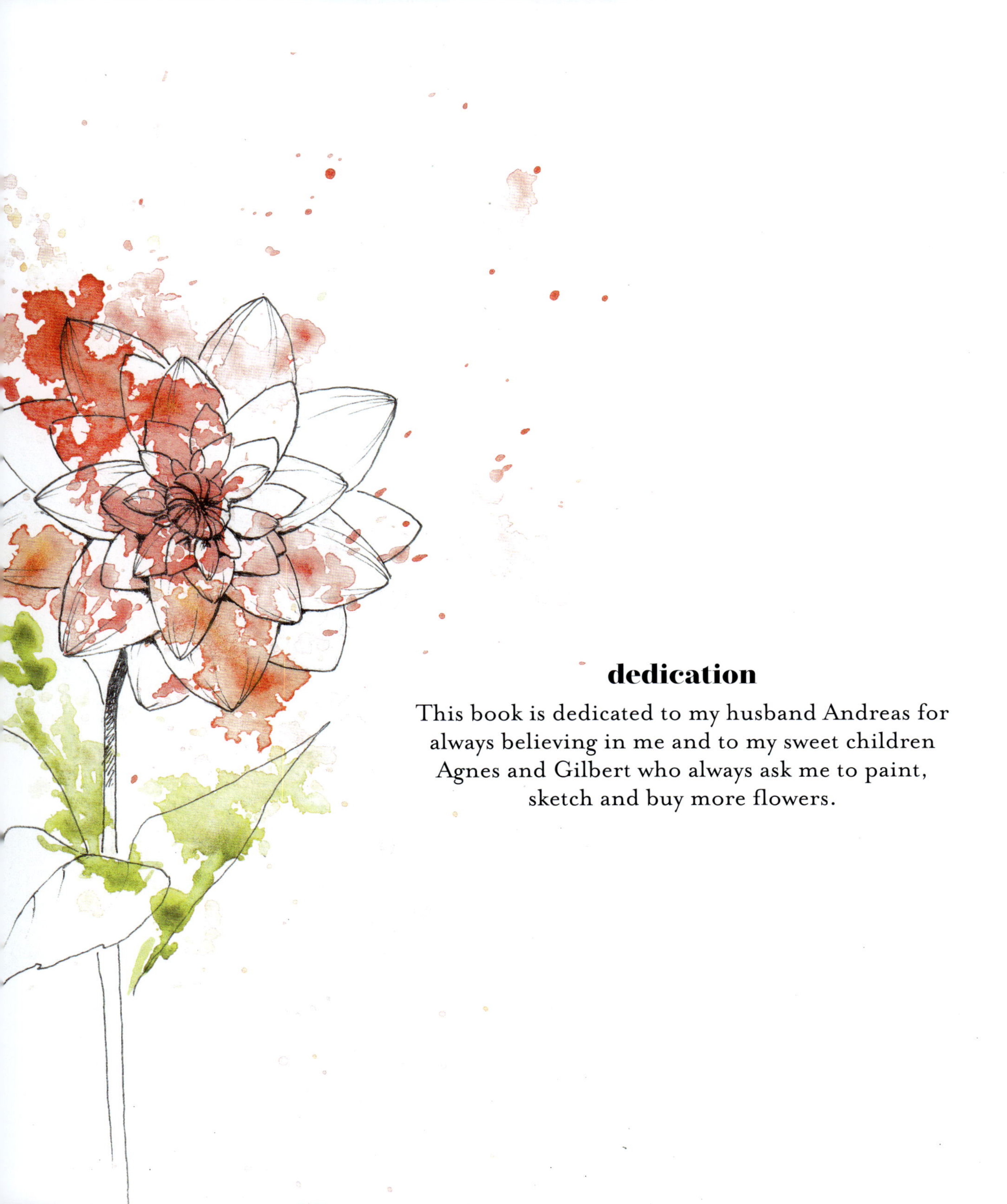

dedication

This book is dedicated to my husband Andreas for always believing in me and to my sweet children Agnes and Gilbert who always ask me to paint, sketch and buy more flowers.

contents

Welcome! 8

part I:
Fundamentals of Watercolor and Ink 11

Supplies 12
A Bit About Choosing Colors 15
Plan For Success 16
Basic Inking Techniques 18
Basic Watercolor Techniques 20
How to Sketch Flowers 22

part II:
Seventeen Flowers in Watercolor and Ink 27

Daisy | The Flower of Purity 29
Plumeria | The Flower of Spring and New Beginnings 33
Iris | The Flower of Hope and Wisdom 37
Gerbera | The Flower of Cheerfulness 40
Cosmo | The Flower of Harmony 45
Tulip | The Flower of Perfect and Deep Love 49
Anemone | The Wind's Daughter 55
Magnolia | The Flower of Nobility and a Love for Nature 61
Sunflower | The Flower of Lasting Happiness 65
Snowdrop | The Flower of Hope, Innocence and Purity 70
Dahlia | The Flower of . . . Well, Almost Everything 75
Poppy | The Flower of Remembrance 78
Lilac | The Flower of Renewal 83
Rose | The Flower of Love, Energy and Admiration 86
Hydrangea | The Flower of Gratitude and Beauty 91
Peony | The Flower of Romance and Luck 95
Hibiscus | The Flower of Romantic Love and the Perfect Woman 99

part III:
Drawing a Harmonious Composition 105

Exercises for Experimenting and Honing Your Personal Style 106
Placement of the Flowers 106
Red and White Tulips in a Glass Vase 109
A Dancing Bouquet of Cosmos and Daisies 114
A Bouquet of Peonies and Lilacs 119
A Field of Poppies 124
A Branch of Spring Magnolias 129

part IV:

Where to Go from Here 133

Share Your Work 134

Make Art a Habit 134

Here Are Five Tips for Facilitating Your Art Habit 136

Here Are Three Tips for Finding Inspiration 136

Don't Be a Copycat 136

Acknowledgments 137

Meet Camilla 139

Index 141

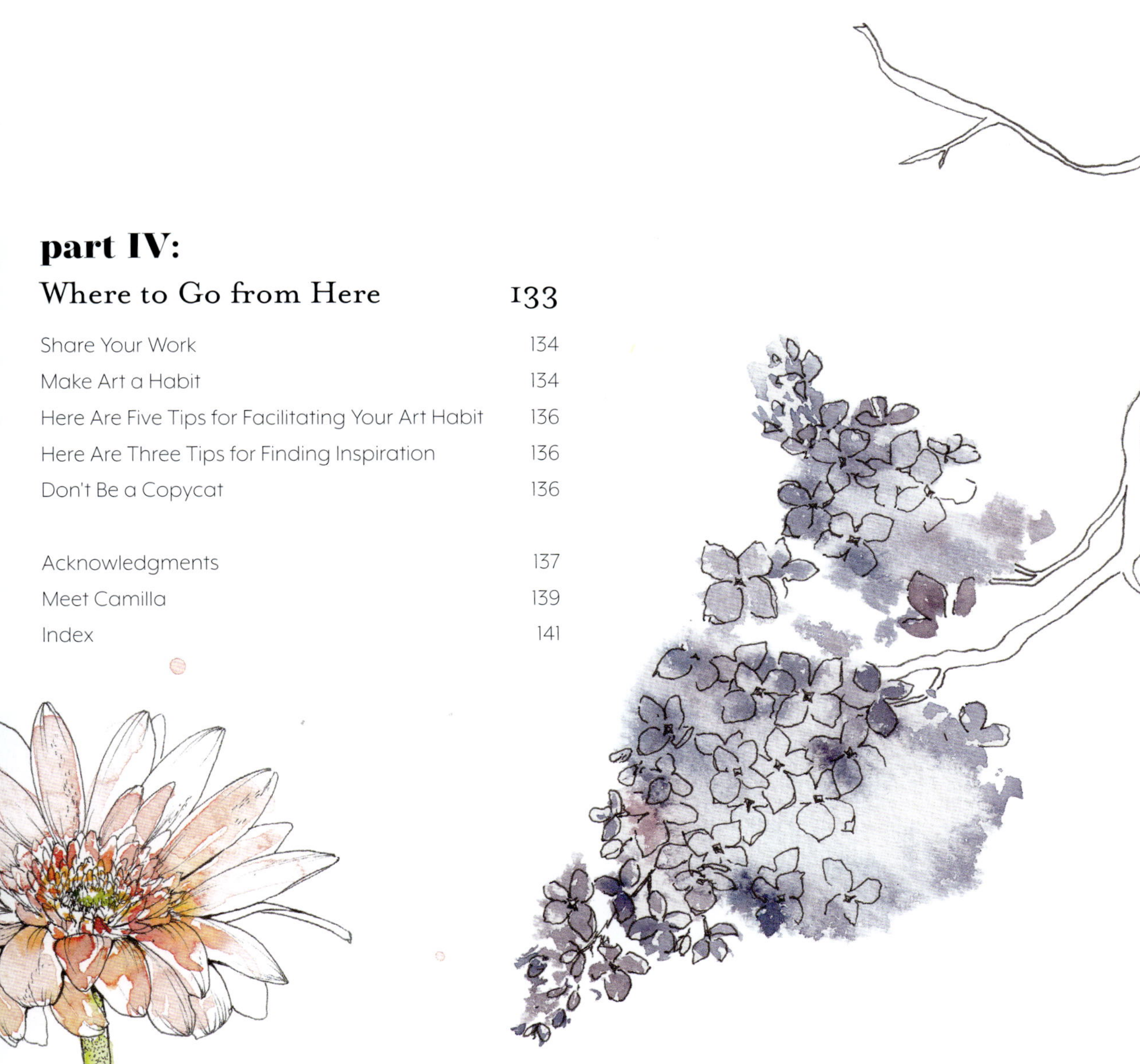

welcome!

Hi! I am super excited to welcome you to this book, because working through these projects will make a huge impact on your life. I know I am setting your expectations high, but hear me out.

Ink and wash (also known as line and wash) as a technique is the perfect way to do quick sketches. The combination of the soft watercolor against the hard lines of the fineliner creates the most beautiful contrast, so you are really in for a treat. You can sketch houses, your lamp or, like in this book, all the flowers around you. I personally love flowers and feel a deep connection with nature while sketching. A sketch is often quick and can be done in less than twenty minutes! Yes, I know it's crazy. You can actually fit this creative time into a busy lifestyle with jobs, schools, laundry, dinner and everything else. By creating regularly, you will change your life—yes, that is a promise. You will get better at focusing and feel more relaxed and present as you grow your skill. You will be so proud of the beauty you create.

Personally, I turned to this medium a few years back when I was pregnant and really tired all the time. I was going crazy with lack of energy and I only had short periods of time before having to nap again. This was a time when sketches in watercolor and ink came in super handy. I loved it. I could do an entire sketch that I loved before having to rest again, and I continued doing this after my baby girl was born. These sketches were the perfect break in between feeding, napping and sleepless nights. We all have reasons for lacking time and energy, but I promise you that this style will fit into your life perfectly.

That sounds good, right? Well, let me give you a quick overview of the book so you know what you've gotten yourself into. First, I'll talk a bit about supplies—don't worry, there are not too many of them and you don't need them all. Afterward, I'll guide you through basic techniques for using a fineliner and then, watercolor. After all, we are actually mixing two different techniques in this book: drawing with fineliners and painting in watercolor. Since we are sketching flowers, it can be nice to have a few drawing basics down as well, so on pages 22 to 25, I'll go over floral observation, basic floral shapes and shading. Those should be all the techniques we need, and then it will be time for sketching.

First, I'll show you how to sketch seventeen different flowers ranging from simple daisies to more complex peonies. This chapter is so much fun that you might just want to start there and refer back to the technique pages when you need them (it's totally cool with me). After you've sketched a lot of nice flowers, it'll be time to combine them in balanced and pretty compositions. So in that section, I'll once more give you a bit of technical instruction, but this time it will be all about creating a harmonious floral piece. Afterward, you get to practice what you learned in five different floral compositions ranging from poppies in a field to pretty posies.

To finish off strong, I'll give you tips on sharing your art and turning it into the best habit ever—but enough chatting. Let's get started!

Camilla Damsbo Brix

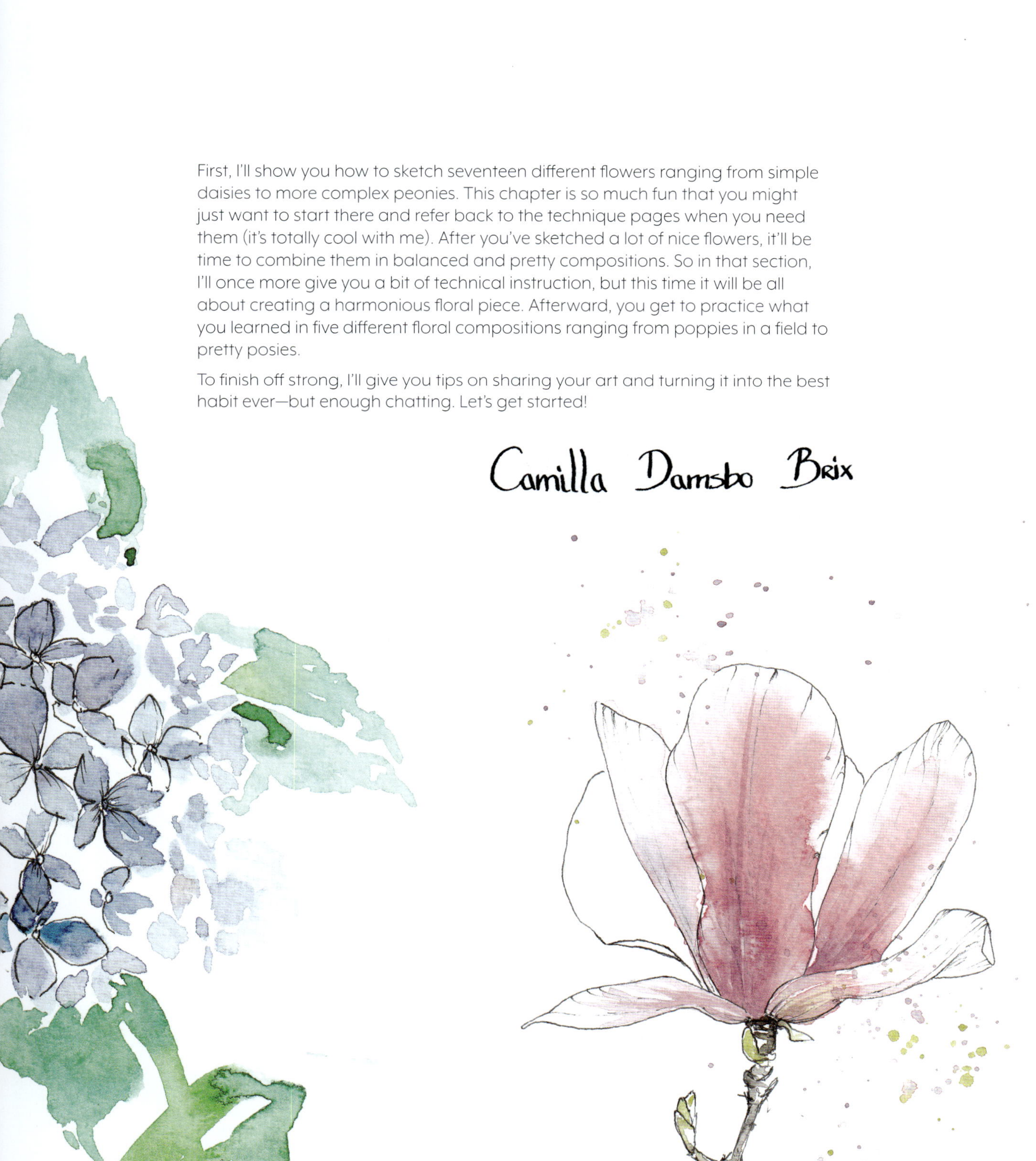

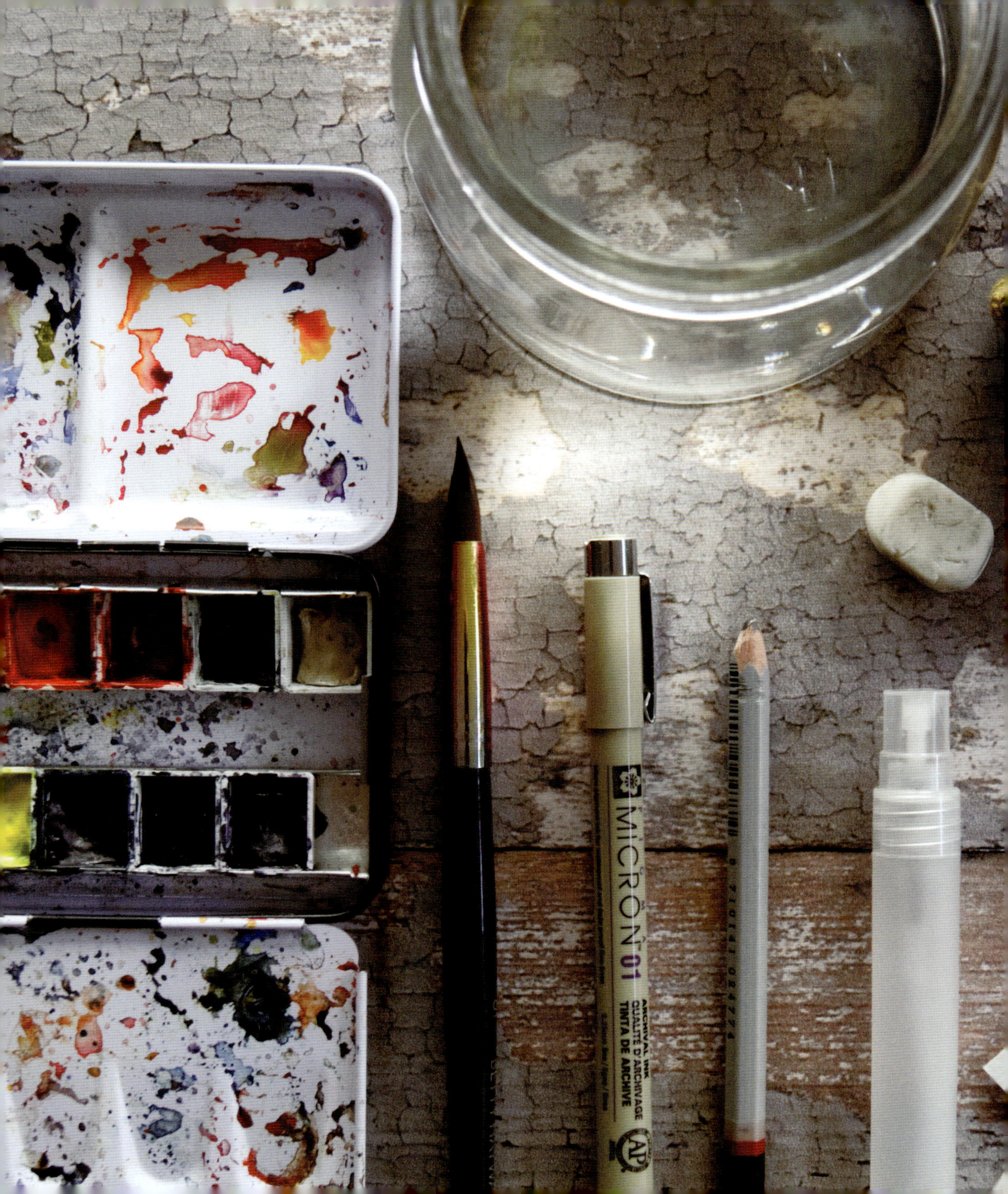
MICRON 01
ARCHIVAL INK
QUALITÉ D'ARCHIVAGE
TINTA DE ARCHIVO

part I: fundamentals of watercolor and ink

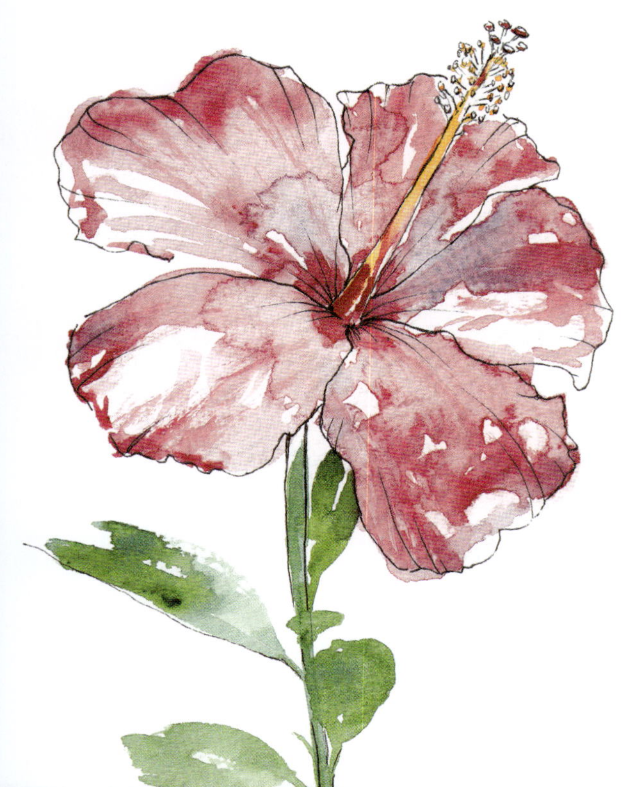

As mentioned in the introduction, you are going to learn two techniques in this book: how to draw in fineliners and how to use a pop of watercolor to make your sketches glow with vibrancy. In this part of the book, you can dive into all the supplies and techniques you need to have a strong base, in order to start sketching beautiful flowers.

supplies

You will need a few basic supplies for the projects in this book, though I tried to keep them to a minimum. It's also important to note that you don't need the exact supplies I use. If you have another type of paper or another color, that is totally cool—go with that and then write the supplies you dream of getting on your wish-list.

fineliners

A fineliner is a type of pen with a tip made of fine fibers or plastic that is filled with pigment-based ink. This means that the ink sits on the surface without bleeding through the paper when you sketch and is usually waterproof. That way, it's the perfect match to watercolor. Fineliners are great for defining shapes, strokes and shadows. When used strategically, they can help lead the viewer's eye right to where you want them to look.

In this book, we'll use black fineliners from Micron and Staedtler in sizes 005, 01 and 02. You might wonder why I use two different brands, and that is frankly because the brand does not matter that much. What matters is that it's waterproof and lightfast. That way, you can use it with your watercolors without too many problems, and it won't fade in the sun. You can usually check if your fineliner meets those requirements by checking the text on the side of the pen.

When deciding which sizes to get, you want to take a good look at your paper. It kind of goes without saying that small paper like an A6 equals thin fineliners and larger paper like A4 calls for bigger pens. I use smaller pens like 005, 01 and 02 in the book, but the illustrations are also pretty small, drawn on a size A5 paper. You want to make sure to have a variety of pen sizes so you can switch between them for thin details and thicker lines.

brushes

One of the very basic materials, but also one of the most important ones, is the brush. The brush is an extension of your arm, and it's the only thing standing between you and your art. Therefore, you really have to bond and become best friends with your brush. In this book, we use round synthetic brushes in sizes 4, 6, 7, 8 and 9.

Choosing a brand is like choosing a religion, like developing loyalty for PCs or MacBooks. Some like da Vinci brushes and some like Black Velvet®. In this book, I use brushes from Betty Hayways and Panart, but you can use what you already have in your stash. If you don't have a stash, then you can go to a local art store and they will often have a cheap alternative for you to start with.

Of course, like with our pens, size also matters for brushes, and I wish I could tell you which exact numbers to go for. However, it's not as easy as that, because sizes vary from brand to brand, and a size 6 can be very small or very large, depending on what brand made the brush. It's a jungle, really. You want to have a brush for finer details—either a thin brush or a bigger brush with a fine tip—and a medium-sized brush for the majority of the painting. If you want to go big, have a brush that is even larger close by.

There are two special categories in brushes: synthetic and natural hair. Synthetic brushes are often the cheapest. They can hold a fairly small amount of water and paint and they often form a nice tip, which makes them great for details. On the other hand, they have to be loaded often to keep them painting. Natural hair brushes hold a lot of water and color, so they are great for big surfaces. But since we rarely paint big surfaces in this book, I would recommend going with synthetic brushes.

And here's a small (but important) tip for you: Never ever keep your brush in the water jar unless it's to rinse it or get water. This will ruin the fibers on the brush and make it all crooked and weird. If you accidentally put your brush down in the jar to chase your cat off the table, hurry up and get it out of the water! And now you can slap yourself gently over the fingers. Your brush is your best friend and it should be treated like that. Now you can kiss and make up.

paint

Paint is such an important part of this book, so you want to make sure to have some good ones close by. Here are a few tips for you: In this book, I used paints from Daniel Smith, but remember, you don't need to have the same supplies as the teacher. Watercolor paint ranges from the super cheap paint that is filled with chalk to professional quality that is filled with pigment. They range from rather dull and flat colors to vibrant and bright ones. Of course, if you want to get the best, I recommend going with professional paints from brands like Daniel Smith or Winsor & Newton Professional, but you don't need to have them. As long as you don't go for the cheapest paint, you should be fine. If you are just looking to get started, I recommend Van Gogh paint or Winsor & Newton's Cotman series. A half pan from the Winsor & Newton Professional series costs about $11 and the same amount of paints from the Cotman series costs about $5.

Whether you go with pans or tubes depends on how you paint. The tubes are liquid and very pigmented, and the pans are dry paint. The dry paint can be a lot easier to control in a smaller sketch like the ones in this book because you get to decide how much water you add. With the tubes, they are already wet and you need to add even more water to get them to flow. I actually use tube paints for the projects in the book, but I squeezed them into pans and let them dry, and you can easily do that too.

I gathered here a list of the colors used in the book. I know you probably don't have all of them, so I made a list of alternatives as well. They are not exact colors, but close enough that you will get similar results.

Color I Used	Alternative Color
Pyrrol Scarlet (warm red)	Vermilion or Perylene Scarlet
New Gamboge (warm yellow shade)	Cadmium Yellow Deep, Sunflower Yellow or other warm yellows
Hansa Yellow Light (cool yellow)	Lemon Yellow or Winsor Yellow
Quinacridone Rose (cool red)	Permanent Rose, Carmine or Rose Madder
Quinacridone Sienna (warm earthy orange)	Burnt Sienna or Transparent Red Oxide
Quinacridone Coral (can be used as both a warm and cool red)	Mix this by using a rose pink and warm yellow
Sap Green (warm earthy green)	Olive Green, or mix this by using a bright Hooker's Green with a bit of red
Green Gold (cool green)	Mix this by using a warm green and a bit of cool yellow
Phthalo Blue (cool blue)	Prussian Blue, Cyan Blue or Cerulean Blue
French Ultramarine (warm granulating blue)	Ultramarine Blue or Cobalt Blue
Payne's Gray (gray with a blue tone)	Mix this by using Ultramarine Blue and Burnt Sienna or by using Lamp Black with a bit of blue
Van Dyke Brown (cool brown)	Mix this by using brown and a bit of Lamp Black
Burnt Umber (warm brown)	Sepia or Burnt Sienna

paper

At a minimum, you need thick paper. So, the first step is to put down that copy paper and walk slowly away from it—now turn your back and run. Copy paper will make you hate watercolor in a matter of seconds after it gets wet, and that's just not worth it. I usually use 300gsm (140lb) paper, but you can go all the way down to 200gsm (93lb). Any weight below that will be difficult to use with watercolor paints. What brand and weight you use is totally up to you. It is a bit of a jungle out there, so I'll just go through the basics here below.

In this book, I use Canson Montval, 300gsm (140lb) cold-press watercolor paper. Just like with the other supplies, there are a ton of brands to choose from. I love the different papers from Canson, but there is a lot to try before finding the one you love. You can go with Hahnemühle or even Arches if you want the best of the best. When you're looking for a brand you like, all you can do is try out a lot of different papers. Everybody is different, and by trying different brands you'll get an idea of the touch and feel of the papers. You might even be able to get samples at your local store to try out.

If you don't use too much water, you can also use a sketchbook with thicker paper—you'll just have to steer clear from the more involved wet-on-wet backgrounds and things like that. I prefer sketchbooks with watercolor paper weighing more than 200gsm (93lb), but if you only work wet-on-dry, you can go lower than that.

If you are going for regular watercolor paper, you will run into the terms "cold press," "hot press" and "rough." In short, cold-press paper is the classic watercolor paper and has a nice texture to it. Rough paper has even more texture, and hot-press paper is super smooth with no texture at all.

I mostly use cold-press paper because I love the feel of the texture, but it can be rather rough on fineliner pens. So, if you want your fineliners to last longer, go for the smooth hot-press paper. This is also the reason I never choose rough paper when working with fineliners.

pencil and eraser

The pencil and eraser are two basic supplies that are super important to take the fear out of fineliner sketches. Go for a pencil that is a bit soft, but not too soft—throughout the book I use a 2B pencil—and a nice, soft eraser that is good for removing pencil lines without ruining paper. The pencil brands I use are Bruynzeel and Derwent, but you can use any pencil, really.

other things you'll love to have close by

Cloth: It's essential to have something to dab your brush into. The benefit of using a cloth is that you don't have to throw it out after every session like you would with paper towels. You can just wash it when you feel it needs it. But if you don't have that, you can just use kitchen towels or something similar.

Water: Have a jar of water at your work station, and if you want to go pro, use two jars—one for cleaning your brush and one for clean water that you only use on the painting. In other words, you'll clean your brush in the dirty water jar after you painted with it, then dip it into the clean water jar before loading your brush with a new color. This ensures that the paint colors do not get all mixed up. Of course, make sure to change the water if it gets too dirty.

Palette: I like to have a ceramic palette close by. It's the perfect thing for mixing paints. Your palette can be as simple, like a white ceramic plate, or as elaborate as you like. Just head to your local store or preferred online retailer to look for a ceramic palette. Plastic palettes can be used as well, but the paint will gather in small droplets and be harder to mix.

Brush Holder: A place for you to place your brushes can be handy. It can be a fancy one that looks like a cute cat or simply a piece of wood—you decide.

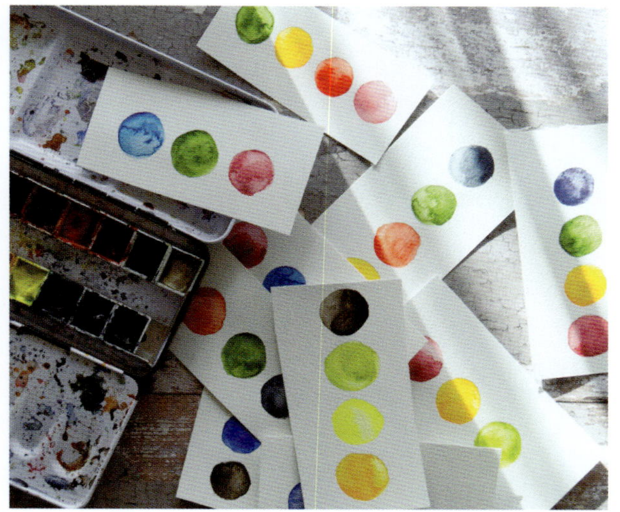

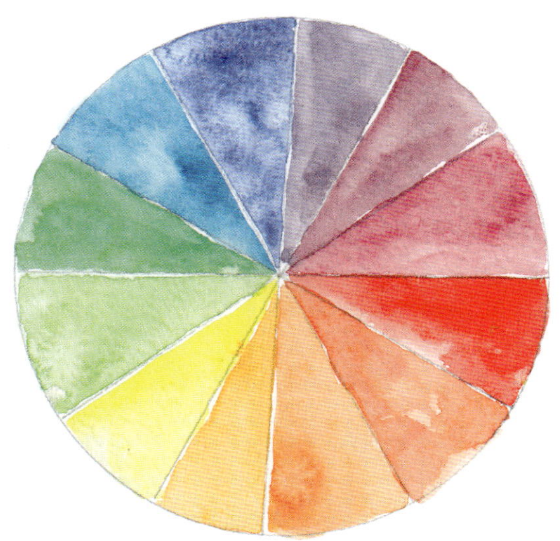

a bit about choosing colors

Before we dive into the projects, I want to give you a bit of a rundown on choosing colors. This is going to be super helpful for you throughout the book and especially after, when you are starting on your own compositions. Choosing colors is actually a very scary process to many. Throughout the book, I'll be indicating how to use your colors, which colors to choose and if they should be pure or mixed together. But just for the fun of it, here is a quick overview.

the practical guide to mixing

First of all, why does one mix colors? You can get a lot of colors premixed, but you can never get as many shades as you can with mixing. Also, by using a few colors and mixing them as you need, you will get a much more harmonious painting. That's because the colors are present in the other colors as well. So for example, the lilac on page 83 that is mixed from rose and blue also has a ton of shades ranging from rose to blue, but also a lot of purples and violets mixed from different amounts of the same rose and blue. This will really tie it together beautifully.

To mix lilac, first take your palette and find a clean well (a well that has no paint in it). It has to be clean or you will get your colors mixed with whatever was on the palette last. Then, clean your brush and load it with blue and put it into the palette. Then clean and load your brush with rose and place it next to the first color in the palette. Mix them evenly by stirring the two colors together completely. Then, if you want it to be bluer, add more blue, and if you want it to be more rose, add more rose. Remember to clean your brush in between loading each color. You can also mix them unevenly for a range of colors. Do this by mixing the two colors a bit in the middle and leaving some areas more in one color and other areas more in the other color. That way, you'll have different color variations ready when you paint with them.

A Serene Color Scheme

If you want a super calm color scheme, keeping your painting clean and fresh, use the colors next to each other in the color wheel, like blues going into the greens or maybe reds going into oranges. This kind of color scheme would work really well in lilacs (blues and purples), red roses (reds and oranges) or maybe peonies (reds going into yellows).

A Bit More Drama

If you want a more dramatic color scheme, choose complementary colors, the colors opposite each other in the wheel. For example, use yellow and violet for an iris, or paint red roses with green leaves. Often, you can actually create a lot more interest in a sketch by adding a tiny bit of a complementary color into an already painted petal. An example might be a bit of green in a red poppy petal.

make your colors lighter or darker

In watercolor, we paint just as much with water as paint, and we use the water to make the paint lighter. Using 100 percent water will give a clear view to the white paper, and adding more and more paint will increase the value of the color. When you have 100 percent paint and no water, you have your darkest value. An example from the book is the tulip on page 49. Here, you can see the dark values in the shadows and details and the lighter values in the petals in front.

step out of the mud

If you've painted before, you've probably tried to paint in beautiful bright colors, only to have them suddenly turn into a muddy brown. There are a lot of reasons for that, but here is a quick list of the top three reasons why your painting turned into a brown swamp:

1. You mixed the colors too much on the page. Instead, load your brush with paint and lightly touch the tip of your brush into the water without touching the paint afterward. Then you can let the water spread the color as far as it can.
2. You mixed complementary colors by accident. Next to each other they are stunning, but when they are mixed, they create neutrals.
3. Check your water. Is it turning brown? As I said above, we paint with water as much as paint, so replacing the murky water might be the easiest quick fix.

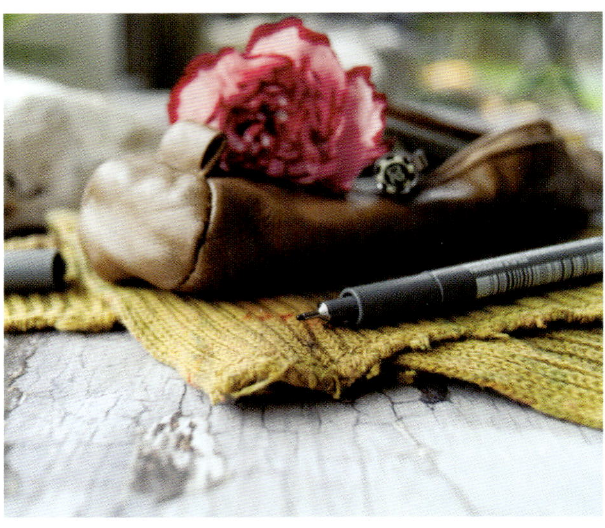

plan for success

What is your sketching strategy? You might not have even given this any thought, and that is totally fine. Maybe you don't even need to. But if you are brand new at mixing watercolor and fineliner, I strongly recommend giving your strategy a few minutes of thought.

There are a couple of reasons that this will make your life easier (and don't we all want that). First of all, fineliners can be kind of scary. They are very much black and can't be erased like a regular pencil. So, when you are sitting there with your white paper, it can be nice to take the edge off with a bit of planning. The second reason is just as good. No flower or composition is the same. There can be a few petals or a lot, subtle colors or super strong ones, one flower or many. You can approach it in so many ways, so it's good to think it through just a tad, and I'll show you how in this short section.

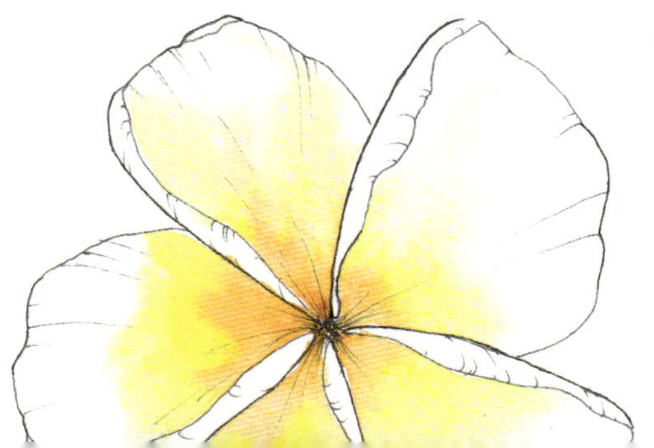

take the fear away

As I just said, fineliners can be a bit scary, but there is a trick that will help you a lot: making quick sketches in pencil first. Take a pencil and a piece of random paper like copy paper, sketchbook paper or even the back of the note your kid brought home from school. Then, just do a few doodles of the flower you have chosen.

Study the flower carefully and sketch it a few times while considering the angles as well as growing states. To go deeper into sketching, check out the "How to Sketch Flowers" section on page 22. When you feel comfortable with the shape, you can go to the watercolor paper, or whatever you want to use, and make your drawing.

Here, you can use your pencil once again, by redoing the sketch on the watercolor paper. If you want to stay on completely safe ground, you can transfer the sketch with a tracing board. A tracing board is a sleek pad that lights up. With it, you can attach your drawing, then put your watercolor paper on top and the light will shine through the drawing so you can see it on the watercolor paper and you can trace the sketch onto it. If you don't have a tracing board, you can tape the sketch to a window and then attach the watercolor paper on top. That way, you'll be able to see the sketch below and transfer it to the watercolor paper. If you can't see the sketch, then just go over it with a thick fineliner and it'll be much easier to see.

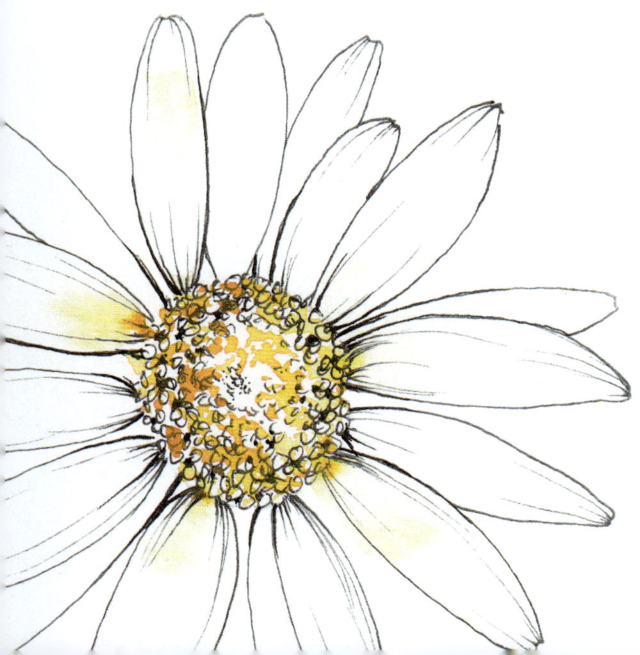

think before you ink

When you make your plan, there are two things to consider: how to start and how you imagine it'll look when you lift the final brushstroke. Here, the question is super simple: Do you grab the watercolor or the fineliner first? Both will give you different results and you want to think about what works best with the flower in front of you. We'll be going into a lot more detail with this in the following chapter, so this is just an overview.

Fineliner First: Let's start with the fineliner. Using fineliner first produces a very controlled look that is true to the reference. Be careful not to overwork your watercolor afterward (the struggle is real) and also make sure that your fineliner is completely dry before adding watercolor. Otherwise, it will bleed, which is just annoying.

Watercolor First: When you start out with watercolor first, you will get a looser look because you don't have a guide to follow. It can be difficult to control the water and paint, but it can give you some amazing results that look fresh and spontaneous. Then, when you doodle the fineliner on top, you will add definition to your painting. Just make sure the paper is completely dry before doodling, or the pen will stop working on the wet surface.

where you want to end

Is it a bit hard to imagine where your sketch is going? Then, you can ask yourself a few questions to help you make decisions beforehand:

1. Do I want one flower or a bigger composition?
2. Which angle do I want to sketch?
3. Which state of growth do I want to show? Is it the bud, the full bloom or perhaps the withered flower? All are beautiful in their own way.

These are just the first thoughts before your first sketch, but if you want more insight into doing balanced compositions, then go to page 106 for more on that.

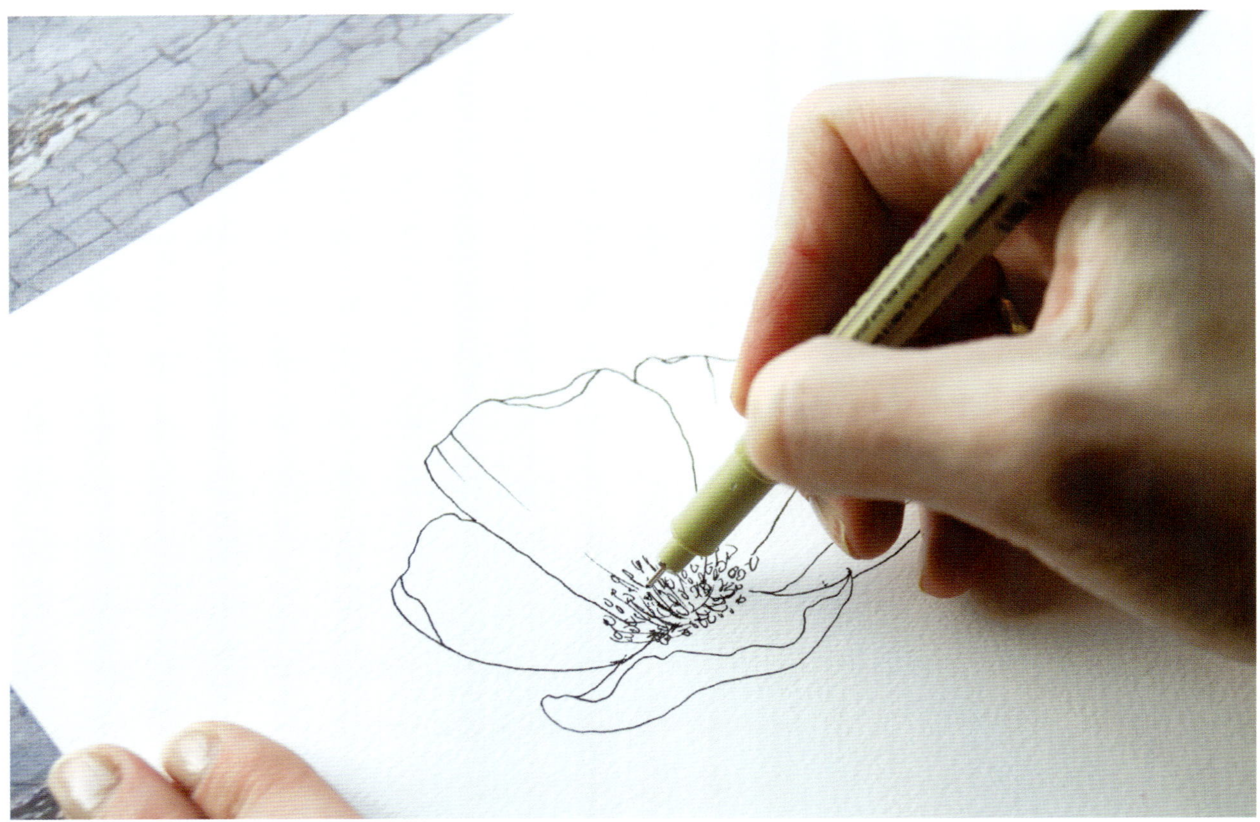

basic inking techniques

Before diving into the sketches, it might be nice to get some of the basic techniques down, such as what size fineliners you want to use, how to create that messy and sketchy look and how to vary the line to create interest and life. Earlier in the chapter, we learned that we have to make a choice about how to start, whether with fineliner or watercolor. In this section, I'll share with you how to start with the fineliner, and then we can talk about the watercolor in the next section.

perfect imperfections

When you want your florals to come to life, you want to let go of one of your biggest enemies when we do our sketches. She is lurking behind your cup of tea, and she is called Perfection. So many of us have a tendency to go for the perfect hairstyle, the perfect interior design or the perfect line for our floral sketches. But I want to push you a little bit to embrace imperfections for a while. Imperfect lines create life, it makes your drawing breathe and it makes it so much more dynamic. Dynamic lines are lines that are broken, have varying thicknesses and don't make the perfect outline. After all, there are no perfect shapes in nature, only dynamic and natural ones. You can create these lines by working fast and holding your tool with a looser grip. As soon as you catch yourself working slowly and creating lines with no life, speed up and loosen your hand.

does size matter?

Apologies for the cheesy headline, but yes, size matters. So which size should you choose? First of all, tools go hand-in-hand. So, if you have a big paper like an A4, go with big fineliners like 04, 05 or even higher, and if you have a small sketchbook, go for the small fineliners like 005, 01 or 02. You'll know which fits your paper. If your lines look too bulky on the small paper, go for a smaller fineliner and if the line is so thin that you can barely see it, go for something bigger.

You want to have a couple of different sizes, because different steps in the sketch call for different-sized fineliners.

- **The Outline:** Here, I often use a medium-sized fineliner like a 01. This way, I can create confident lines that are visible, but not too bold.
- **The Details:** After the outline, comes the details—you know, the curves, small dots and stuff like that. You want to go with a smaller fineliner. In this book, I used a size 005. That way, you get the contrast between the bold lines and the fine details.
- **Shading:** Finally, we have the shading. There are different ways to create shading (I'll tell you more about that later), but one way to do it is to strengthen some of the lines you already created with a thicker fineliner. Here in the book, I use a size 02.

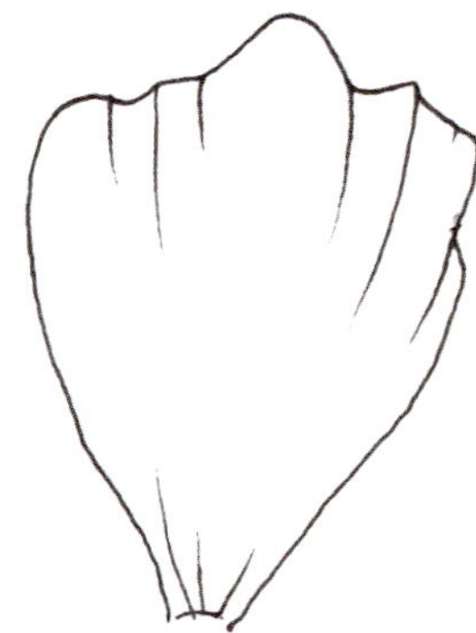

line variation

When using a fineliner, as opposed to a brush or a dip pen, there is not much variation in the line, but you can still use line variation a little bit. If you press the fineliner to the paper, the line will be as bold as it can be and then when you drag it across the paper while lifting it slowly, it will make the line thinner. You can also cheat a bit and draw a couple of times on the same line. Just make sure to not overwork it.

This small trick is super valuable when you want to add your lines. Keeping detail lines thick at the outer edge of the petals and then thinner toward the center will help guide the viewer's eyes toward the focal point, almost like tiny arrows pointing to your center of interest.

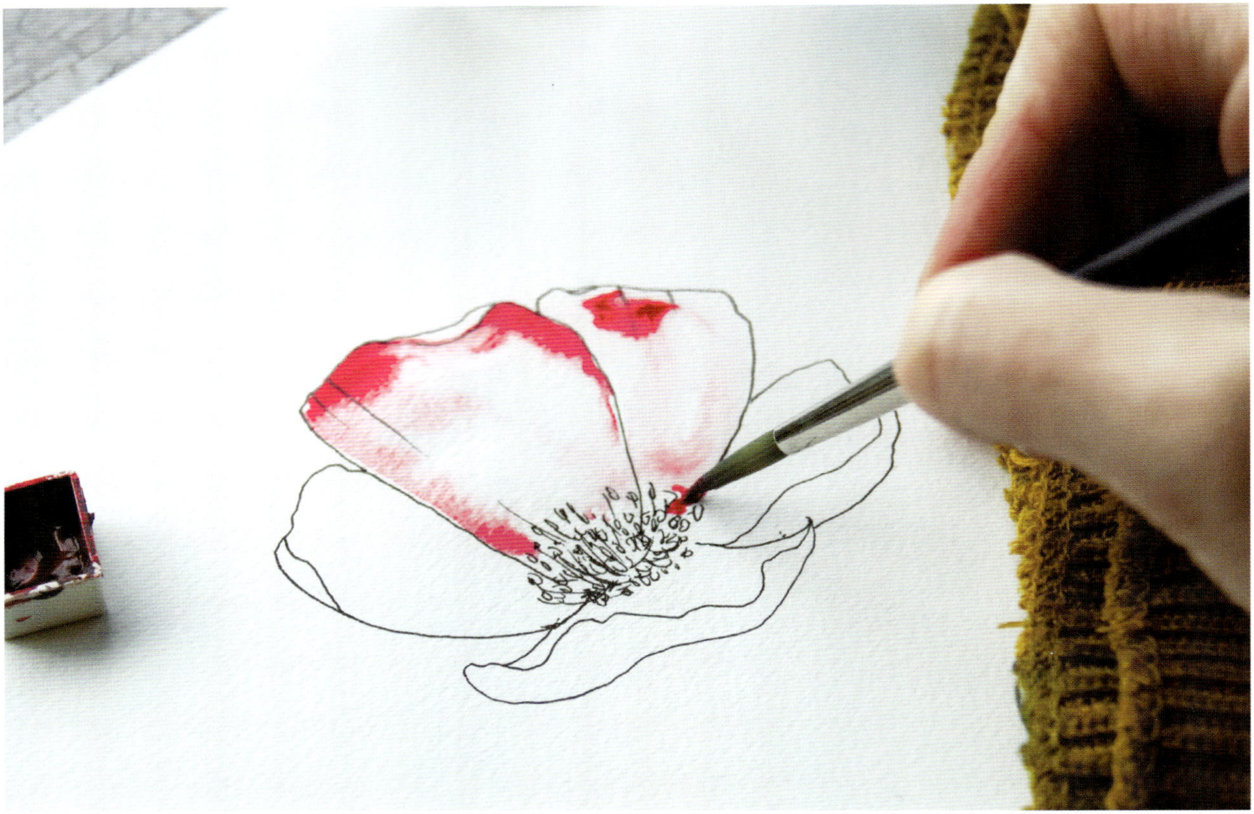

basic watercolor techniques

We have talked a lot about those important ink lines, but adding that perfect pop of color in just the right way is just as vital. I absolutely love this step because this is where we, in a few strokes with the brush, can add a depth of color, vibrancy and life.

As with everything we talked about until now, you can do this in any way you feel like. After all, this is all about enjoying the process and not focusing too much on the exact methods. But I do want to let you in on my own techniques. It's not a secret like the recipe for Coca-Cola®, but it is just as effective in my opinion.

wet-on-dry

Painting wet-on-dry might just be the most common and easiest way to paint. It's almost like drawing with a pencil and we have a lot of control over the watercolor. No paint goes into corners we don't want, and we can even create small intricate details.

How to Do It

This technique is very simple. You paint with wet paint on dry paper. Start by loading your brush with paint, and then just draw with the brush like it was a pencil. Can you feel how you can control the lines and keep the paint from running?

Layering

Watercolor dries up to be about 10 percent lighter than when we put it on the paper, so layering is important. You can definitely add more layers on something you already painted. Just make sure it's completely dry. Then, when you add your second layer, you can either make it wet-on-dry or wet-on-wet. If you decide to do a wet-on-wet layer, you will get a soft, lightly colored layer, and if you decide to make a second layer wet-on-dry, you add less water and your color will become brighter and more vibrant. A second layer in wet-on-dry is perfect for details and shadows, as you will see on page 49 in the tulip project.

Drybrushing

A handy little wet-on-dry texture trick is to use drybrushing. It is exactly what it sounds like. You work dry: dry paper and a pretty dry brush dipped in not-too-wet paint. Then, gently apply the dry brushstrokes without water soaking into the paper. This technique is even drier than wet-on-dry painting. With wet-on-dry, you have a wet brush and wet paint, but here, everything is almost dry. It can be handy to have a scrap piece of paper to check if you actually have a dry brush or if it's still too wet. This technique is super useful on petals, leaves and anything really that needs a different texture.

Boost Your Wet-on-Dry Surface With Wet-on-Wet Interest

While your paint is still wet, you can boost the color by using the wet-on-wet technique. Just drip color into the brushstroke and the paint will mingle within the boundaries of the stroke. The color will only go where there is water.

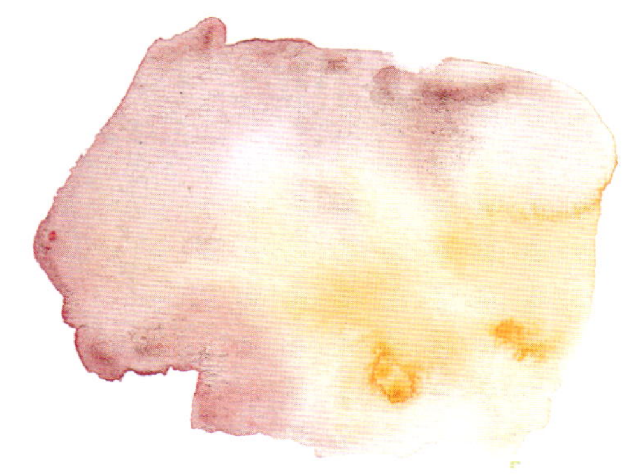

wet-on-wet

Wet-on-wet is a pretty incredible technique that I personally love. This is where watercolor shows its magic side. This watercolor technique is THE perfect companion to fineliners! The combination of the hard lines and the soft watercolor is just divine.

How to Do It

This technique is super simple. You paint with wet paint on a wet surface—either your wet paper or already-wet paint. As long as the surface is wet, you can add paint. Be sure to stop when it starts to dry, or you'll get blooms in your wash (or make them on purpose because they look pretty).

Don't Be Scared

Painting wet-on-wet can be a little intimidating because you need to get a sense of how much water goes with how much paint to get the effect you want. A good rule of thumb is to keep your surface shiny, but not wet.

Just a Quick Tip If You're Using a Sketchbook

Don't add too much water! This technique does require thicker paper like 200 to 300gsm (93 to 140lb), so if you only use a thin sketchbook below 200gsm (93lb), you might want to stay clear of wet-on-wet.

paint mixing techniques

Effectively mixing multiple techniques in a painting may sound obvious, but it's not! Some petals I wet first and then paint wet-on-wet. With some other petals, I start with a wash of water, then have them simply touch an adjoining painted petal: the wet paint in the adjoining petal then flows freely into my water-washed petal, flooding it with color. Yet other petals are painted completely wet-on-dry. Some petals are even painted in a mix. This will create a super organic look that leaves us with a lot of white space (and we love that). It's easy to overthink, so try to just start with one petal, adding water and paint, and then go from there.

the importance of white space

Try closing your eyes for five seconds and listen. Unless you listen to music, your washing machine or a very noisy cat, you will experience silence. White space can be compared to silence and is a vital component in design and art (and in your everyday). White space is what makes your painting breathe. Period. It can also give the sketch highlights, details and even make for an interesting texture.

What Is White Space?

White space is all the parts of your painting where you can see the white of your paper. There is no good white paint in watercolor unless you want to go with gouache or white gel pens or something similar that can be used on top of your watercolor. That's because watercolor is transparent by nature and putting a transparent white paint on white paper wouldn't make sense. So white is just paper, as simple as it may sound.

How Can You Create White Space?

A good place to start is to not overdo the paint. Only use a little paint in your wet-on-wet washes so it does not cover the entire area you're painting, such as a petal. Another way to do it is to be sloppy when wetting the petal. Keep a few dry spots and the paint will stay clear of them, leaving white space instead.

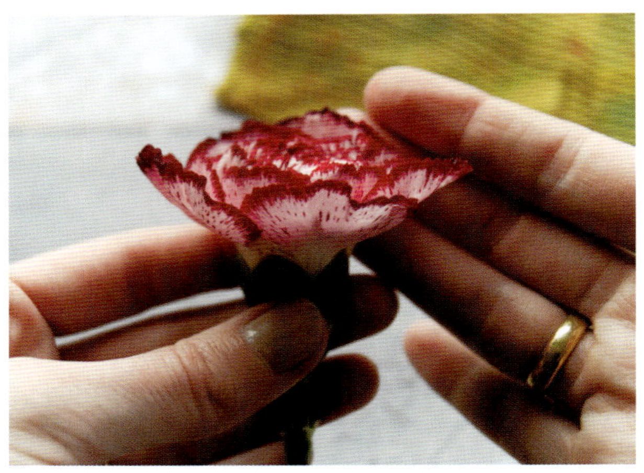

how to sketch flowers

Every time we approach a new flower, we want to sketch it first. All flowers are different, and even if they share characteristics like the amount of petals or similar leaves, they all have something that makes them special. Think of it like a portrait—we all have two eyes, a nose and a mouth, but somehow, we all still look very different. So, what you are aiming at is to capture the essence of the flower, showing what makes this flower unique.

observe the flower

To draw is to see. That's what I was told in school when I was a little girl learning to handle pencil and paper, and it's not entirely wrong. The biggest part of drawing is to tell our brain what we want the pencil to do.

So now, I give you a little task. First, find a reference of a pretty bloom.

Then, look at your flower and ask yourself these questions:

- Is the flower made of different shapes?
- How many petals are there? Do they overlap? Do they curl? Are some of them foreshortened?
- What does the center of the flower look like?
- How fat is the stem?
- How do the leaves fall, and how are they placed on the stem?

Now that you've observed your reference, you are ready to grab a pencil and a piece of paper and do your thing.

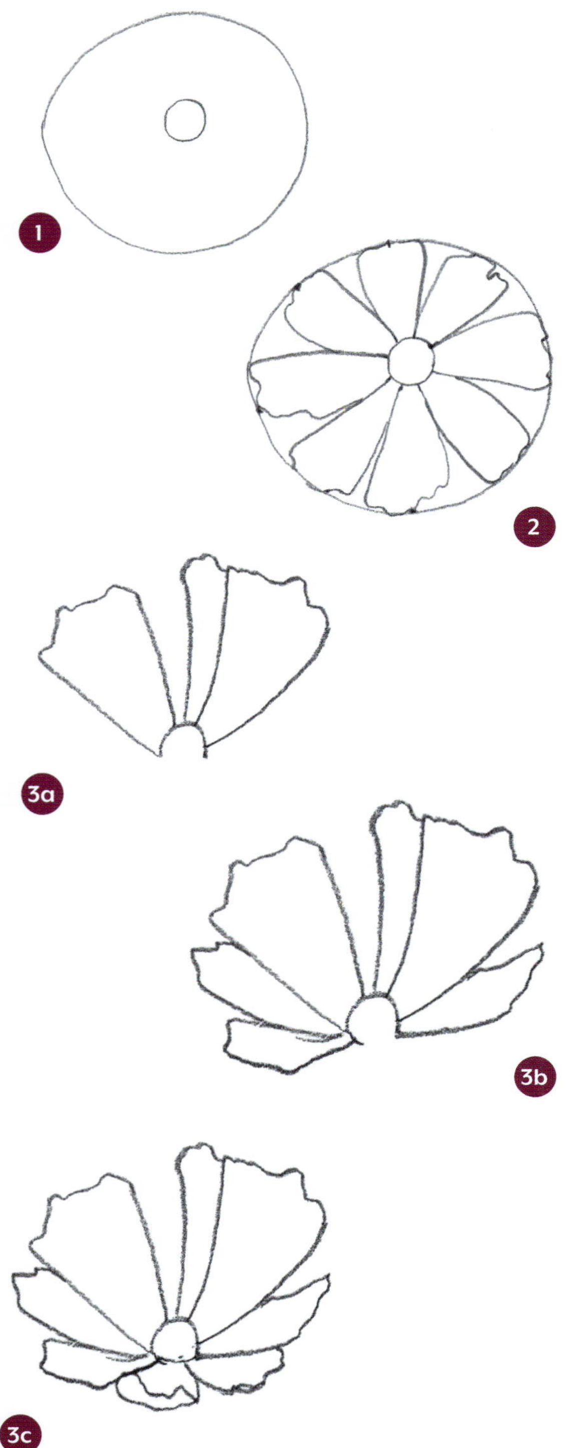

Sketching Flowers, Leaves and Stems

Sketching Flowers

The Basic Shape

Take a good look at the shape of your flower. For this example, I used the cosmo. You can see the circle in the middle of the flower head, and then you can draw a circle around the middle to show the edge of the petals (1). These two shapes will help you guide your drawing.

Placing the Petals

Do a count and then add small marks on the inner circle where you think the petals fit. Adjust until you feel it looks right. You can do the same on the outer edge as well, and then you just need to connect the dots by drawing the petals in the space between the two circles (2).

Foreshortening

When you see a flower from the side, some of the petals will look super short. That is because they are closer to you. Let's take a look at the cosmo again, now from the side:

- The petals at the back are long and wide (3a).
- Then, we go closer to the sides and they are long, but a lot thinner. That is because some of the petal is hiding from our eyes (3b).
- The petals closest to us are wide but also short. The part closest to the flower is hiding from us (3c).

We can show the foreshortening with the fineliner size 005, so don't be scared of it. In fact, it's better to love these perspective lines. They give your flower life, movement and dimension—so what's not to like?

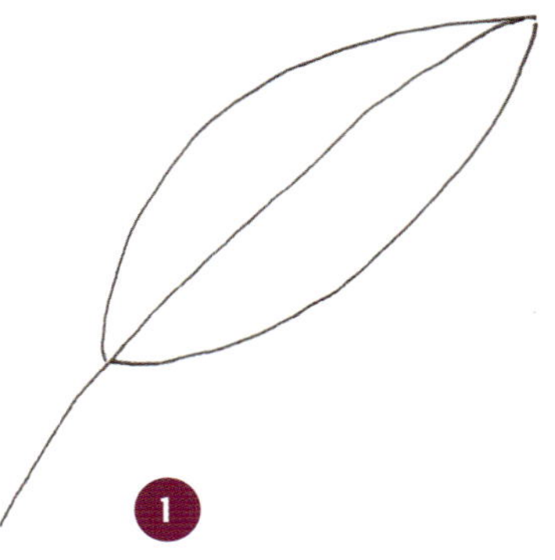

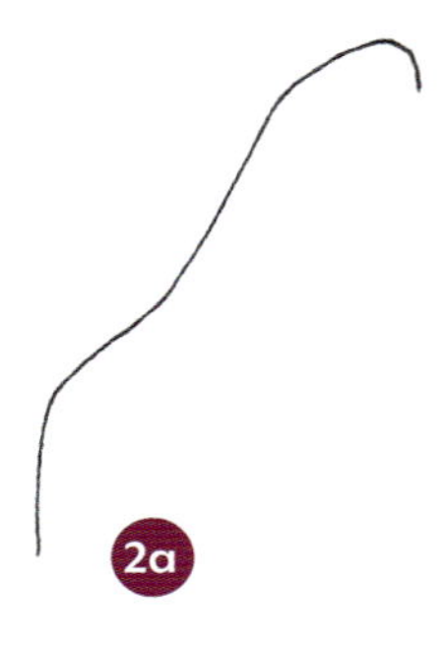

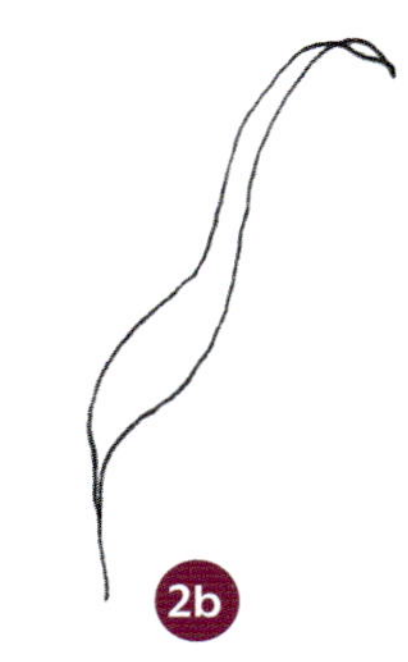

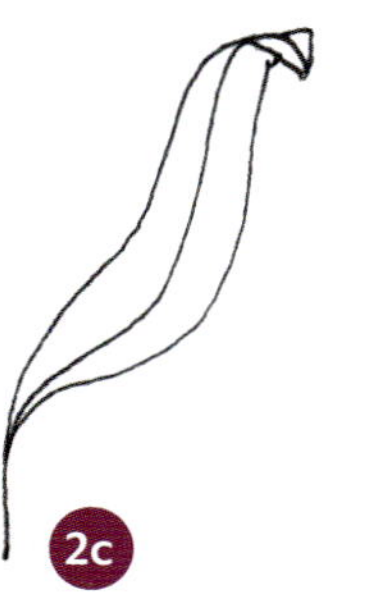

Sketching Leaves

Leaves often have a pretty basic shape, but as soon as they start turning a bit, they can seem intimidating. First, let's break it down, and that will make it a lot easier.

Basic Leaf

You have your basic leaf-shape here (1)—two rounded lines meeting in both ends. Inside the leaf, you can find a midrib going from the bottom to the top and out from their veins. Every leaf is different, so take a good look at your reference. And remember that basic leaves often are foreshortened just like the flowers.

Curled Leaf

When you have a curled leaf (2), you want to start with the midrib. Then, you can sketch the edge closest to you first and end at the tip of the midrib. When you have that edge, you can place the other outer edge of the leaf. Finally, you add the line that is missing in the bend.

Sketching Stems

I always like to make my stems dance. I do that by adding a few twists and turns to them, even if they are not always in the reference. But by adding a bit of movement, you can really breathe more life into the flower. Of course, a cosmo will move more than a peony, but you get my point. Basically, you draw two lines close to each other. You can make them straight up and down or give them curls and bends depending on how much movement you want to give them.

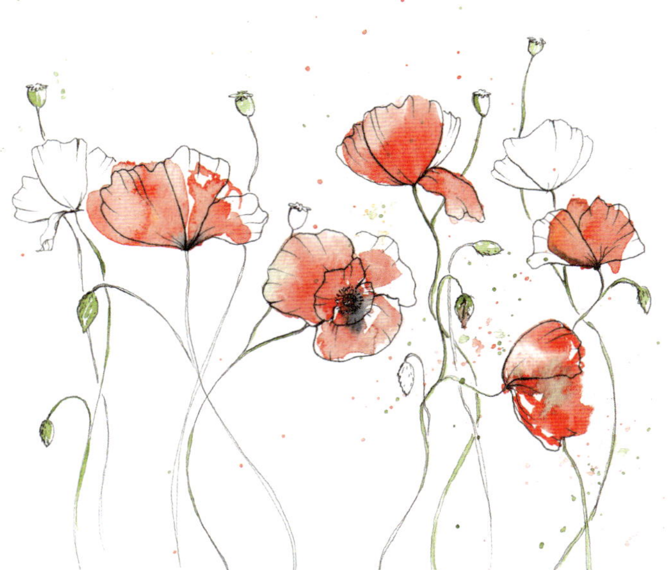

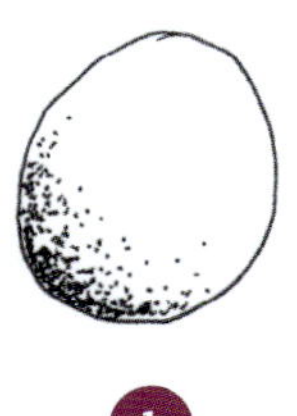
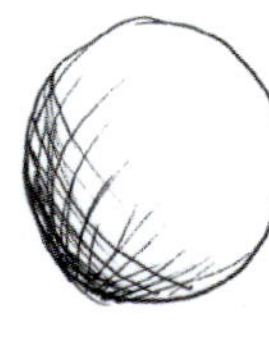
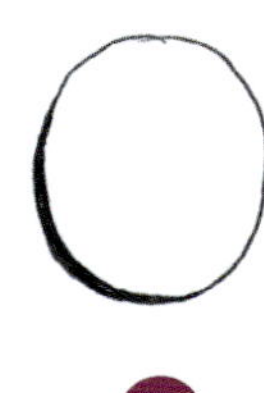
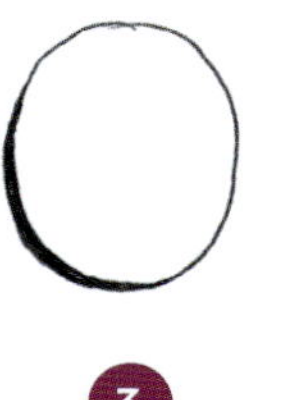
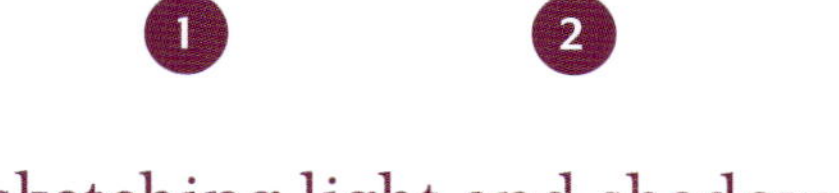

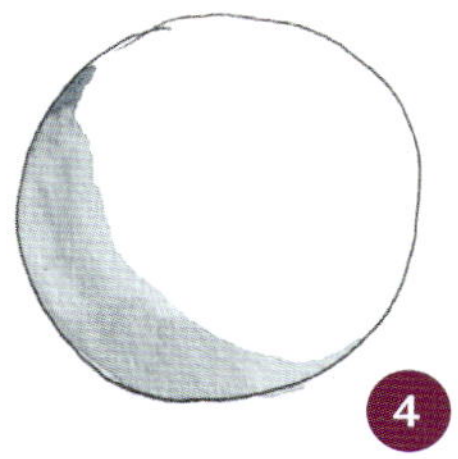
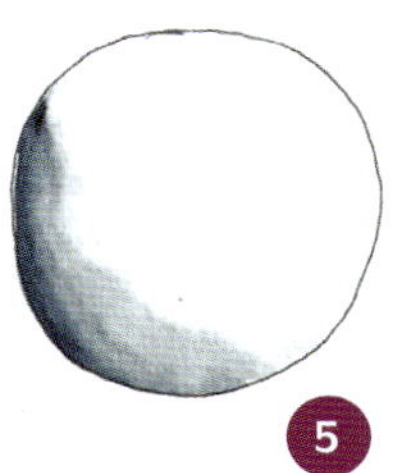

4

5

sketching light and shadow

Since the sketches in this book are meant to be very basic sketches, you don't want to go too much into detail with light and shadow, but it can be really useful to know where they are. Then, it's a lot easier to either draw it in fineliner or show it in paint afterward.

Value

Instead of light and shadow, which can be a little intimidating, think of them as values. You can go from white paper to very dark. If you look at your reference like that, you'll be able to see very light areas and very dark areas—those are your light and shadow. The rest is midtones.

A quick tip: Turn the reference into black and white on your phone or computer. That way, you won't get disturbed by colors, but can focus on the values instead.

Going from Light to Dark

Now that you found your lightest and darkest area, all you need to do is make the transitions. And there are so many ways to do that.

Shadows Using Fineliner

When doing shadows in fineliner, you can either do them before or after the watercolor wash. I prefer to do it after because then you know if the watercolor might give you some natural tones of shadows that you can use.

Stippling (1): Use small dots to show the shadow, with very few dots closest to the light and a LOT of dots in the darkest area.

Crosshatching (2): Use lines that crisscross in the direction of the petal. Make the lines closer to each other when going toward the darkest area.

Drawing Very Dark Lines (3): If you have areas in complete shadow, then just fill in the shape and draw it completely black. This will give drama and be a beautiful contrast to the soft watercolor.

Shadows Using Watercolor

To make shadow in watercolor, make sure you let your first layer dry completely before going in with shadows.

Hard Shadows (4): Shadows with hard lines are usually seen in bright sunlight. This type of shadow is created by painting a shape similar to what the shadow is mirroring. Don't touch the edges—let them be hard.

Soft Shadows (5): To create soft shadows, you will use a technique called feathering. A soft shadow happens when there is a smooth transition between the shadow and the color of the petal. Give the area in shadow the deepest version of your color as possible. Then, soften the edge with a damp brush where you want the shadows to go into midtones.

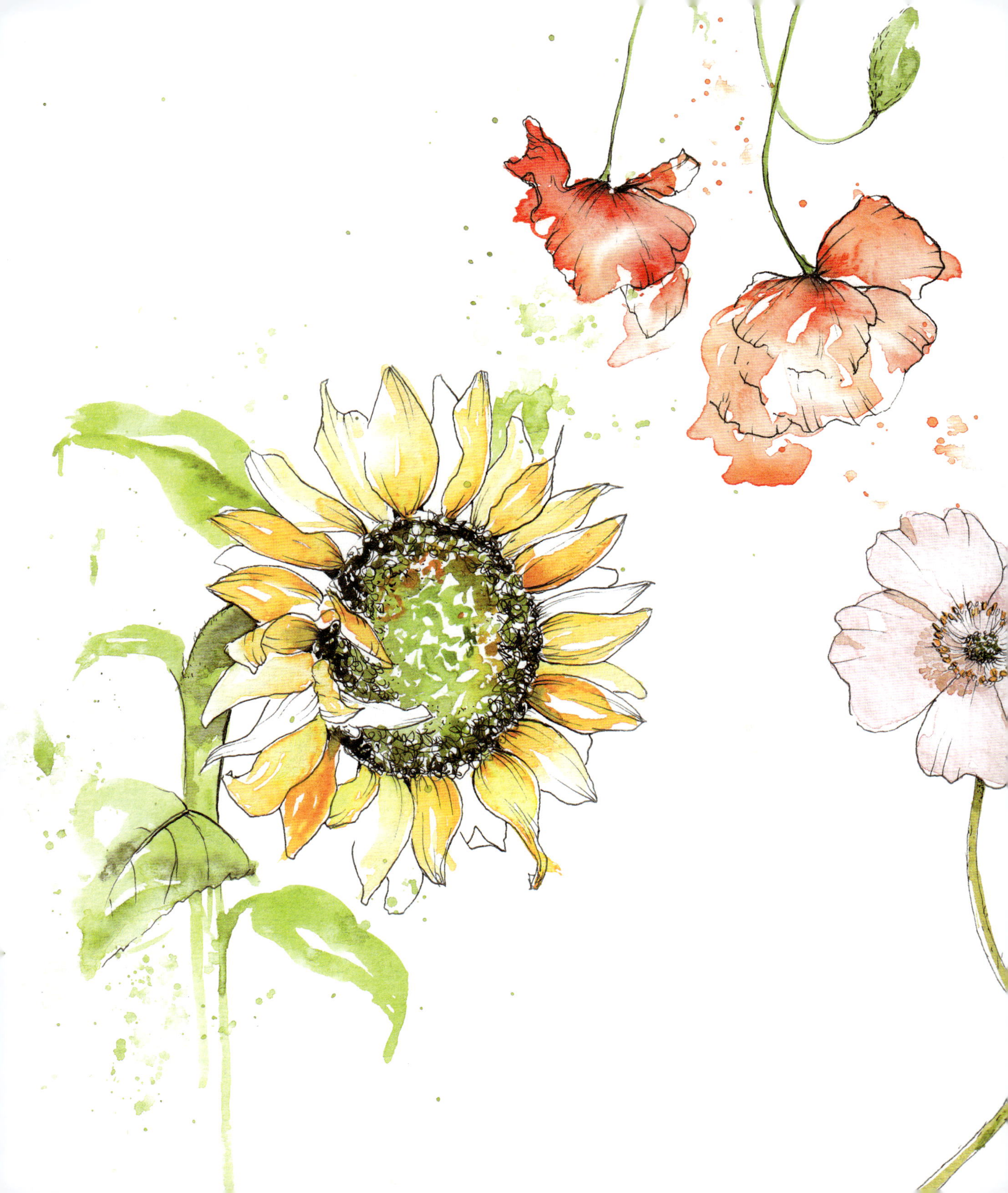

part II: seventeen flowers in watercolor and ink

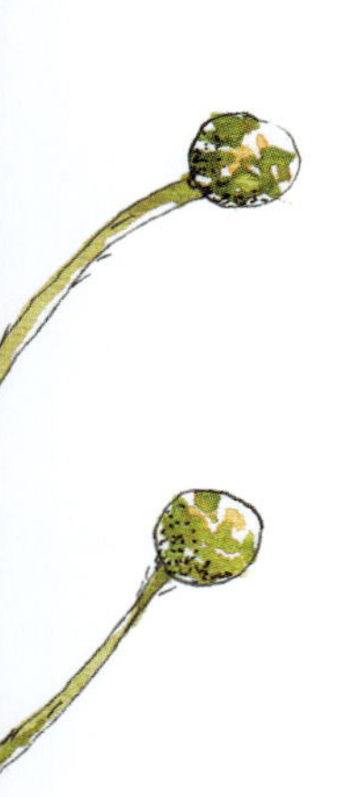

Congratulations! You finished all the techniques and now you have come to the fun part—the part of the book where you can get out your supplies and start sketching. If you are a complete beginner, I suggest you start from the top and work your way down. I am introducing new methods as you progress, and you'll notice that no project follows the same formula. I am doing this to encourage you to experiment freely with the techniques and find a combination of line and wash that fits your own style. In this chapter, you'll learn techniques like using your fineliner to create petals with bends and curves, using the wet-on-dry technique to create shadows and detail lines, using interesting wet-on-wet backgrounds to emphasize white flowers and so much more. But enough talk. When it comes down to it, the best way to learn is just to do a lot of sketches. And the best part is that this is super fun and not at all like school. Sketching flowers is the best and most relaxing thing ever!

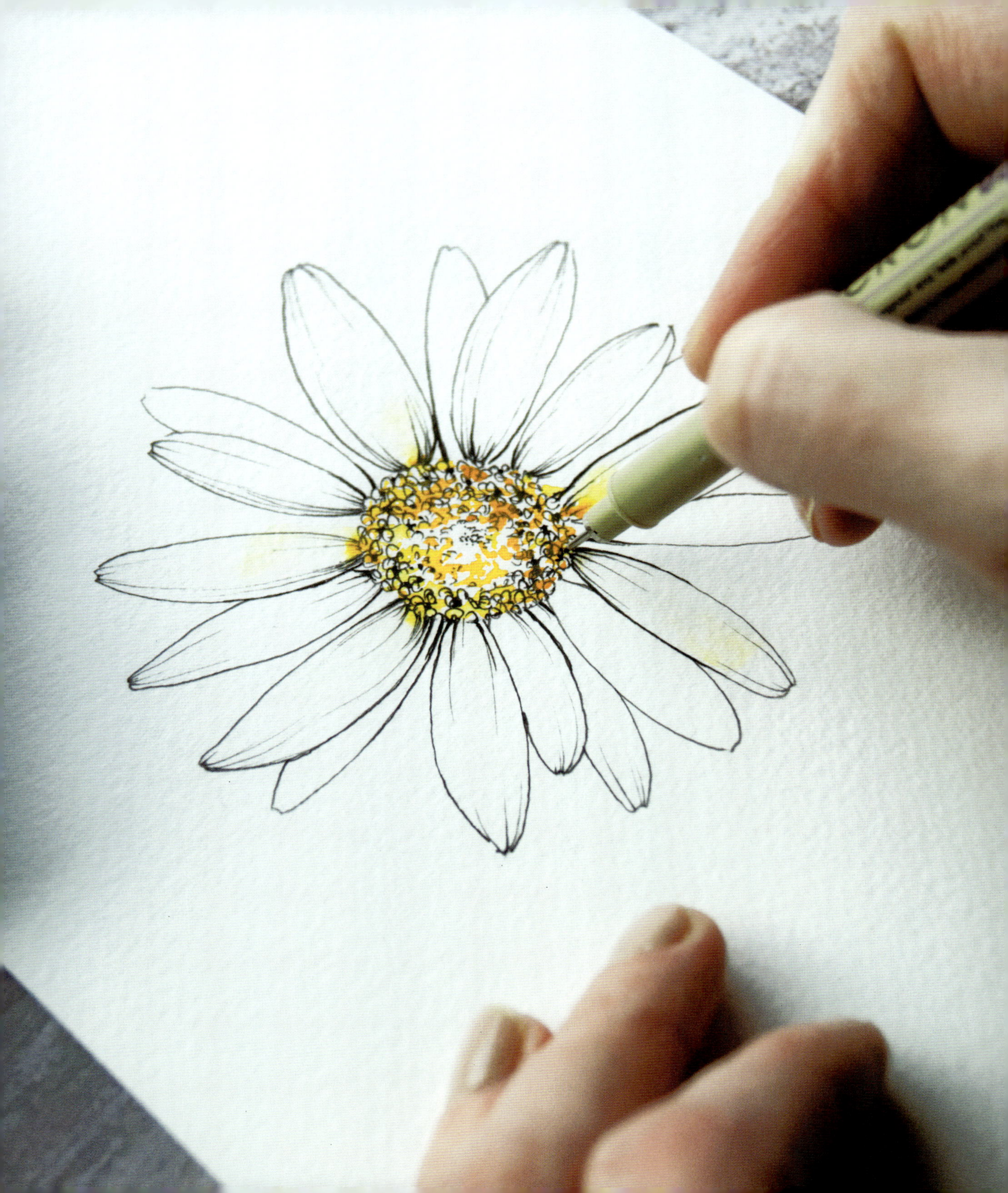

daisy

the flower of purity

A few years back, I drove through the country with my husband and kids and suddenly, I saw the most breathtaking field—a field of these yellow and white blooms. I had to stop the car, snap several photos and hurry home to paint. In this step-by-step, you'll learn how to sketch your first flower of the book, the very simple and elegant daisy. Here, you will get a good feeling of the most basic approach to line and wash by using the fineliner first and then a pretty wash.

Materials

Pencil and eraser

Paper: Canson Montval 300gsm (140lb) cold press

Fineliners: sizes 005, 01 and 02

Watercolor brush: size 4

Water and cloth

Color

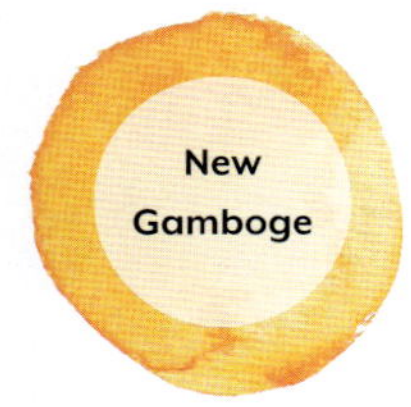

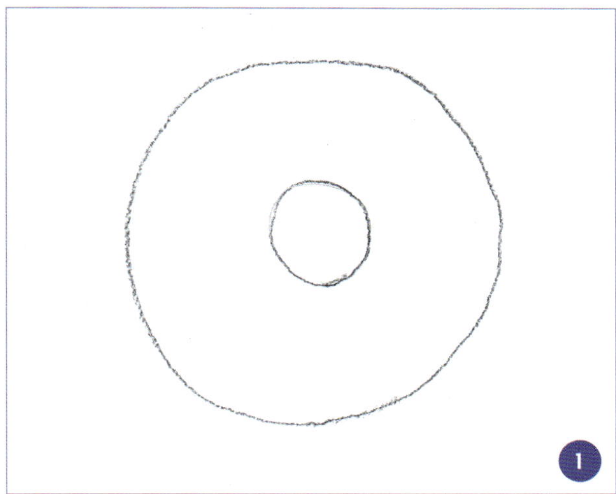

Step 1: Let's start by making it easy for us. As explained in the "How to Sketch Flowers" section on page 22, draw two circles in pencil, a small one for the center of the daisy and a bigger one for the outer edge of the petals. This will be your guide for the drawing.

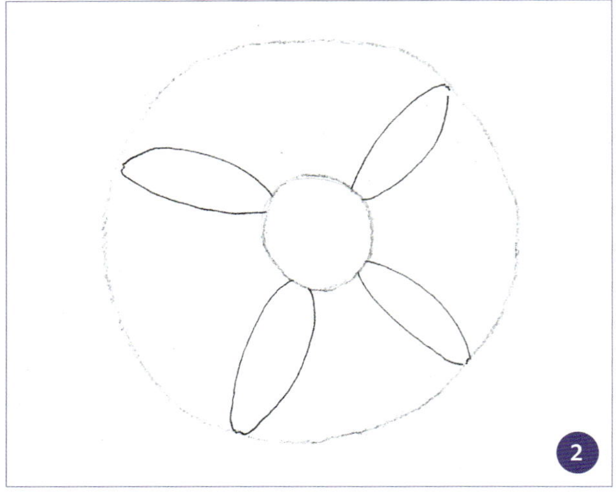

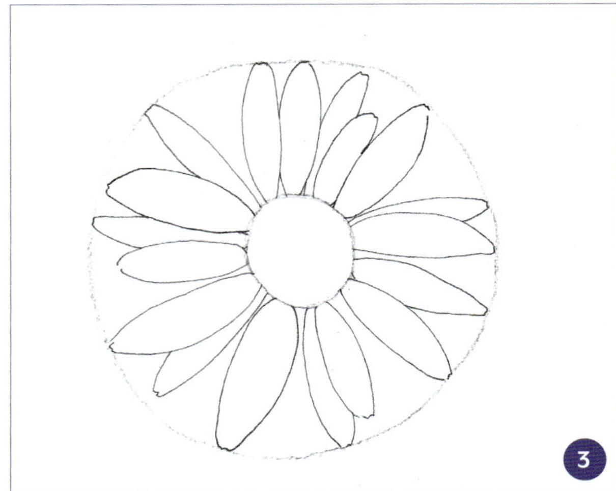

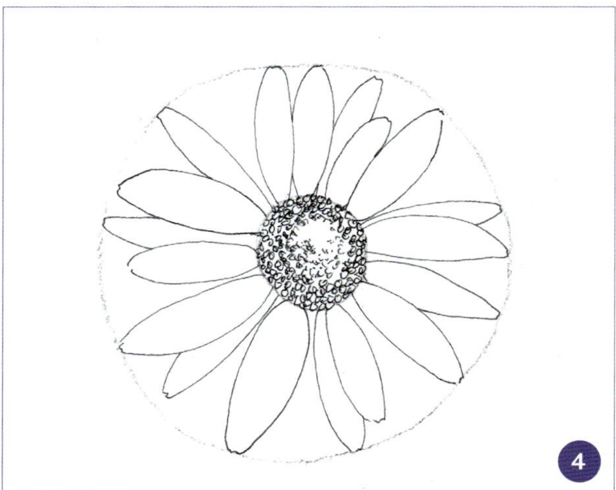

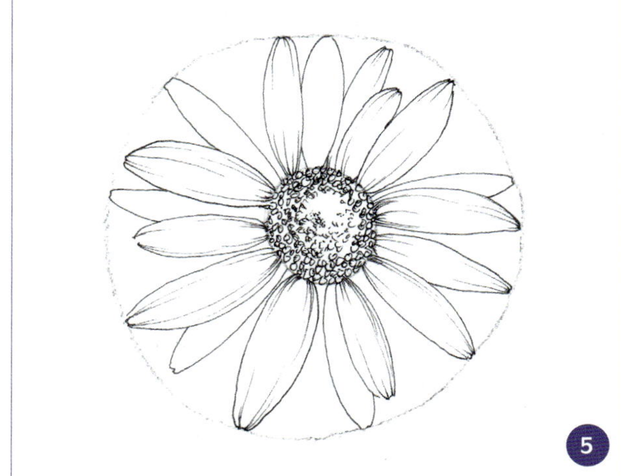

Step 2: Take your 01 fineliner and draw the first four petals. They should be spread evenly around the flower. Start by drawing the petal from the small pencil circle and then, when you get to the outer pencil guide, make a small bend in the line and move back to the center.

Step 3: Now draw the rest of the petals with the same fineliner. Make some petals overlap to give your flower a bit of depth. Also, make some of the petals shorter than the rest—this will make it look less perfect and more like real life.

Step 4: After drawing the petals, it's time to work the center of the flower. Draw small doodles with your 01 fineliner, like circles and small C-shapes. Make them bigger closer to the petals and smaller as they approach the center. Leave an area free of doodles to give the illusion of a highlight.

Step 5: It's time to get some shape into your flower. Take your 005 fineliner and draw long, slightly curved lines starting either from the outer edge of the petal or the inner edge. They should curve in the direction of the petal, thereby shaping it. Try making the line a bit thicker at the beginning and thinner toward the middle of the petal (see page 19 for line variation). You don't have to draw on all the petals. It's really pretty to leave a few plain and white.

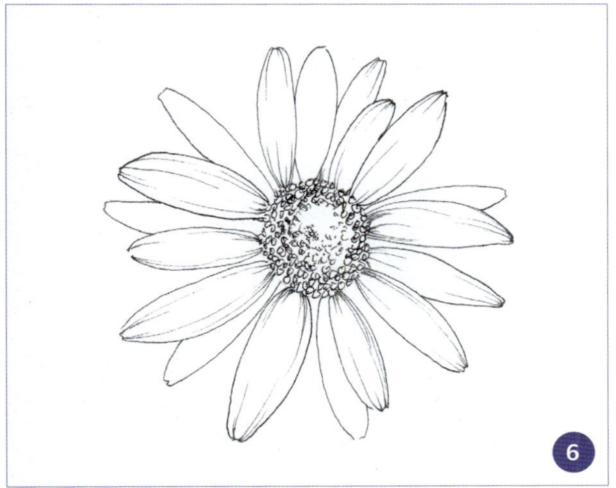

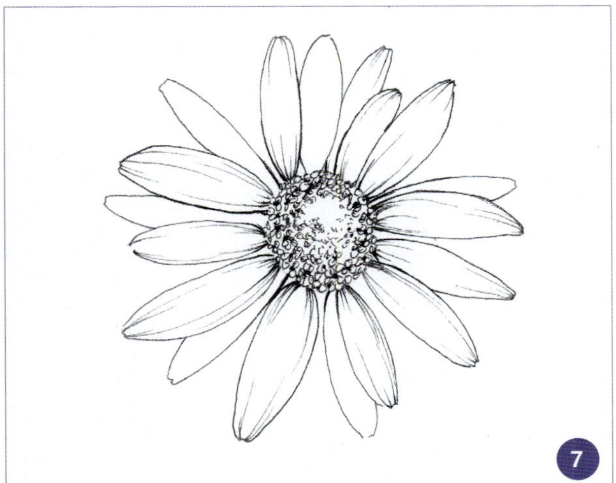

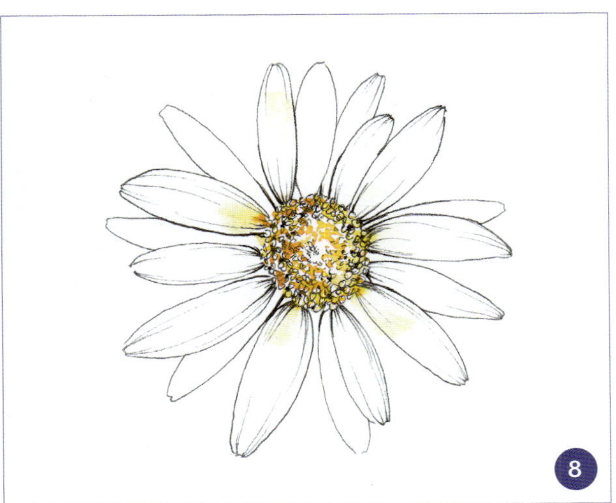

Step 6: Until now, we had our pencil guidelines, but you don't need them anymore. When your ink lines are completely dry, you can find your eraser and carefully erase the pencil. Try to hold your eraser softly and don't press too hard so you don't risk ruining the paper.

Step 7: The last layer with fineliner is a bit of shading. And in this flower, we do this very simply. Grab your 02 fineliner and start in the flower center. Fill in small gaps between the doodles you created earlier to make some shadow and nice contrast. Then, strengthen a few of the lines on the petals as well. Work from the center out, and just strengthen a few. This will give an illusion of shadow from the center. You can also strengthen a few lines between the overlapping petals just to show that the overlap will cause a shadow as well (see page 25 for inspiration on shading).

Step 8: Now it's time to get your watercolor gear out. Take a size 4 brush with a nice tip. Load it with a warm yellow (I use new gamboge) and start adding paint to the center of the flower wet-on-dry. Use the tip of your brush and make small dots with the paint instead of big strokes.

Let's try the wet-on-wet technique here: While it's still wet, rinse your brush and then load it with clean water. Now wet a few of the big petals. Start from the outer edge and work your way toward the center so the water just kisses the yellow a little bit. This will cause the yellow to flow into the white petal.

Now you can leave it to dry and admire your first sketch. Well done!

plumeria

the flower of spring and new beginnings

Even if the plumeria is an elegant and very simple flower, it is very meaningful around the world and always symbolizes something positive. That is probably why they are often seen in pretty floral garlands—I mean, if a flower garland isn't a party starter, then nothing is. With the plumeria, we are going a bit further with the wet-on-wet technique to create that beautiful soft yellow shade in this bloom. You will experience how a yellow is not just yellow and how a mix of cool and warm can create depth and glow.

Materials

Pencil and eraser

Paper: Canson Montval 300gsm (140lb) cold press

Fineliners: sizes 005, 01 and 02

Watercolor brush: size 7

Water and cloth

Colors

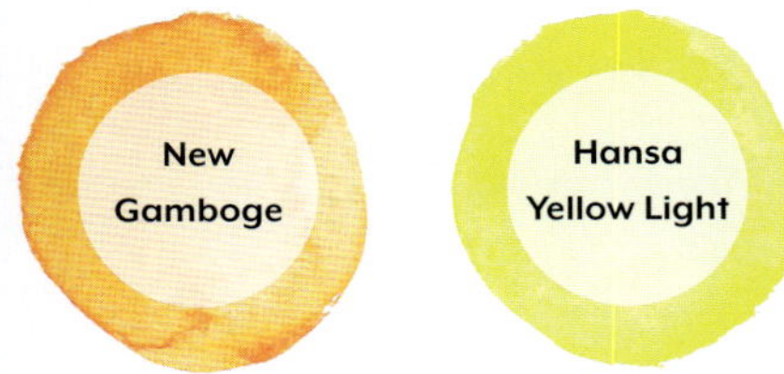

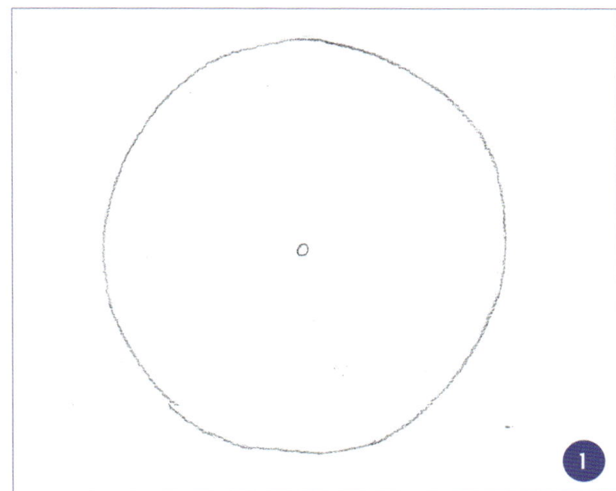

Step 1: Draw a very tiny circle in pencil and surround it with a bigger one. This shows the center of your plumeria and the outer edge of the petals.

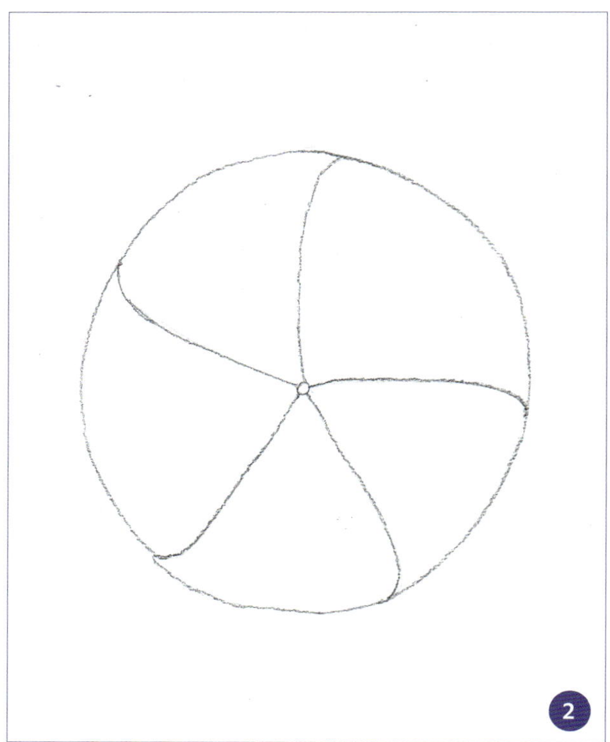

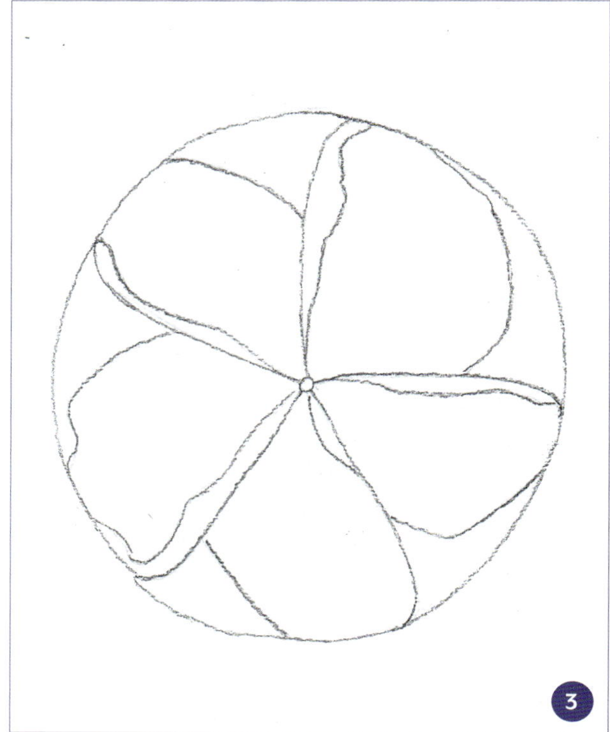

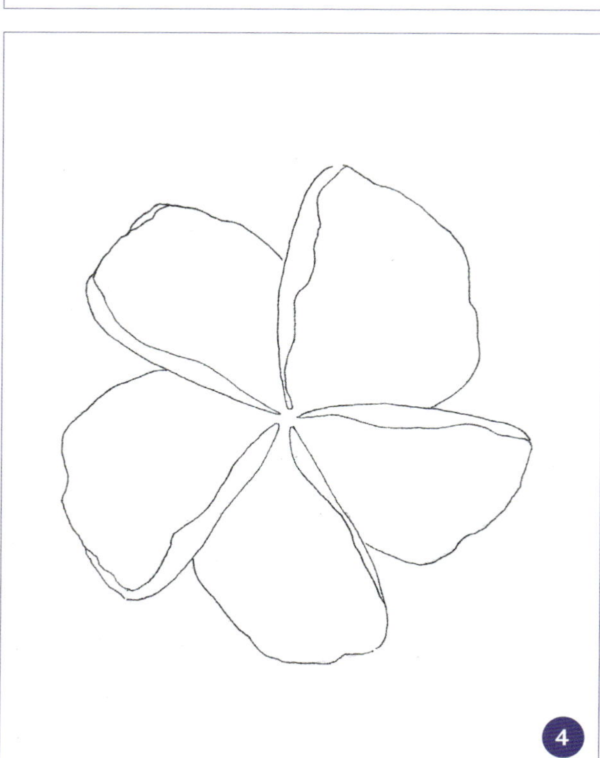

Step 2: Now, you can begin drawing the petals. Draw a straight line starting from the inner circle, ending in a small curve at the outer circle. Draw four more lines so they are equally spread in the circle.

Step 3: Now finish the petals with the rest of the outer edge and a bit of a curl. The curl is just a crooked line on the inside of the petal following the left side of the petal.

Step 4: When you have the sketch ready, you can draw in the outlines with the fineliner. I use a basic 01 for this outline. After you are done, you can remove the pencil lines with an eraser, as well as the small circle in the center.

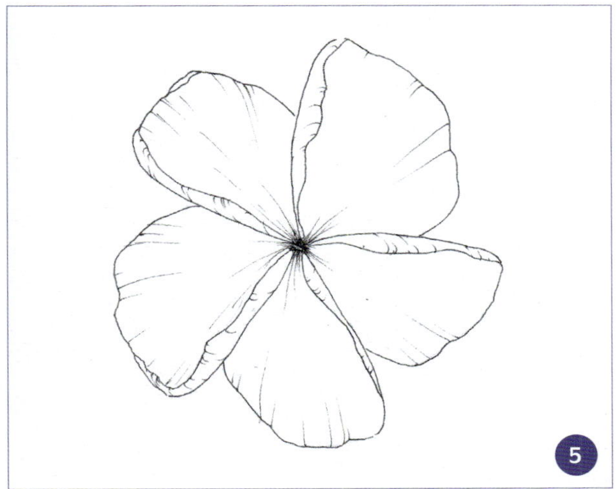

Step 5: Now we are ready for the details and, in this one, we are using the 005 fineliner for that. The plumeria has some pretty smooth petals, so don't do too much here. Start adding lines in the petals from the center and from the outer edge. You have a bend in the petal edges, and here you can use the lines to show the curl. Start at the crooked line and slowly shape the curl with thin C-shaped lines bending downward. You can also add a few lines from the outer edge to meet the crooked line.

Step 6: Use the 02 fineliner to draw on the left side of the petals to make those lines stronger. This line variation will give an illusion of dimension.

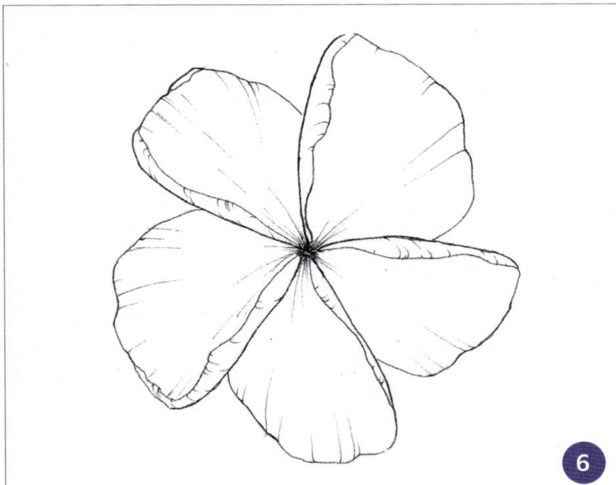

Step 7: Now it's time for paint! Yay! Wet one petal with just enough water so that it's shining but without water puddles. Then dip your size 7 brush in new gamboge and carefully dip the paint in the part of the petal closest to the center. Let the paint flow a bit into the water. Then load your brush with Hansa yellow light and add that to the middle of the petal between the warm yellow and the area without paint. This will give it a nice glowing and warm center.

Continue doing this to all the petals and you are all done!

Great job! Now it's time to admire your plumeria and maybe draw a few more to make your own flower garland.

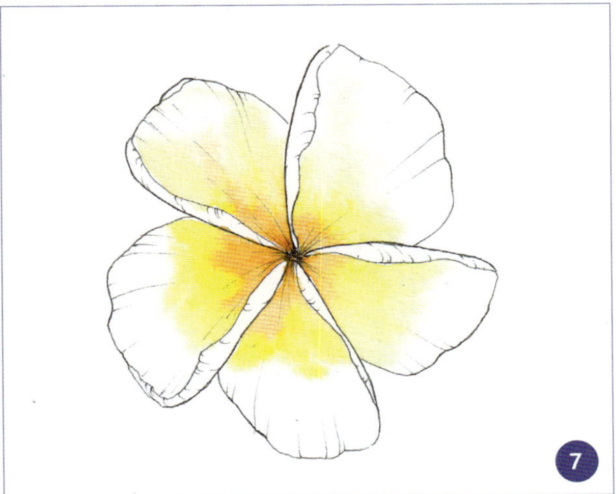

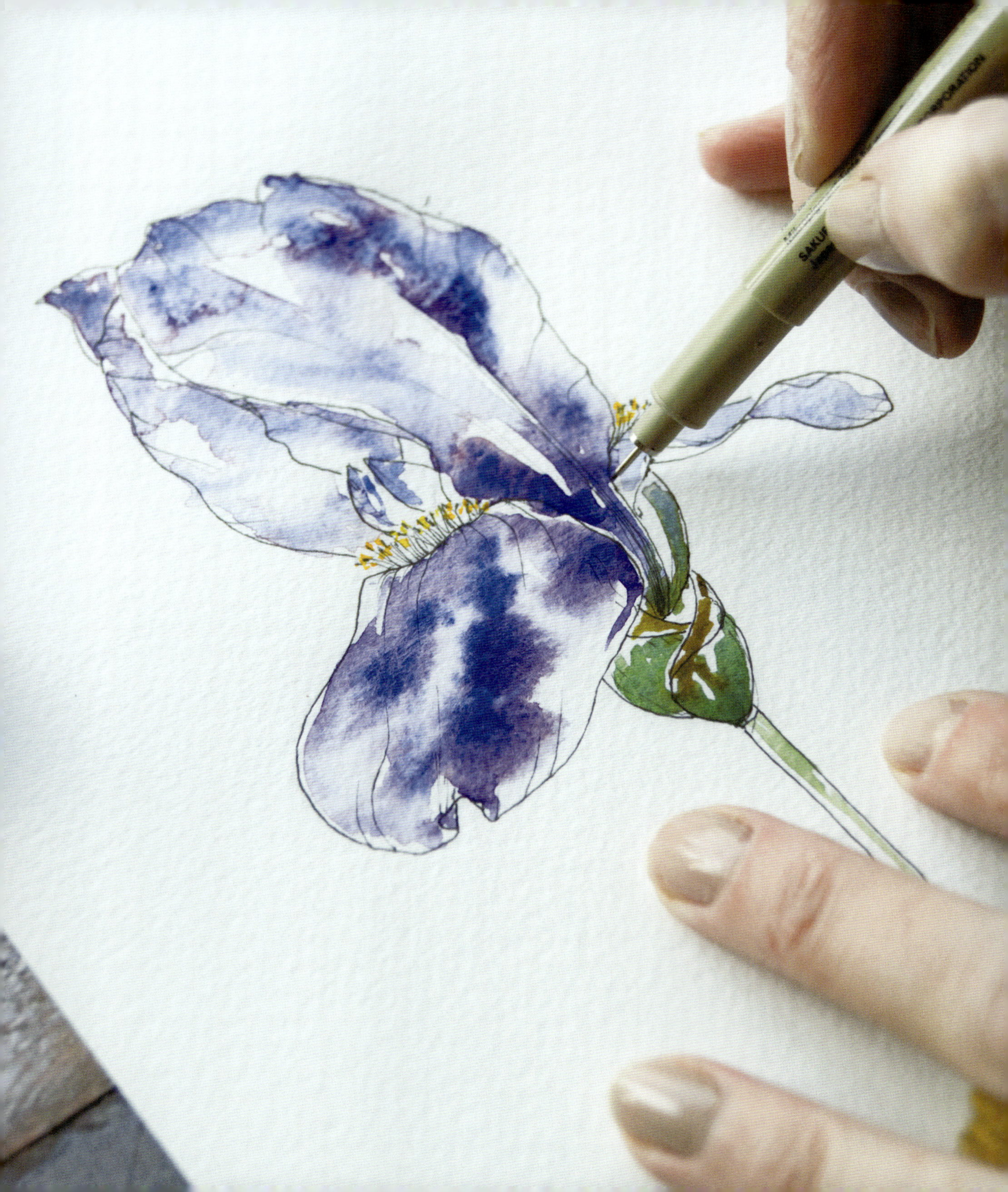

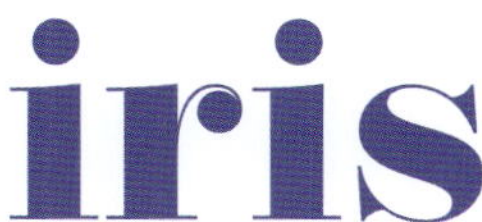

the flower of hope and wisdom

I know the iris can seem a bit scary at first—well, not scary like zombies or clowns, but its rather strange shape can look intimidating. I still wanted to feature this flower in the beginning, because even tricky flowers can be made easy by observing and sketching them in pencil. So, in this step-by-step, we are going to take the scary out of an intimidating shape, create some stunning texture with wet-on-wet watercolor and do a bit of color mixing. I can't wait to show you this!

Materials

Pencil and eraser

Paper: Canson Montval 300gsm (140lb) cold press

Fineliners: sizes 01 and 005

Watercolor brushes: sizes 4 and 9

Water and cloth

Palette

Colors

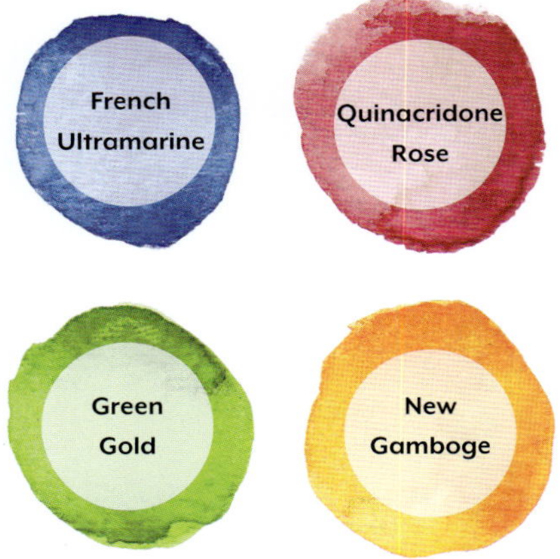

Mixes

The blue color is French ultramarine with a bit of quinacridone rose.

The green is a mix of green gold with a bit of the French ultramarine to give it a blue tone.

The brown is a mix of green gold and a tad of quinacridone rose to muddy it up.

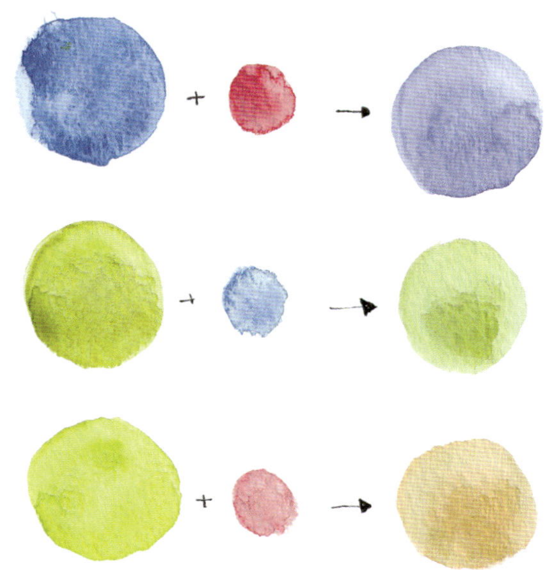

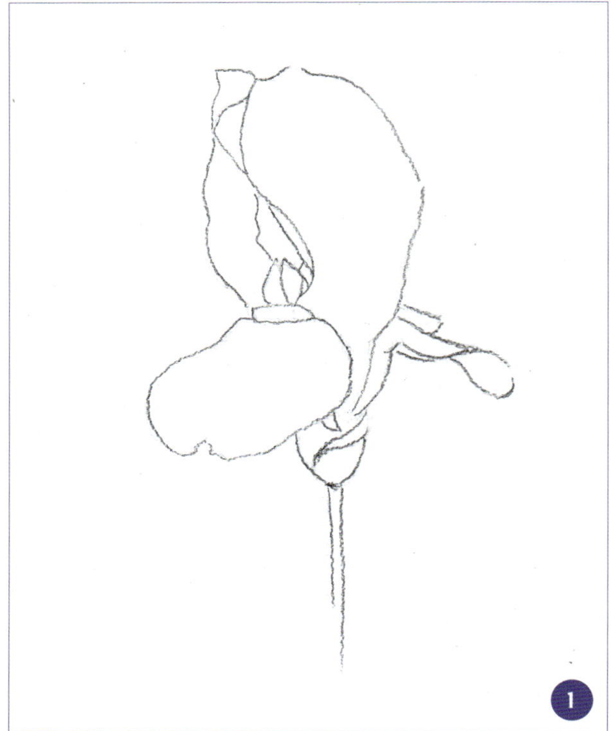

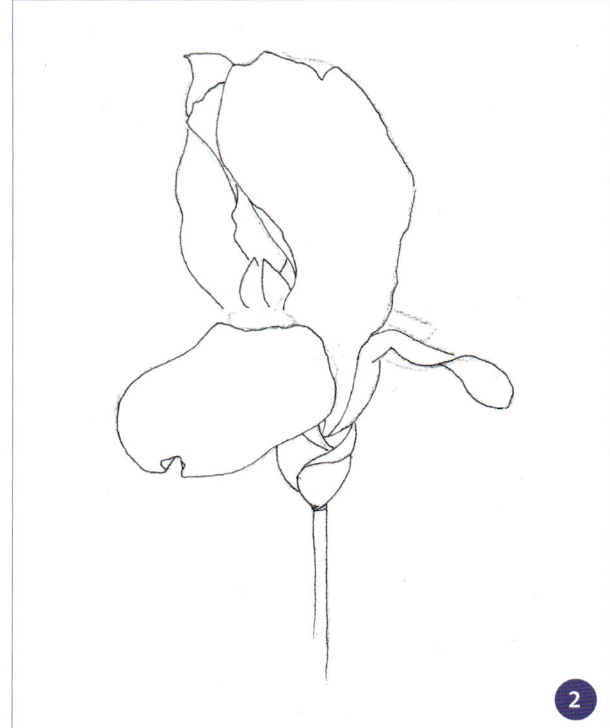

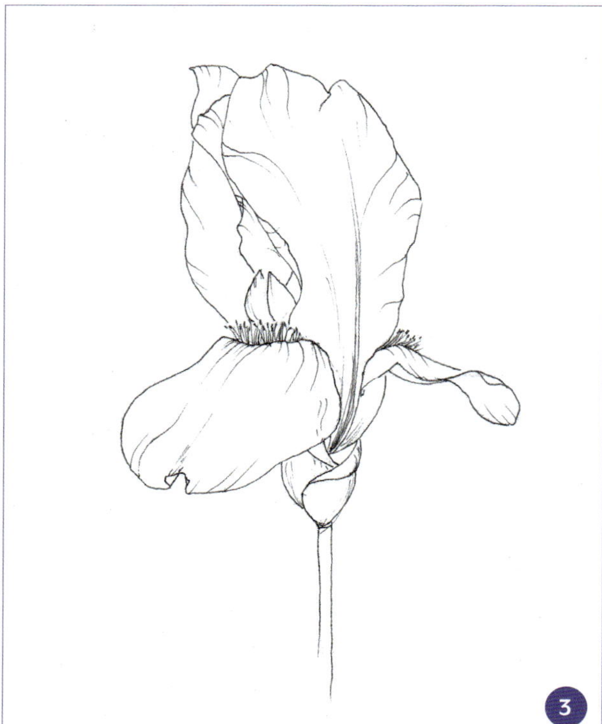

Step 1: First, grab your pencil and do the (close to) lifesaving sketch. Start with the big folded petal in the front and then place everything according to that. It's easiest if you take the biggest petals first and then work your way down to the hairs and the stem. If something feels off, just erase and try again. To take even more pressure off, you can do the sketch on copy paper first for practice.

Step 2: When you are happy with your sketch, use your 01 fineliner to do the outline. Leave out the detail of the small hairs. They are so delicate that you want to use a thinner fineliner for them.

Step 3: Now, grab your 005 fineliner and draw the details in the petals. These are the lines showing the direction of the petals and the small hairs in the center and right side of the iris.

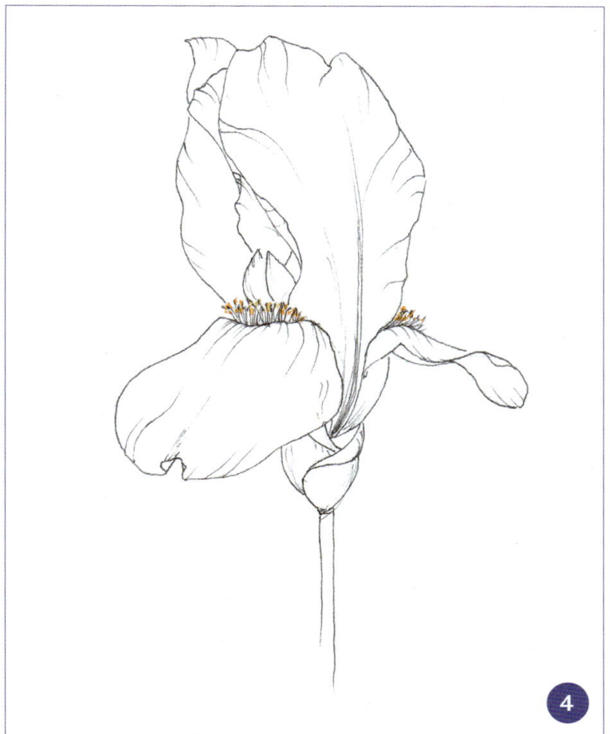

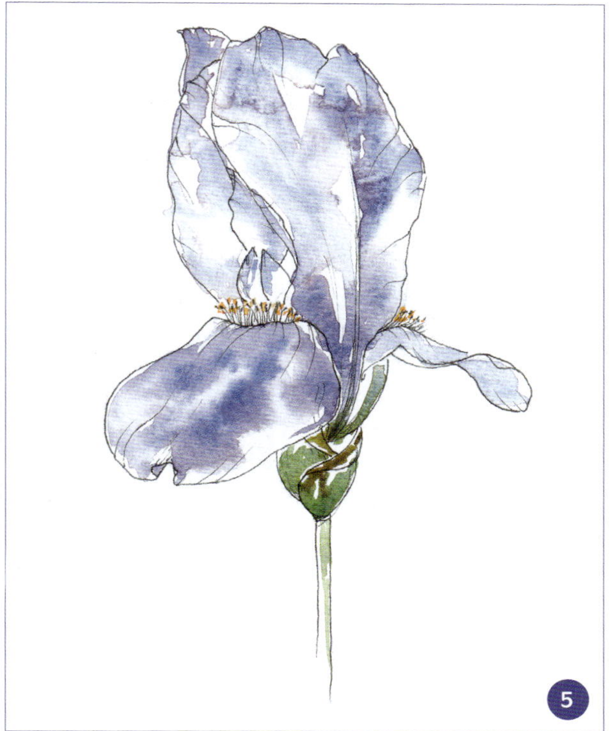

Step 4: You can put even more focus on the hairs now because it's time to color them up. Grab a thin brush—I like to use a size 4 with a fine tip. Load it with a nice thick mixture of new gamboge and carefully paint tiny ovals at the end of the hairs. Let it dry completely before continuing.

Before starting Step 5, make sure you have your colors mixed (see page 37 for your mixes).

Step 5: For the petals, I promised you wet-on-wet (find the technique on page 21), so start by wetting the big petals with your size 9 brush and drip in the mix of French ultramarine and quinacridone rose, leaving some spaces white for effect. Don't be scared of the color looking bluer or more rose at some points. The different colors just add to the interest of the final drawing.

While the petals are still wet, you can paint the stem in a mix of green gold and ultramarine blue. The curled and brown part of the stem is painted in a mix of the green gold and a bit of quinacridone rose. This is all done wet-on-dry and close to the still-wet petals so that the green softly flows into the blue.

Woohoo! You finished yet another flower. While the iris dries, you can go and make yourself a cup of tea. Make it a good one, because you earned it. Then, come back to see how the paint has dried up and created a beautiful drying texture.

gerbera

the flower of cheerfulness

Somehow, the gerbera always reminds me of my younger days when I worked as a florist in a supermarket. We always put this pretty bloom in the bouquets, and I think it's become a modern-day classic. With its bright colors and clean shape, this is a flower that spreads joy and cheerfulness to your heart and home. In this tutorial, we are going to practice the different things we learned so far, like painting wet-on-dry, leaving white space on some of the petals and drawing detail lines to show the direction of the petals. Since this flower head is seen from an angle, we will also try our hand at drawing foreshortened petals, and then those lovely detail lines will come in handy.

Materials

Pencil and eraser

Paper: Canson Montval 300gsm (140lb) cold press

Fineliners: sizes 005 and 02

Watercolor brush: size 4

Water and cloth

Palette

Colors

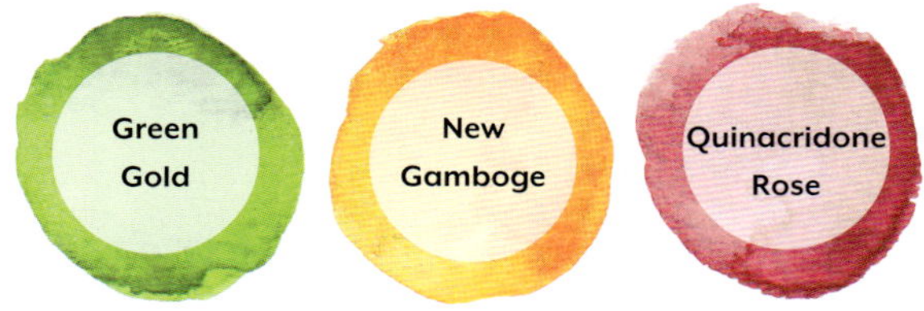

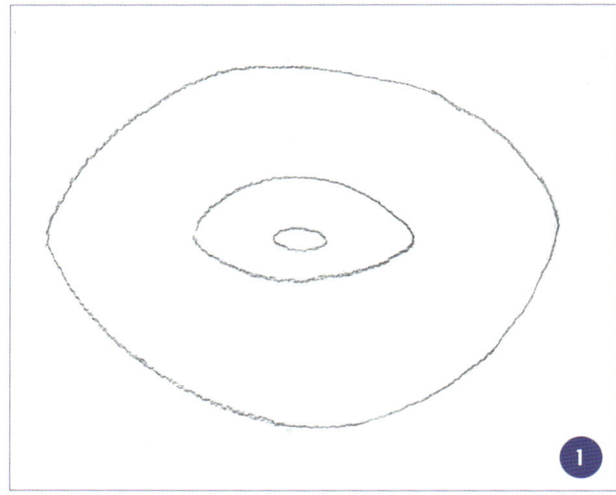

Step 1: Draw three flat ovals in pencil. They should be tucked into each other with equal space around the edges, almost like oval rings in water. When it comes to sizes, make the inner circle 0.4 inch (1 cm), then the next circle 2 inches (5 cm) and the big one 6 inches (15 cm).

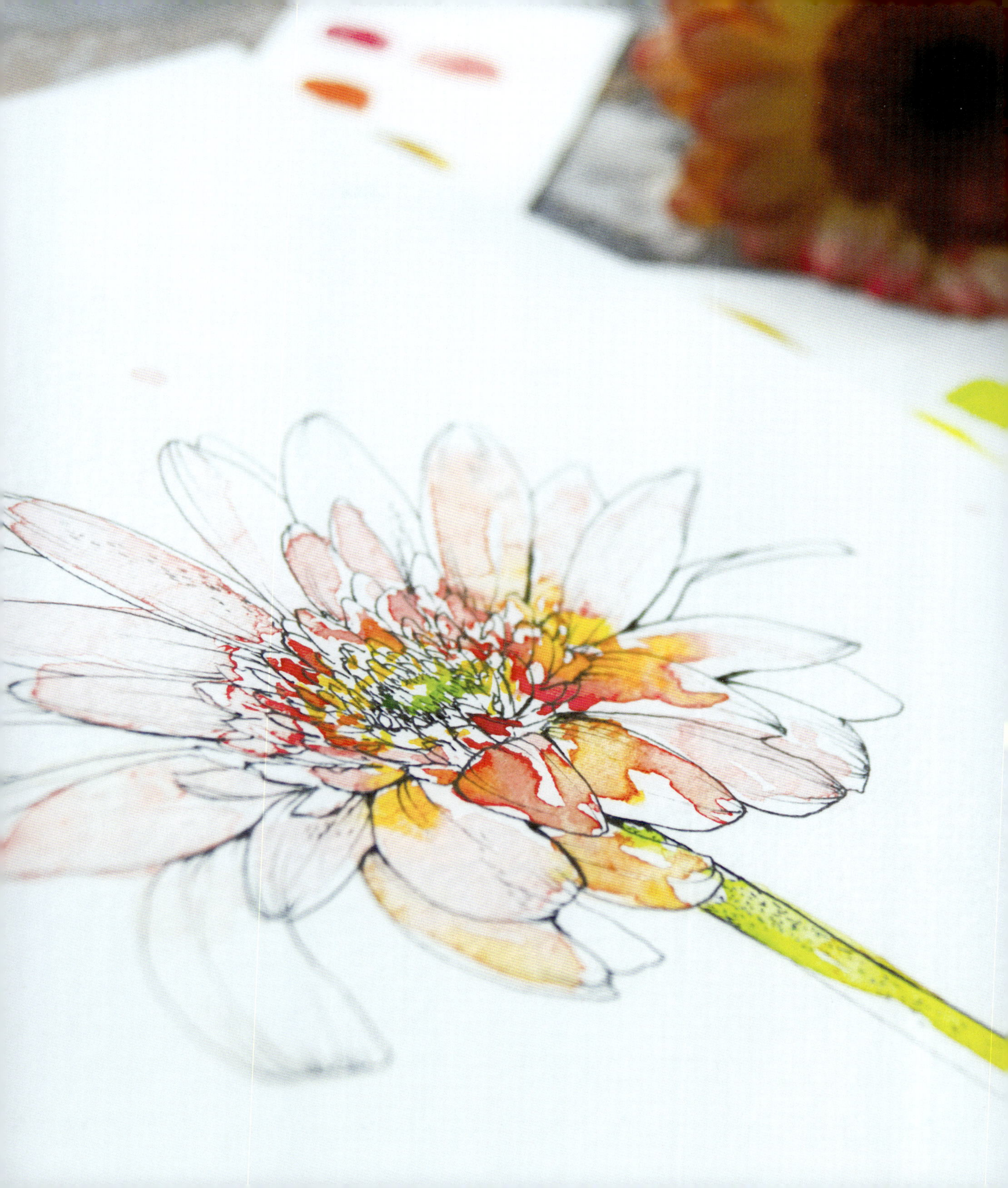

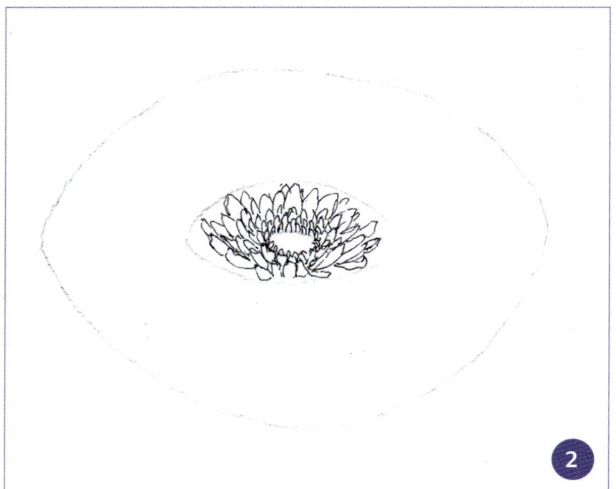

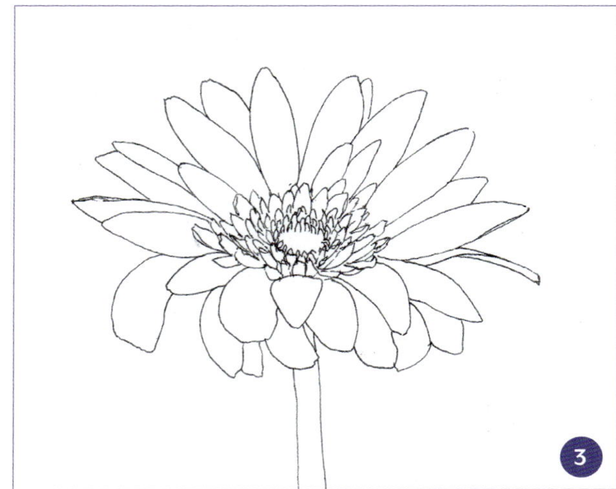

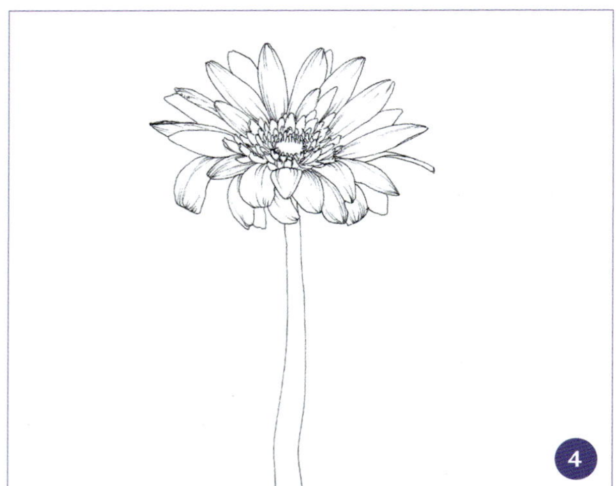

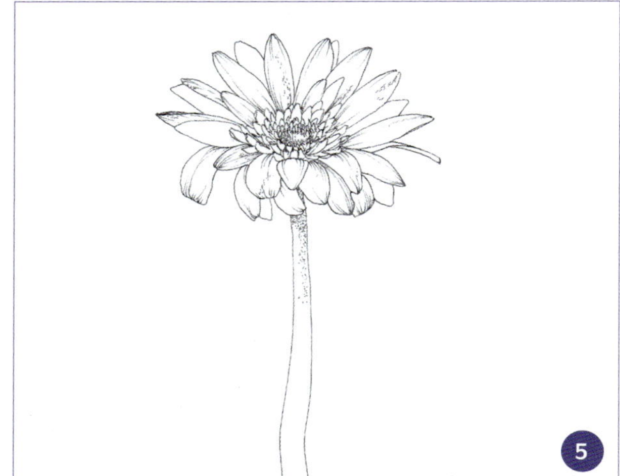

Step 2: Draw the small inner petals from the smallest oval out to the middle oval using your size 005 fineliner. Closest to the center, keep the petals small and build them up in size as you go outward. Think of the small petals as half ovals and remember that you can only see the whole petal on the ones closest to the center. The rest are tucked behind. This flower is tilted a bit so some of the petals are foreshortened (see "Sketching Flowers" on page 23 for tips on this).

Step 3: When you are happy with the small petals, it's time to work your way out to the big petals. Start with a few medium-sized petals and then just fill in the gaps with big overlapping petals. Have some in the front and some in the back. Make the petals in the back full, the ones on the sides longer and shallower and the ones in the front bend toward you, which makes them short and wide. Draw two loosely parallel lines for the stem. If you like, you are welcome to do this in pencil first. Regardless, gently erase the pencil lines when your fineliner petals and stem are complete.

Step 4: After you have drawn all the petals, it's time to shape them. Draw lines that shape the petals just like you've done before. Start from the back and work your way forward with your 005 fineliner. Leave some petals blank. Make sure that your lines follow the curve of the petal (especially when it's foreshortened in the front).

Step 5: Now, use your 005 fineliner to add small areas of lines and dots on the stem and some of the petals. This will give them texture and life.

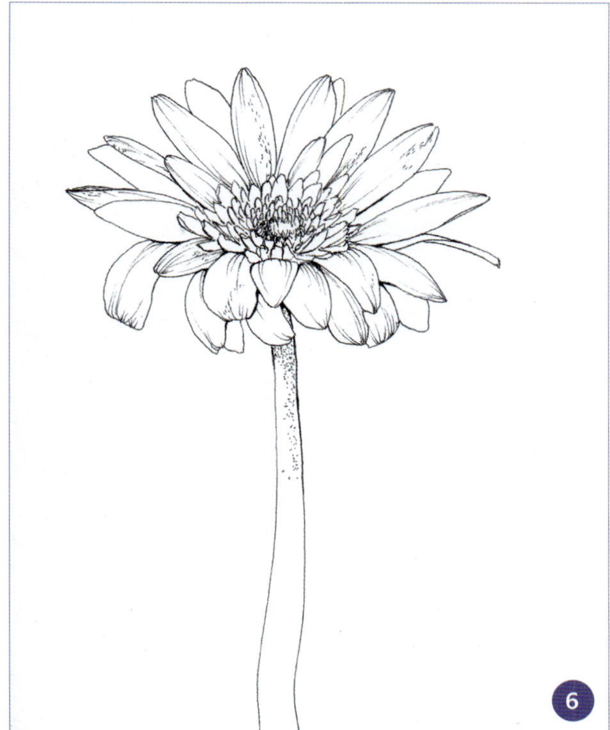

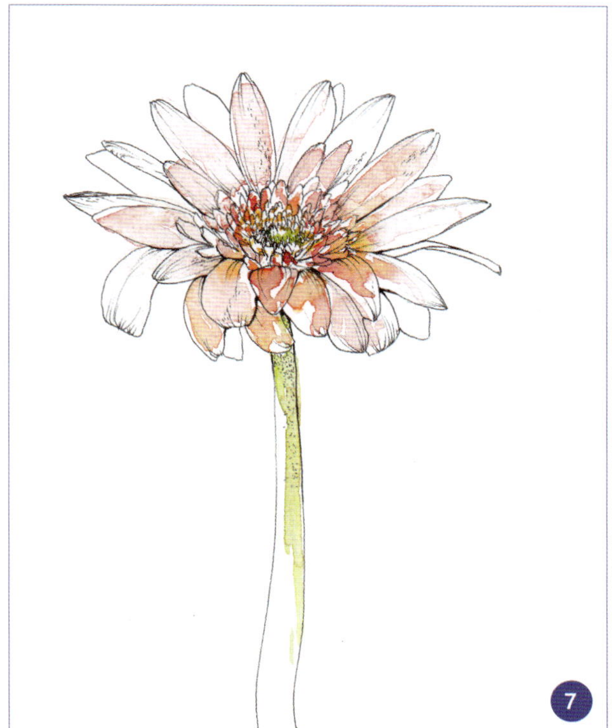

Step 6: This step is almost invisible, but as you know, the power is in the details. Add darker lines with the 02 fineliner to create even more dimension. Focus on the areas below the petals closest to the forefront, as this will make them pop.

Step 7: Now you can finally add the magical pop of color. Start in the center with the green gold. Add it in small dots, wet-on-dry, using a small brush (I used size 4). Quickly load your brush with new gamboge and dab that in as well to let the two colors dance together.

While it's still wet, load your brush with a mix of quinacridone rose and new gamboge. Start painting the smallest petals first and work your way outward. As you get closer to the biggest petals, you can use less paint and more water. Keep working wet-on-dry, or add extra pure paint to the wet areas to boost the colors even more. Leave a few petals without paint. Finally, paint the stem wet-on-dry using the green gold. Let a bit of the color from the stem flow into the petals to create a slight shadow.

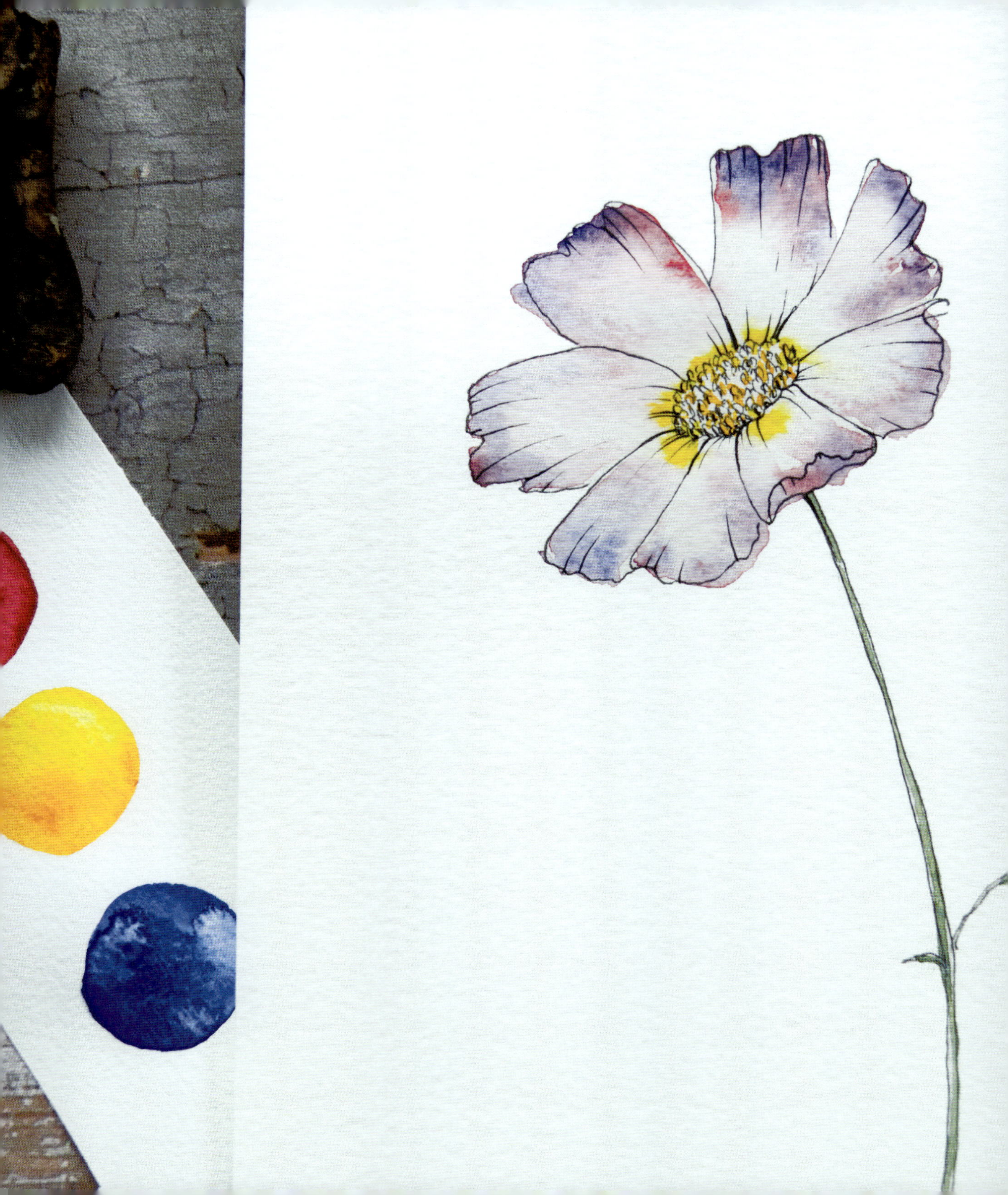

cosmo

the flower of harmony

The cosmo is one of my favorite flowers of the summer. The big, bright blooms just shine through all the greens and demand attention. I can't wait for you to sketch this beauty. After you finish this project, you'll be able to mix a beautiful vivid violet hue, make a clear focal point and sketch a breathtaking flower—pretty impressive, I'd say.

Materials

Pencil and eraser

Paper: Canson Montval 300gsm (140lb) cold press

Fineliners: sizes 01 and 02

Watercolor brush: size 6

Water and cloth

Palette

Colors

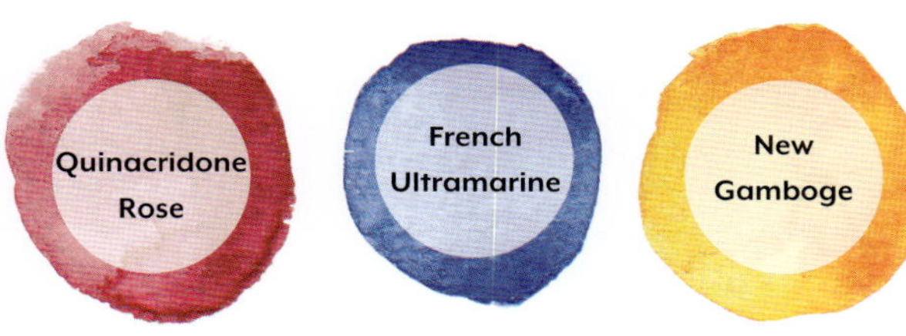

Mixes

To get the beautiful violet, I mixed the quinacridone rose and the French ultramarine in equal parts.

To get a green that looks cohesive with the other colors, I decided to mix that as well, using new gamboge and the French ultramarine in equal parts.

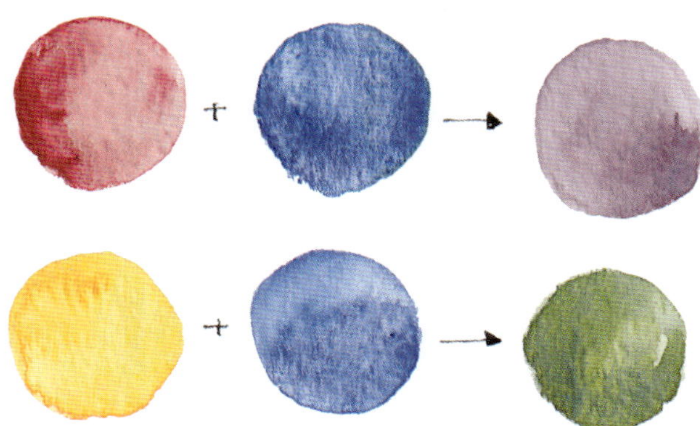

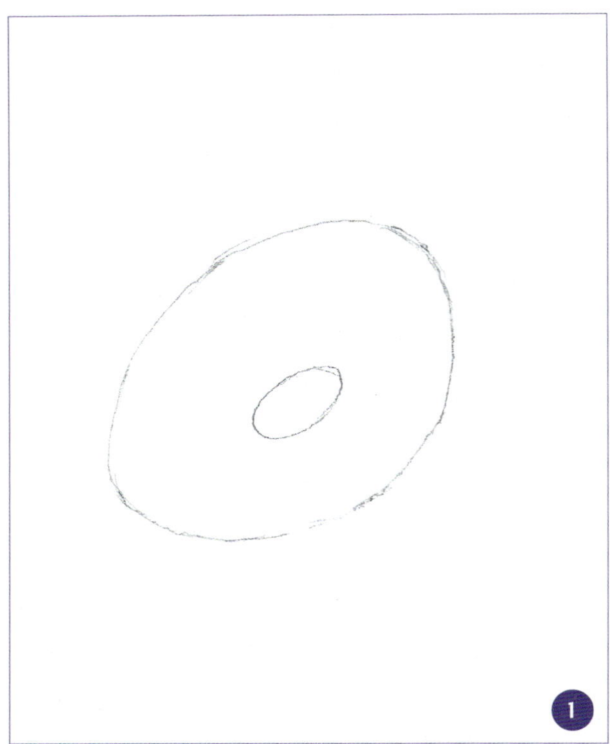

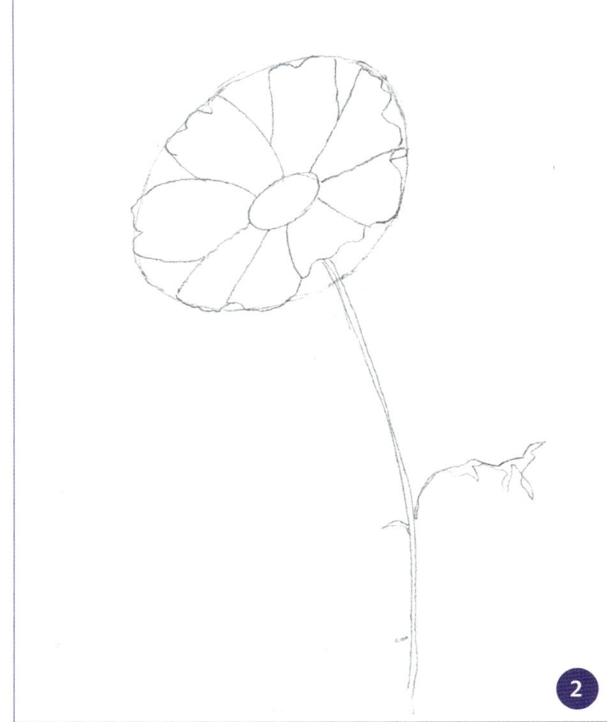

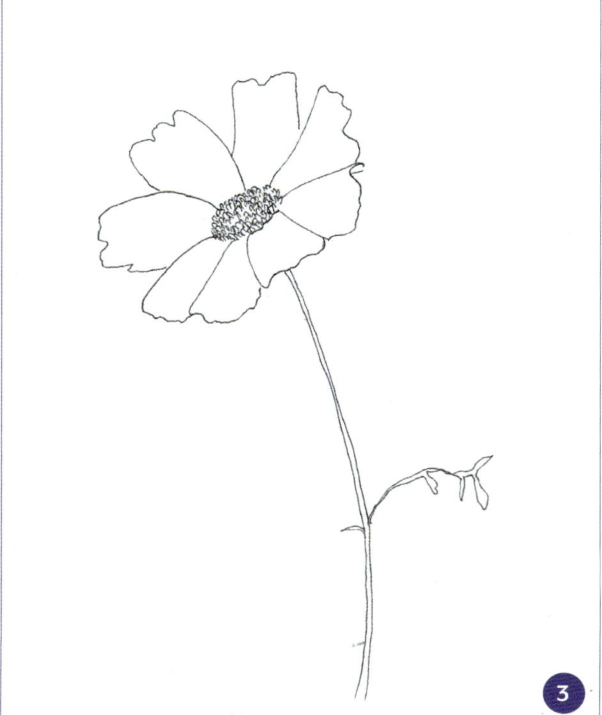

Step 1: We start by sketching the guidelines for the flower head. Draw two ovals in pencil. Let the inner oval be around 0.4 inches (1 cm) and the outer oval be around 2 inches (5 cm). Let them tilt a bit to the side and draw the outer oval so the top line is farther away from the center than the bottom line.

Step 2: Now you can sketch the flower with pencil (see "How to Sketch Flowers" on page 22). This cosmo has eight petals and one long, curving stem with a small branch protruding from it, at approximately the halfway point. The petals in the back are fully visible and overlapping each other and, as they get closer to the viewer, they get foreshortened. There are even some beautiful bends in the edge of some petals, creating life and movement.

Step 3: Take your 01 fineliner and start in the center to add a few doodles. These can be small ovals or cone shapes. Just make sure they are not perfect but more on the sketchy side. You don't need to draw every detail to show that it's the center of the flower. Then, get started on roughly outlining the petals, working from the center out. When you are loving your lines, you can remove the pencil with your eraser.

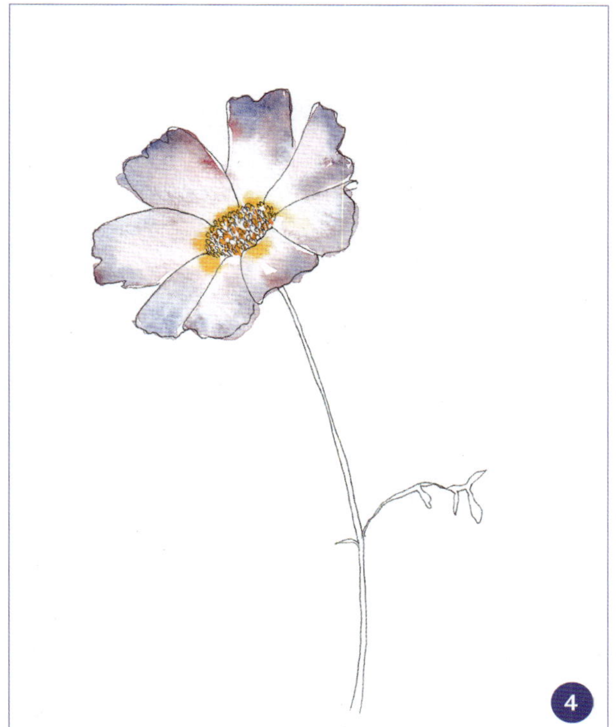

Step 4: When you are done drawing all the petals, it's time to find your paint and choose your colors. Use a scrap piece of paper to test your colors and make sure they are wet and ready to go. Wet one petal at a time with your size 6 brush and drip in the color (here, I used the violet mix). Let it flow freely to create its own texture. Repeat this step with all the petals. And don't worry if they run into each other, because that will be just as beautiful. While the petals are still wet, you can grab a bit of new gamboge. Add it very carefully wet-on-dry to the center, leaving lots of white space. Let the yellow paint kiss the wet petals in a few places to mix softly with the violet.

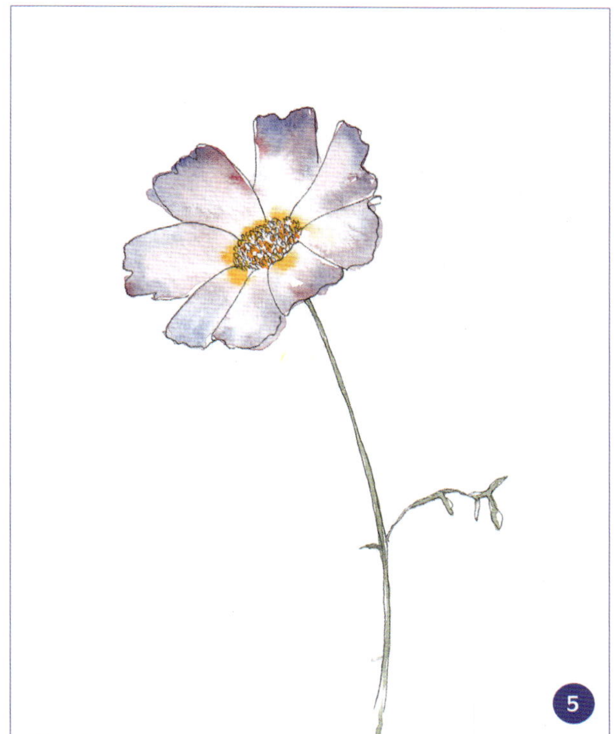

Step 5: Using the green mix, give the stem a bit of color too, but don't be too precious about it. After all, we want people to look at the flower, not the stem. Now you can wait for the cosmo to dry.

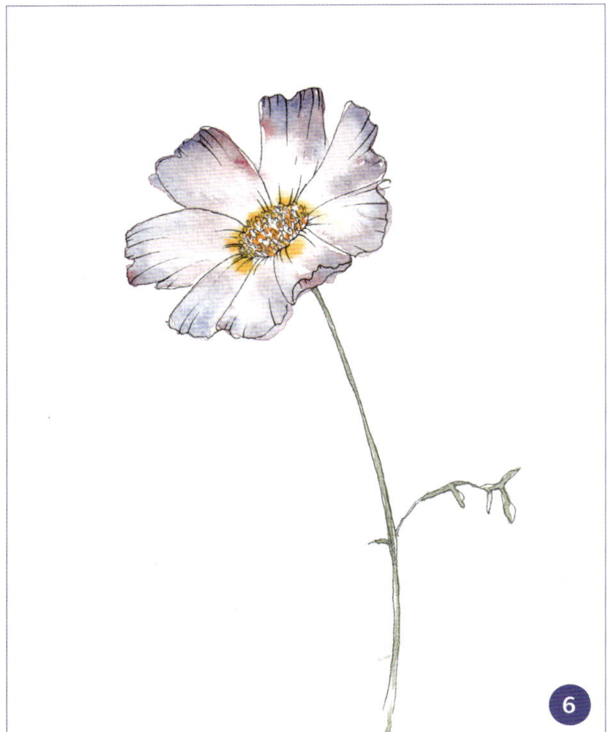

Step 6: Add detail lines with your 01 fineliner. Start from the outer edge of the petal and work your way in. Press harder with your fineliner when you start the line and slowly lift it while you move it across the petal. If it's hard to do the lines, see the section "Line Variation" (page 19).

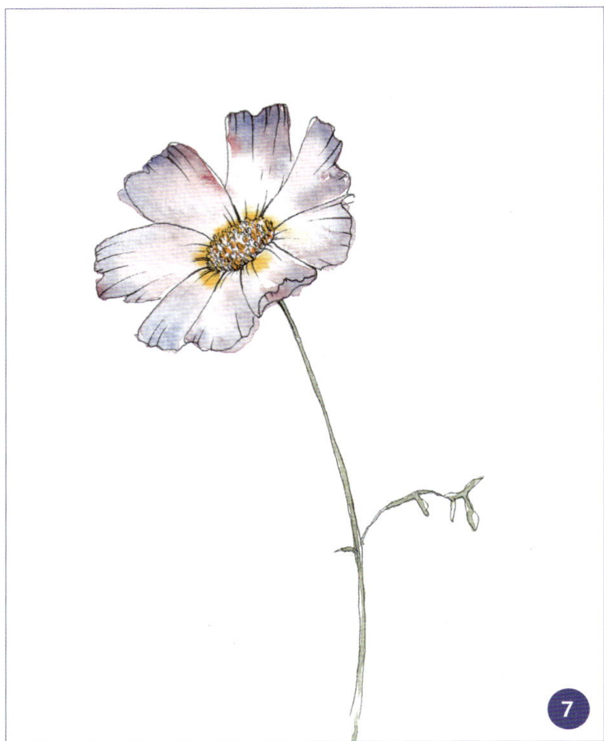

Step 7: Strengthen the lines with an 02 fineliner where the petals overlap to give them an even stronger definition.

Celebrate! You just sketched the most beautiful flower of harmony. Now you deserve a cup of tea while you upload your creation to Instagram and wait for the likes to fly your way.

tulip

the flower of perfect and deep love

I don't know about you, but I absolutely adore tulips. The bright colors make them so cheerful, and as they grow and reach for sunlight, they almost look like graceful ballerinas. In this tulip, you are going to try something new—well, new at least if this is the first time you are trying to layer watercolor. I have heard quite a few people say that they are scared of layering because they risk overworking the piece, and to be honest, that threat is real. But if you use it thoughtfully and do it with a plan in mind, it is THE key element to creating beautiful and vibrant colors.

Materials

Pencil and eraser

Paper: Canson Montval 300gsm (140lb) cold press

Fineliners: sizes 005, 01 and 02

Watercolor brushes: sizes 4 and 7

Water and cloth

Palette

Colors

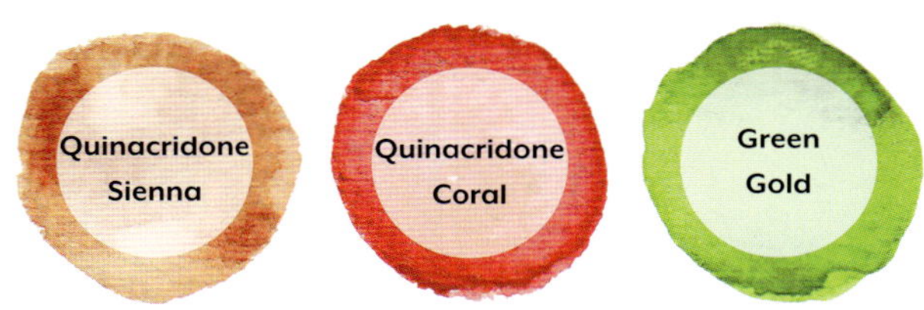

Mixes

To get the shadow color, I mixed quinacridone sienna and coral. If you want it cooler, just add more of the coral. To warm it up, just add more sienna to the mix.

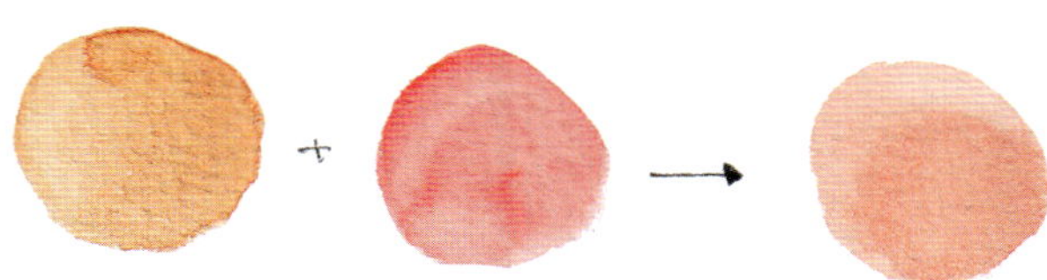

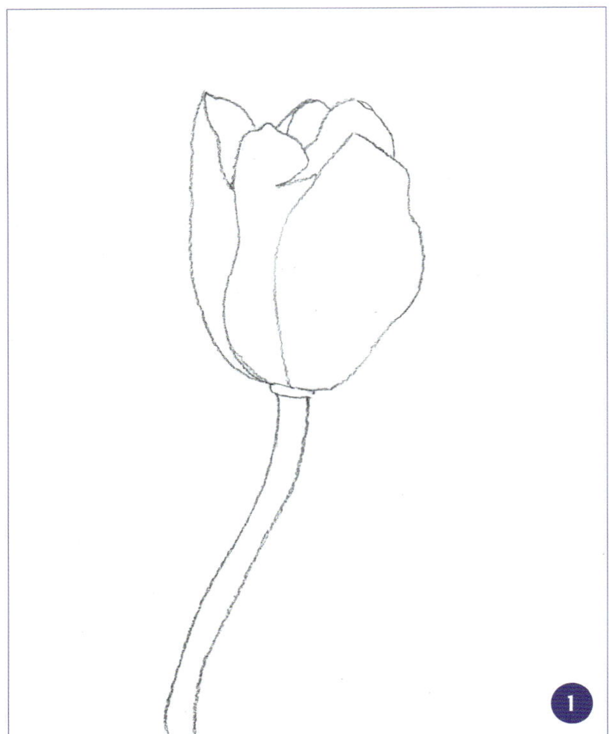

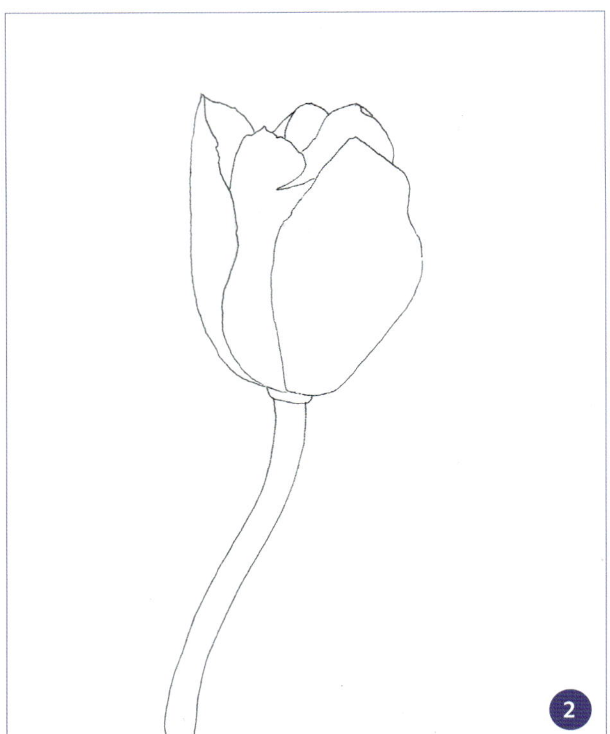

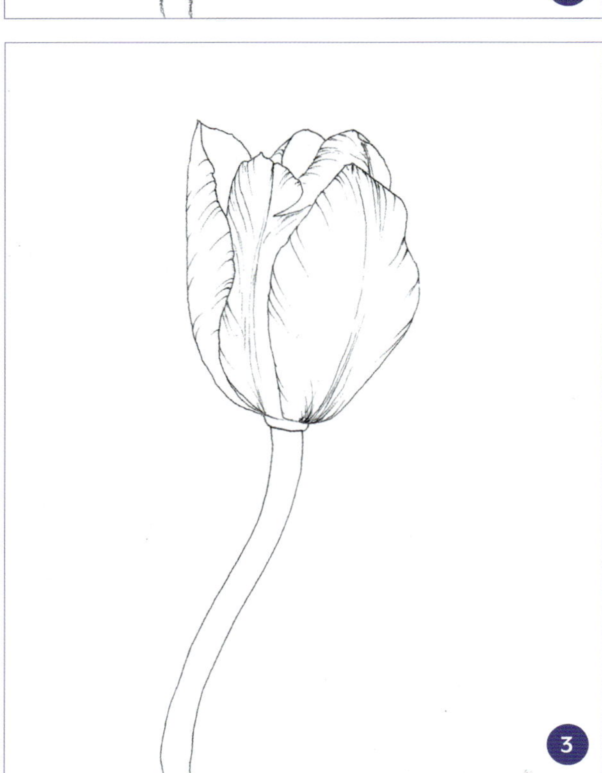

Step 1: The tulip has a very iconic shape with its tall, lean petals hugging each other almost like a group of close friends. Grab your pencil and start by drawing the biggest petal closest to you. Then, add the other outer petal. Now you have the basic shape of the tulip and you can draw the inner petals so that they fit the outer shapes. Also add a few bending lines to show a stem.

Step 2: Use your 01 fineliner and create a rough outline. Don't worry about this line being imperfect, because that just adds to the charm. After you make your outline, you can erase the pencil line.

Step 3: Now it's time to practice your linework. Grab your 005 fineliner and start drawing the beautiful texture on the petals. Start from the outer edge of the petal and draw a line that curves in the direction of the petal. Be random about placing the lines closer or farther apart and remember that less is more. The tulip has a vein in the middle of the petal and you can hint that as well by drawing a longer curved line in the middle of the petal. Add more lines to the petals in the front to make them stand out.

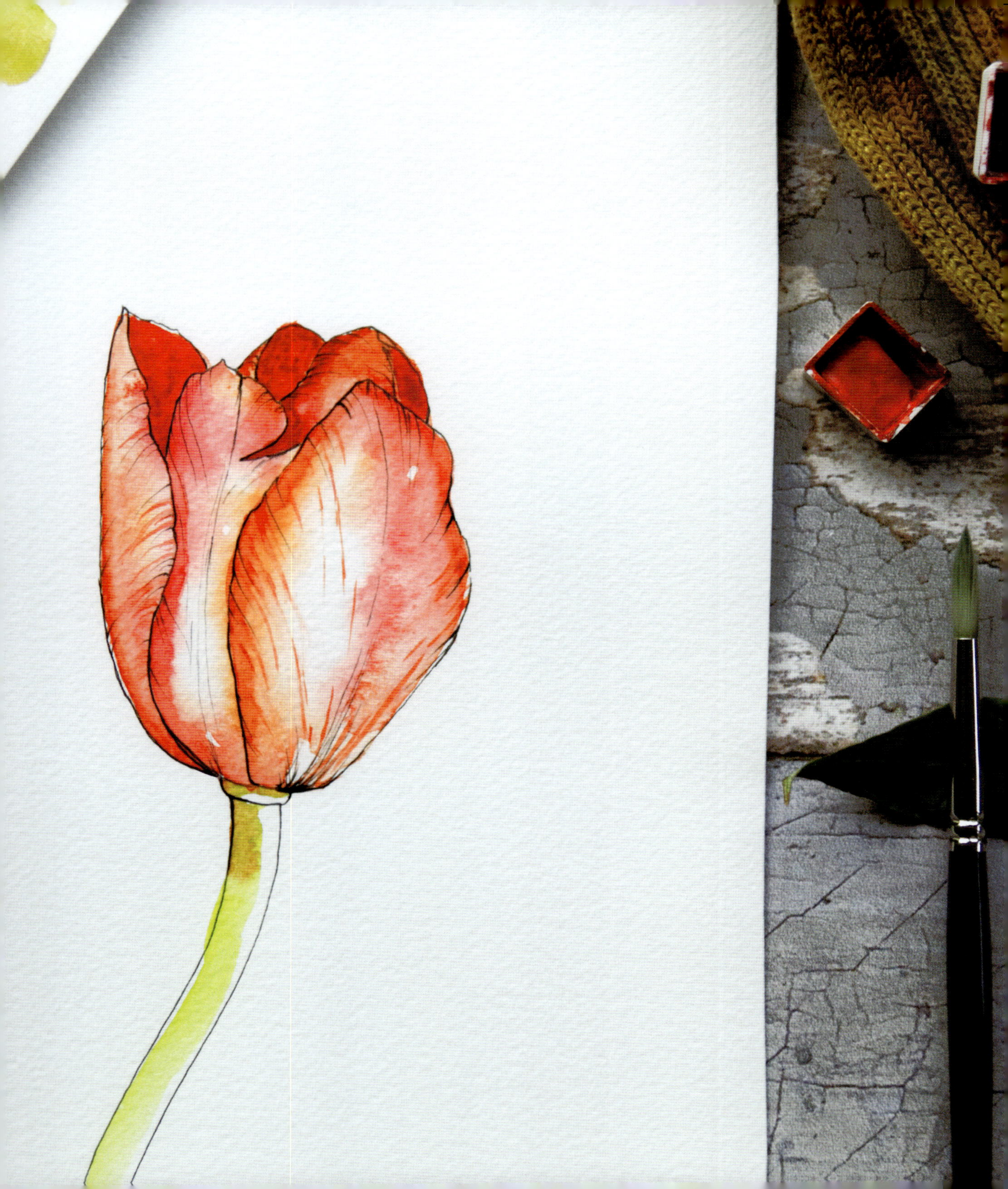

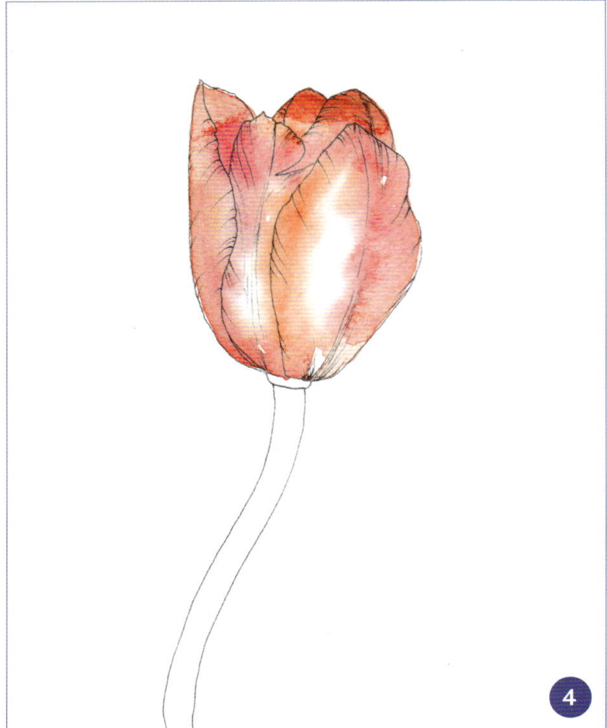

Step 4: Your flower is now ready for the first wash. Wet the entire flower head with your bigger brush (I use size 7) and add color to the wet area. On the petals, drip in pure quinacridone sienna and quinacridone coral and make sure to leave white space (see page 22 for more on white space).

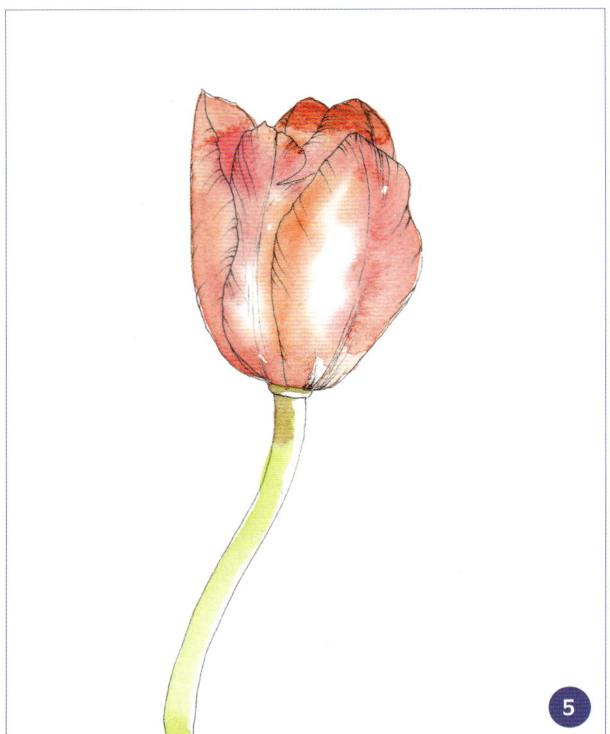

Step 5: After the flower head is dry, you can paint the stem in a beautiful green. I used a green gold to get a yellow tone. While it is still wet, you can drip in a bit of coral at the top of the stem to create a small shadow. Just be careful—green and red are complementary colors, so too much mixing will muddy them up. Put the drawing away for a while to let it dry.

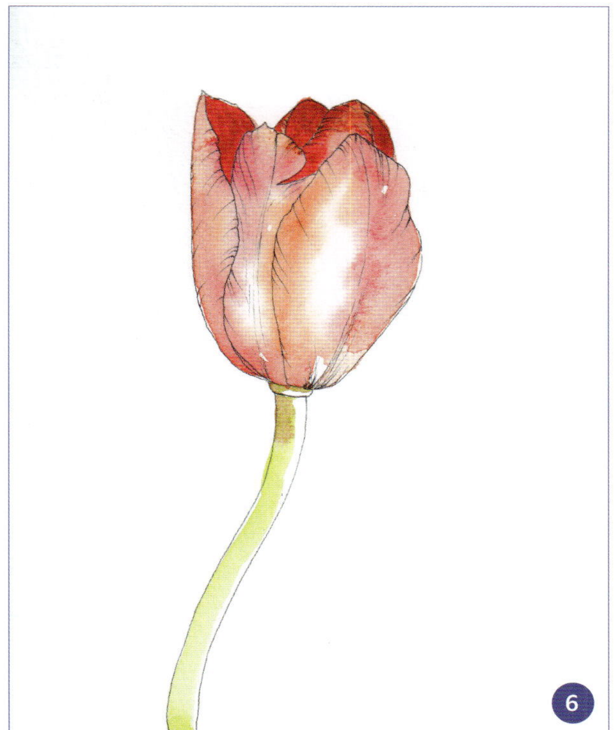

Step 6: When it's dry, you can get some dimension in your flower by adding another layer of color. Yay! Layers! Mix a combo of quinacridone sienna and quinacridone coral with more coral so it's on the cooler side. Paint the petals in the back wet-on-dry with a smaller brush (I use a size 4). This shows the shadows on the inside of the tulip.

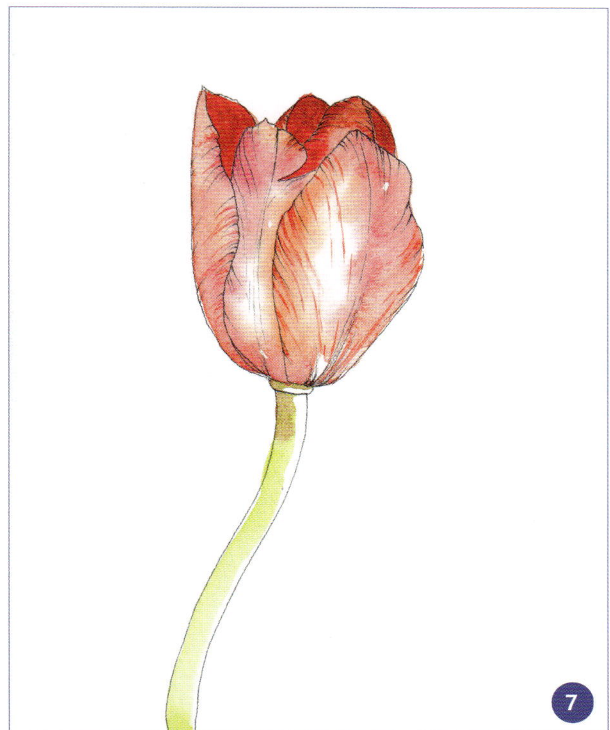

Step 7: While waiting for the shadows to dry, you can add texture lines to the two front petals. Use the smaller brush for this and work only with the tip. Use a mix of the quinacridone sienna and quinacridone coral with a little water. Here, you can just be loose with the mixes by either using pure paint, a mix of quinacridone sienna and quinacridone coral or both—you decide. Vary the placement and length of the lines—just make sure they follow the curve of the petals.

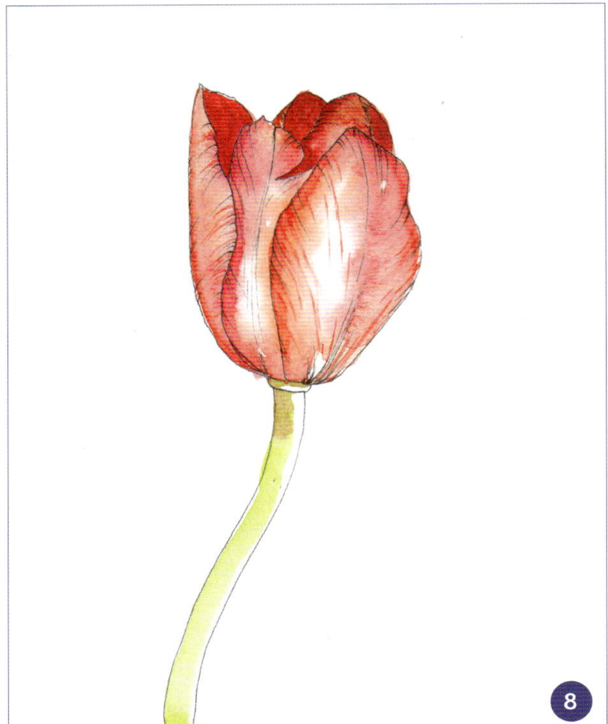

Step 8: When that has dried, you can add shadows to the front petals as well. Paint the shadows under the overlapping petals as well as on the edge of the curved petals. Add a bit of paint to the edge and carefully feather it out (see page 25 for this technique).

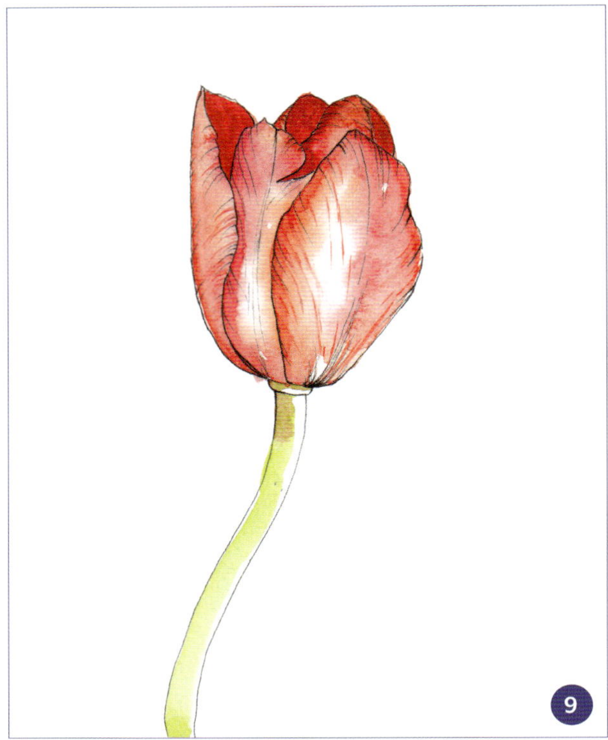

Step 9: Now, we are ready for the final touch, which is creating some line variation. So, grab your 02 fineliner and make a few of the lines thicker. Use it sparingly and just to add a bit of interest to the lines on the front petals. This will make them stand out even more.

Well done! Besides sketching a beautiful tulip, you just worked several layers, added a ton of thin lines and even did shadows using feathering. That is pretty darn good—congrats!

anemone

the wind's daughter

Anemones are an extremely beautiful, understated flower with a ton of meanings. In different cultures, they symbolize protection against evil, forgotten love, anticipation and even remembrance. In Greek, *anemone* translates into "the wind's daughter," and to me, that says it all. It's exactly how I look at this graceful flower, and it's exactly what I thought about when making this step-by-step tutorial for you. So we are taking a closer look at this beauty while learning a bit more about creating harder shadows in watercolor.

Materials

Pencil and eraser

Paper: Canson Montval 300gsm (140lb) cold press

Fineliners: sizes 005, 01 and 02

Watercolor brushes: sizes 4 and 8

Water and cloth

Palette

Colors

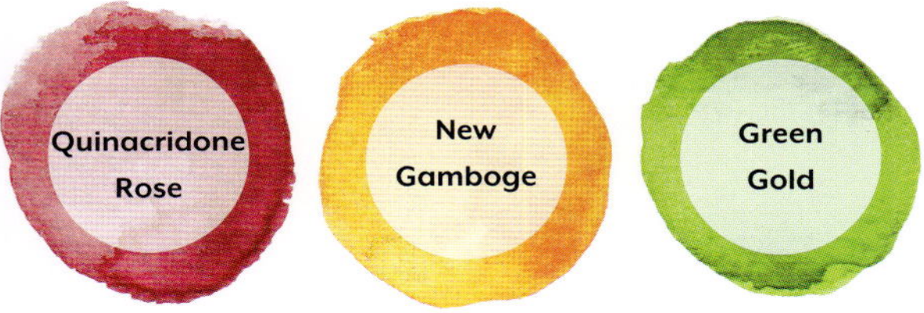

Mixes

The shadows are painted in a watery mix of quinacridone rose and a bit of green gold.

The stem is painted with the same mix, but with more of the green gold and less water.

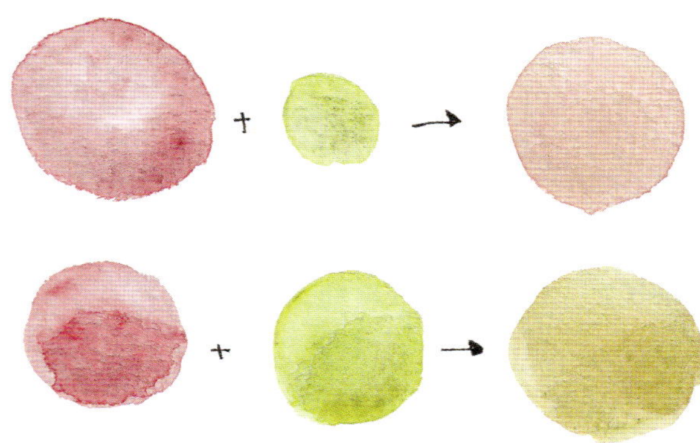

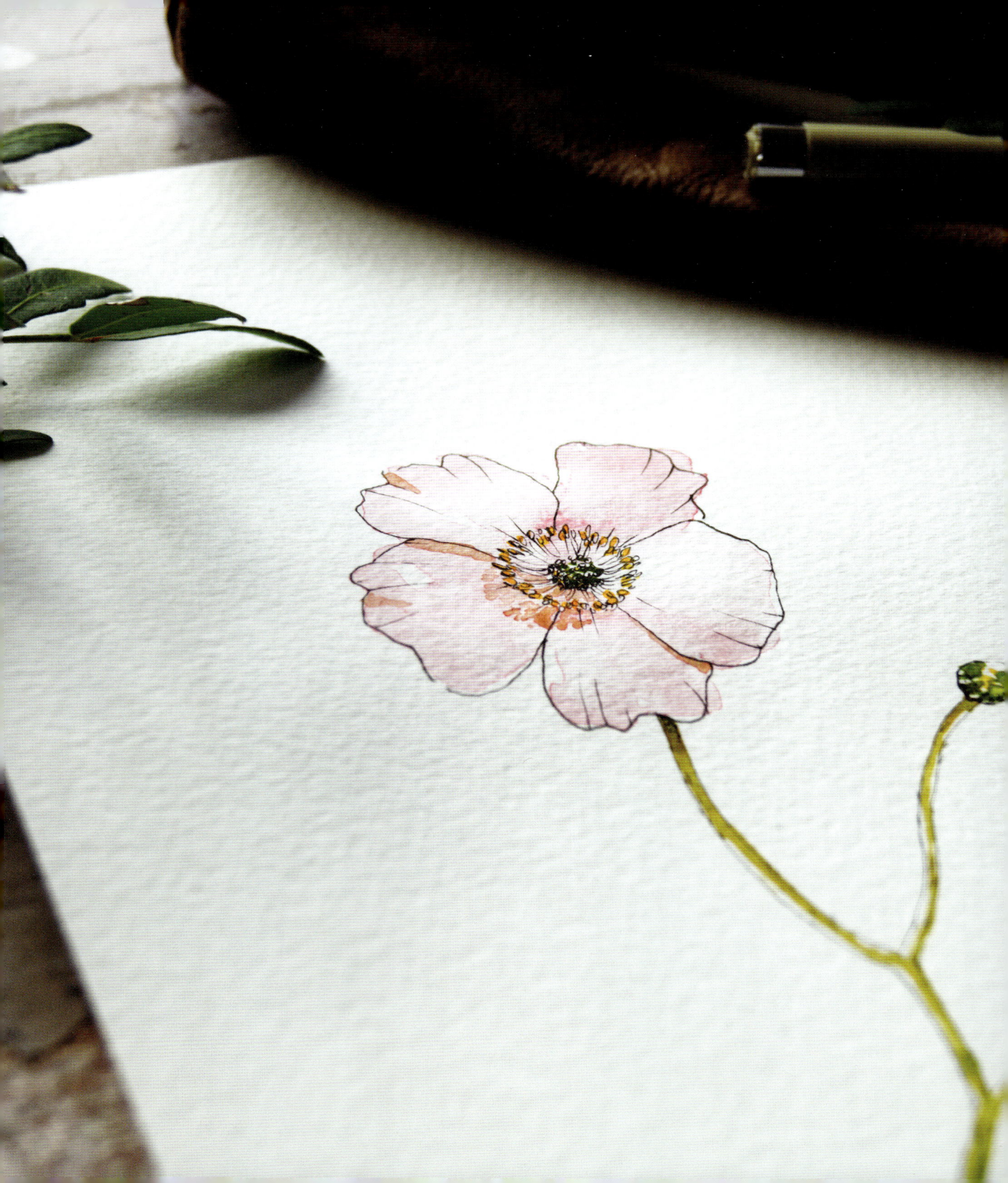

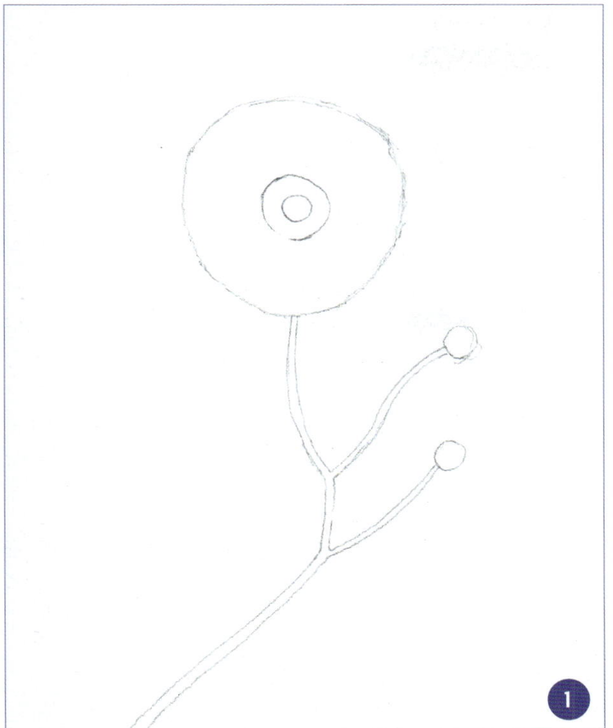

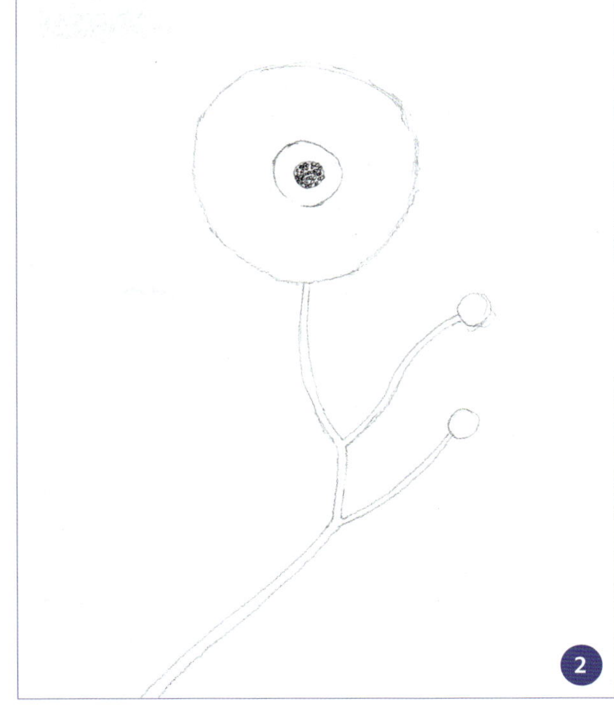

Step 1: Let's begin with our all-time good friend, the pencil, to draw a guide. Start out with your main flower, which is three circles inside of each other. The two inner circles are close to each other and the outer circle is pretty far away, showing the length of the petals. Then, draw two smaller circles to the side below the flower head and connect everything with a stem. Try to give your stem an organic feel. By giving it a few twists and bends, you turn it into the wind's daughter in the middle of a dance.

Step 2: Take your 005 fineliner and fill up your inner circle with tiny circles.

Step 3: Draw small ovals around the second circle. The ones in the back are long ovals, and the ones in the front are small, foreshortened ovals. Connect the ovals and the center with C-shaped lines.

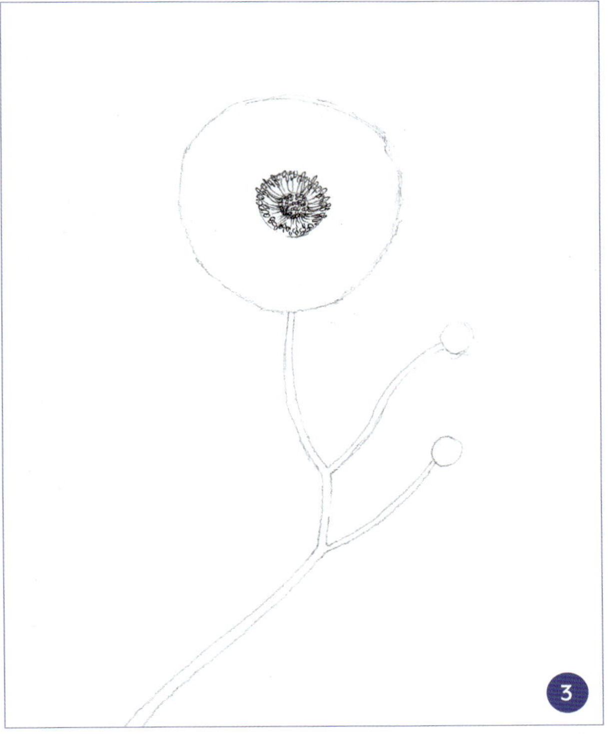

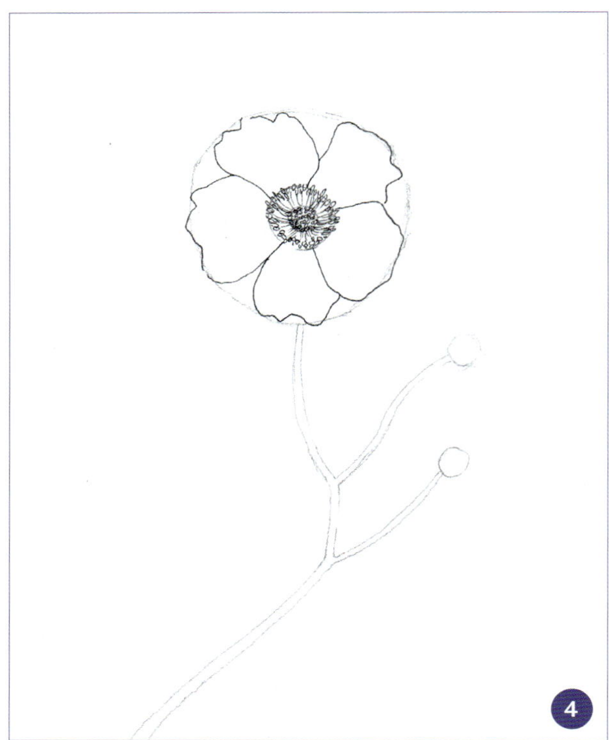

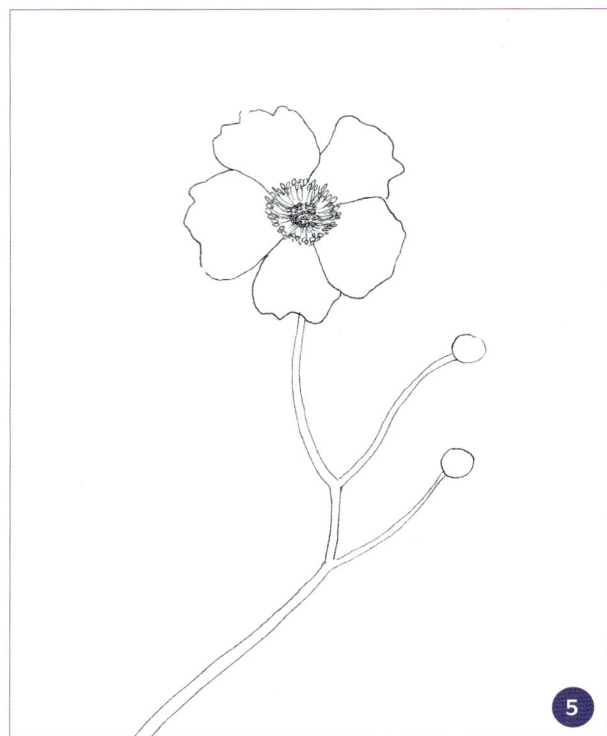

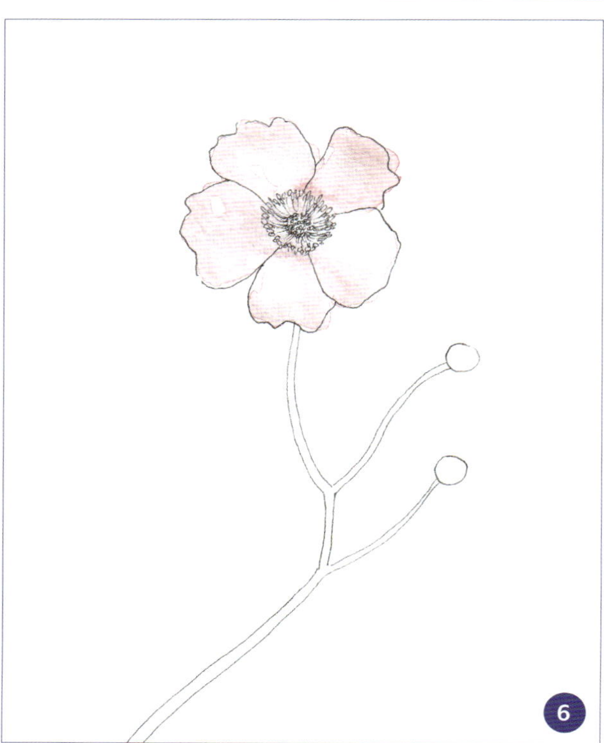

Step 4: Draw five petals with the 01 fineliner like I showed you on page 23. Let them overlap. Adjust the length if you feel your outer circle is too big or too small. You can also draw this in pencil first if that makes it easier to control.

Step 5: Draw the rest of the flower following the pencil lines. Carefully erase the pencil with an eraser. After all, we don't want to disturb the already beautiful dance by ruining the paper.

Step 6: Now, it's time for some color. So, wet the petals and using your size 8 brush, paint them wet-on-wet with a very watery quinacridone rose. To make sure your paint is light enough, drip the pure paint in a palette and add water to that. Then, test the color on a scrap piece of paper before painting your anemone. When you've painted the petals, put your drawing away for a little while; go for a walk or do a dance while you wait for it to dry.

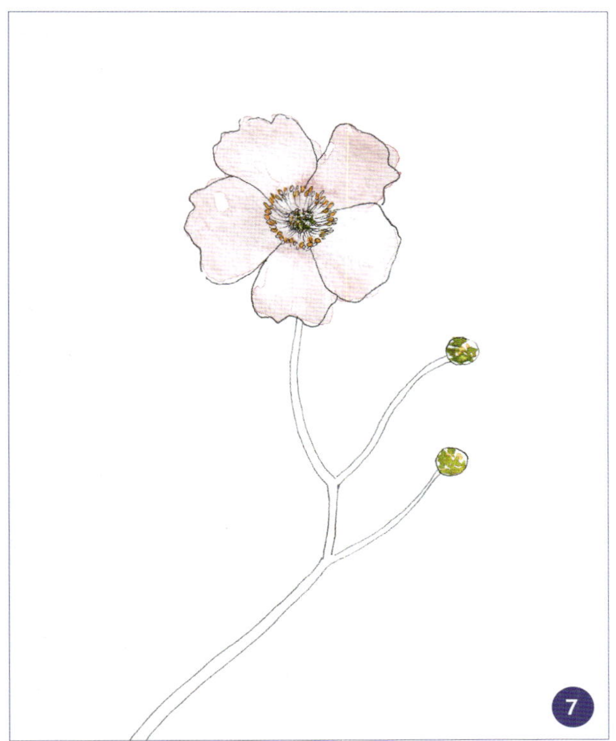

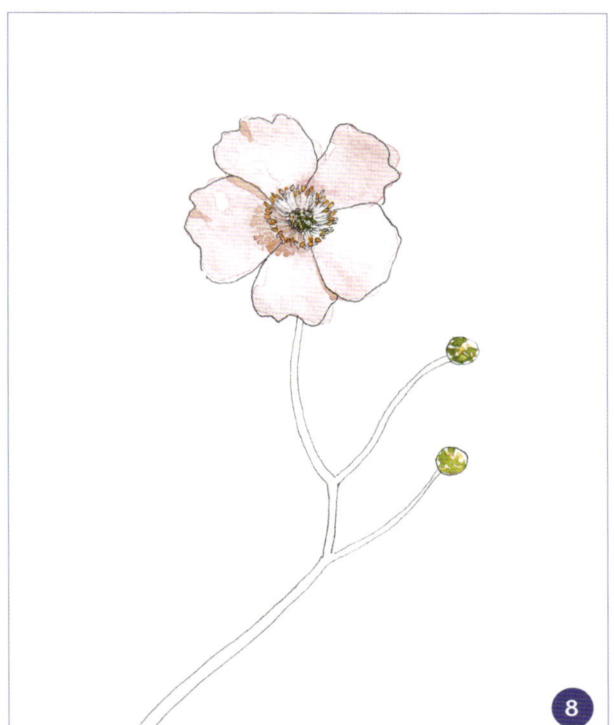

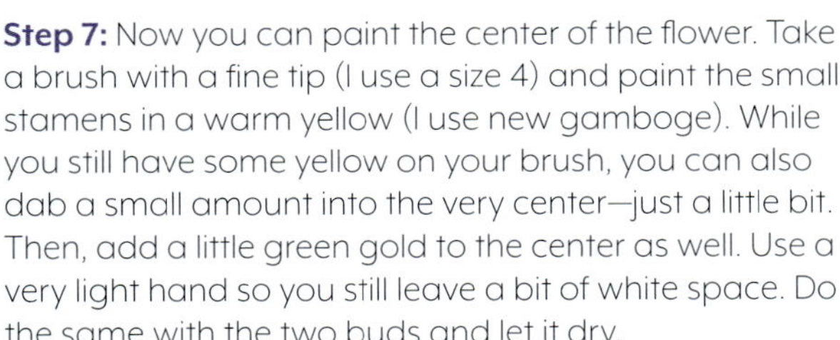

Step 7: Now you can paint the center of the flower. Take a brush with a fine tip (I use a size 4) and paint the small stamens in a warm yellow (I use new gamboge). While you still have some yellow on your brush, you can also dab a small amount into the very center—just a little bit. Then, add a little green gold to the center as well. Use a very light hand so you still leave a bit of white space. Do the same with the two buds and let it dry.

Step 8: Are you ready for some hard shadows? Imagine this anemone has a big bright sun hanging above a little to the right. This will cause the stamens to cast a hard shadow and so will a few of the overlapping petals. Now mix a watery mix of quinacridone rose and a bit of green gold. Keep it very light and, with your thin brush, carefully paint the shadows. It's better to go too light than too dark, so use plenty of water.

Step 9: Now, you actually need a mix of green gold and quinacridone rose again, but with less water and more of the green. Because this time, we are painting the stem. Take your brush and use a few fast lines to get an uneven coloring. Remember we are not going for perfect, just beautiful. While it's still wet, you can drip in a bit of pure color to give it some more interest.

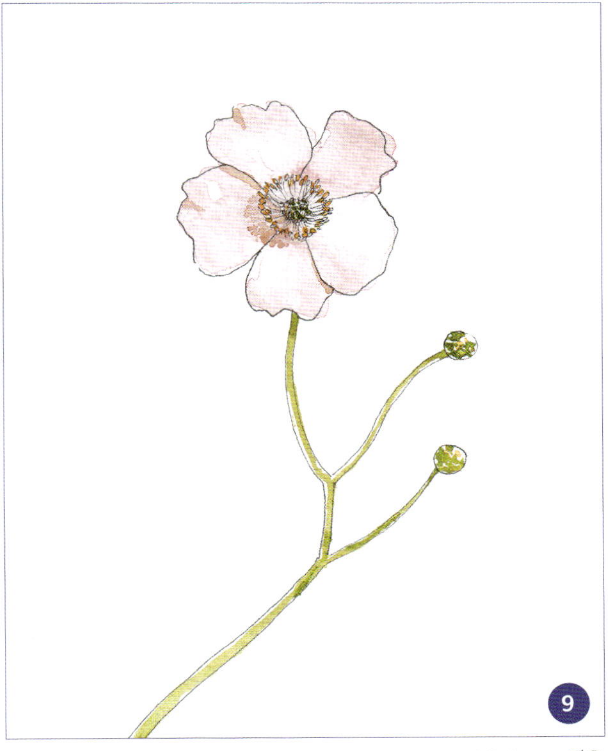

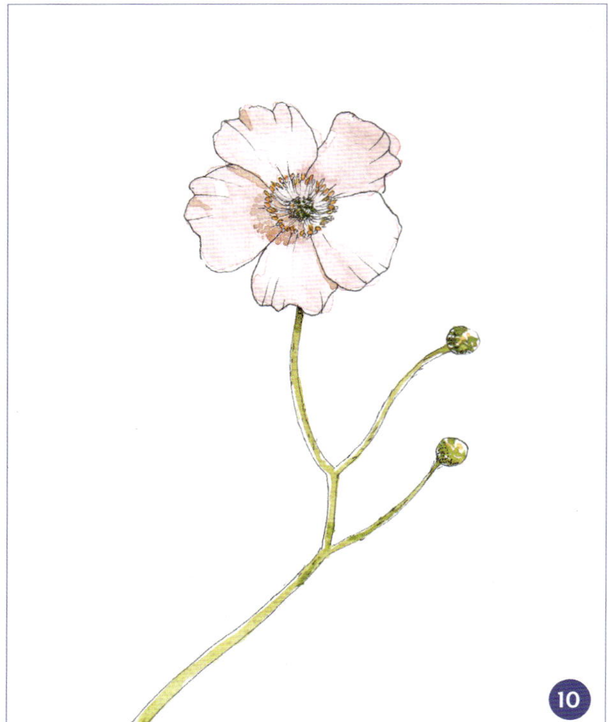

Step 10: When your greens are all dry, you can grab your 005 fineliner and add all the final details. All the petals really need is a few lines showing the curve, and the buds get a few dots where they meet the stem. This is also a great way to add to the feeling of shadow (see page 25 for stippling). Finally, you can give the stems a few random short lines for hairs.

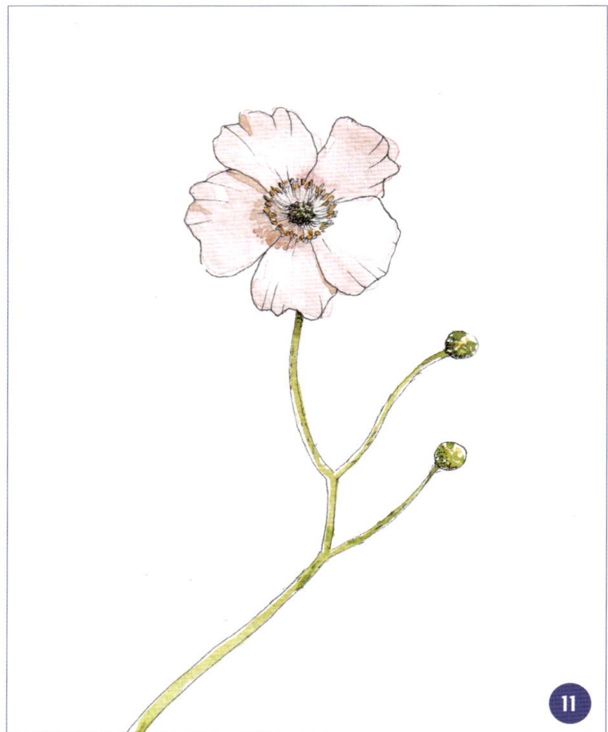

Step 11: Phew! This is the last step, so you are almost there. Just take your 02 fineliner and draw a dark line on the left side of the small oval stamens. This again gives a sense of shadow. If you feel like you need more definition of some lines, you can also go in there.

And wowza, you just painted the most graceful dancer! Well done!

magnolia

the flower of nobility and a love for nature

You have reached one of my favorite flowers of all time. When the magnolia blooms, it is the perfect sign of spring here in Denmark. The lifespan of the flowers is short but sweet, and all we can do is just enjoy the moment while it's there. The only way we can really deepen this experience is by capturing its essence in a drawing. Are you with me? The magnolia is all about spring and light, so in this step-by-step, I thought I'd introduce you to splatters. They are fast, fun and create the most wonderful vibrancy on the page. (And a small pro tip for you: Don't do this next to your husband's computer, because he won't like it.)

Materials

Pencil and eraser

Paper: Canson Montval 300gsm (140lb) cold press

Fineliners: sizes 01 and 005

Watercolor brushes: sizes 7 and 4

Water and cloth

Palette

Mixes

To get the color on the petals, I used the quinacridone rose with a tiny bit of French ultramarine. It gives the rose a blue tone, but you don't have to do this.

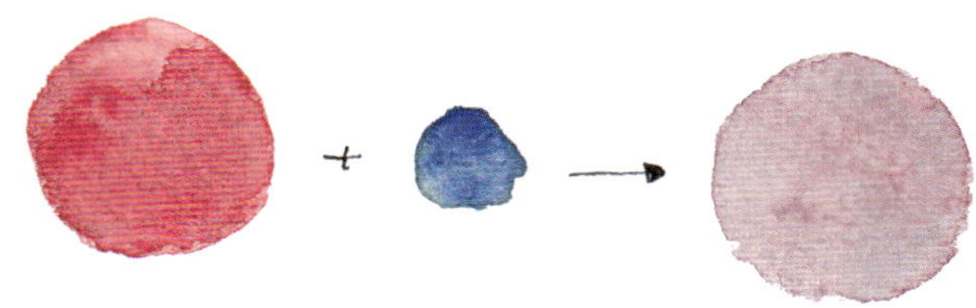

Colors

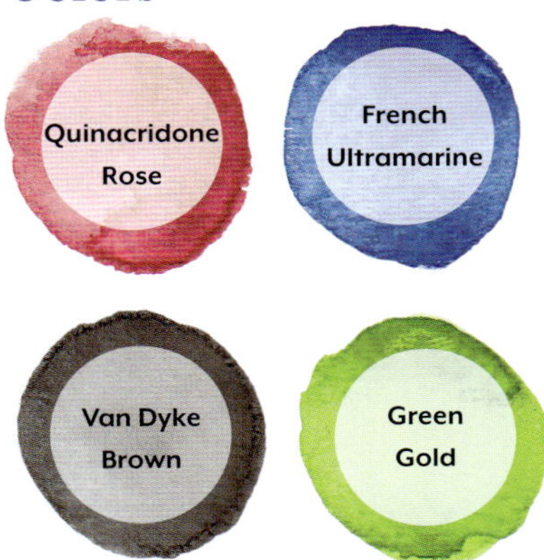

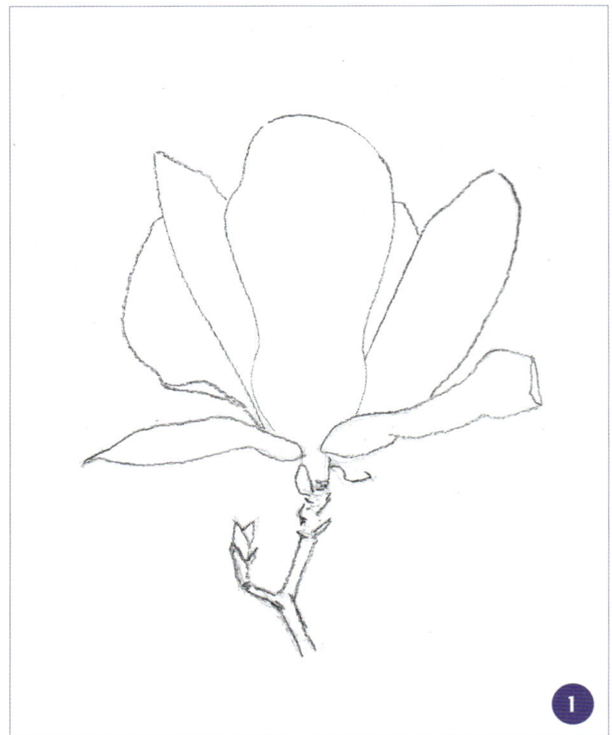

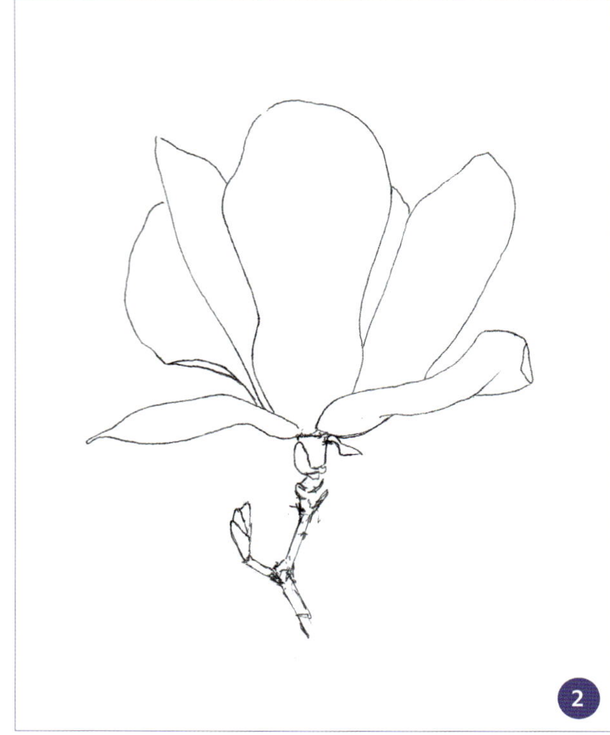

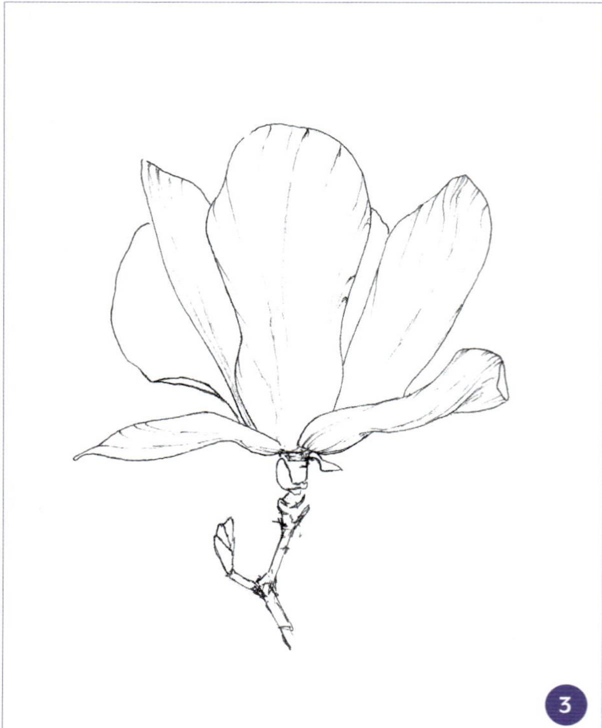

Step 1: Make a quick sketch in pencil. Start with the big petal in the middle, and then draw the narrow petals next to it. When you get those down on the paper, you can easily place the rest. Make sure to draw a branch with a small bud as well. The magnolia is actually a tree, so make your lines sturdier than you would with a flower stem.

Step 2: Do a quick outline using your 01 fineliner. Keep it especially rough and sketchy around the branch to get a wood effect with plenty of texture. Erase the pencil lines.

Step 3: You've done this so many times now, so if I say it's time for detail lines, you automatically grab your 005 fineliner, right? Shape your petals with it and show the direction of the curl.

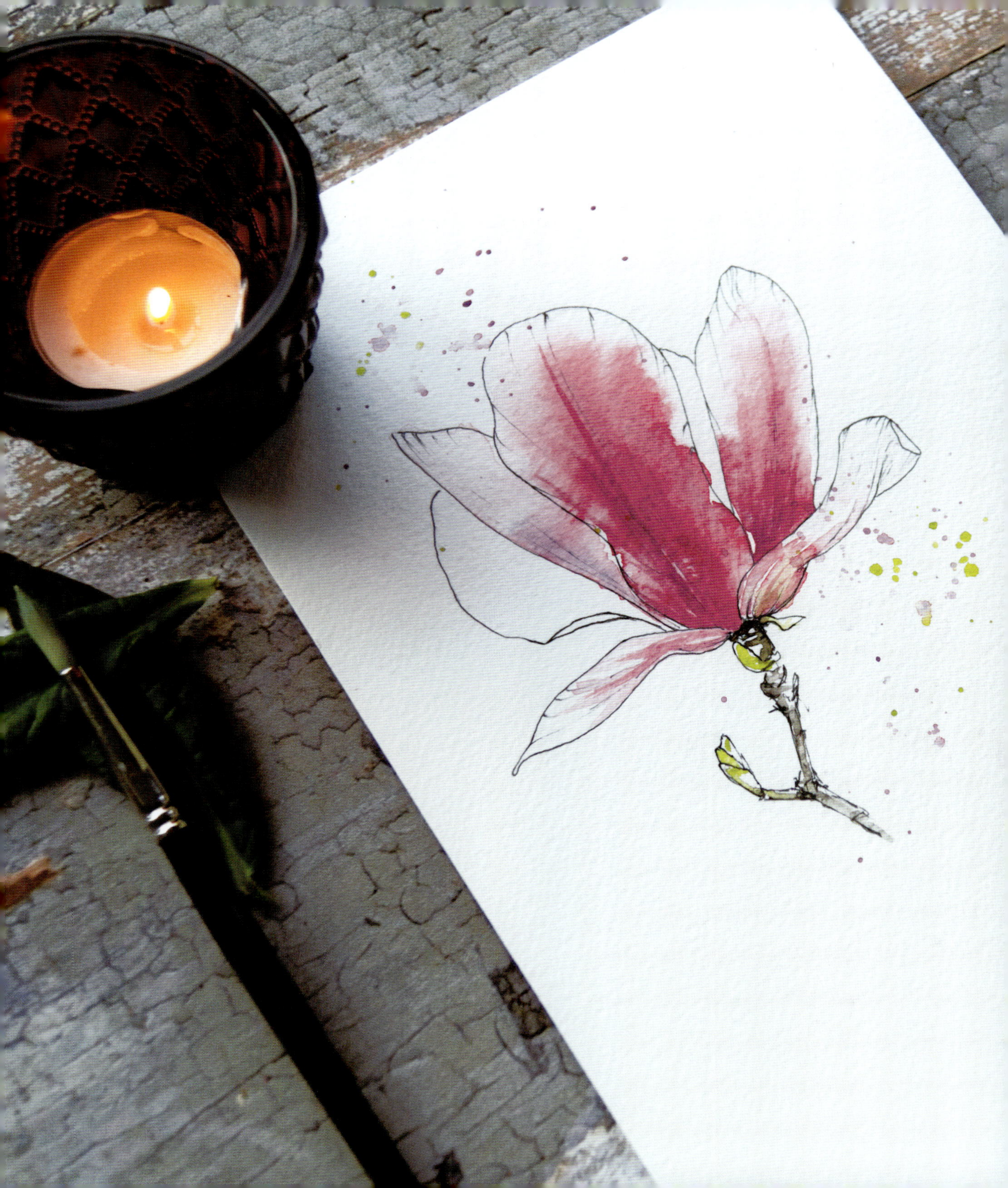

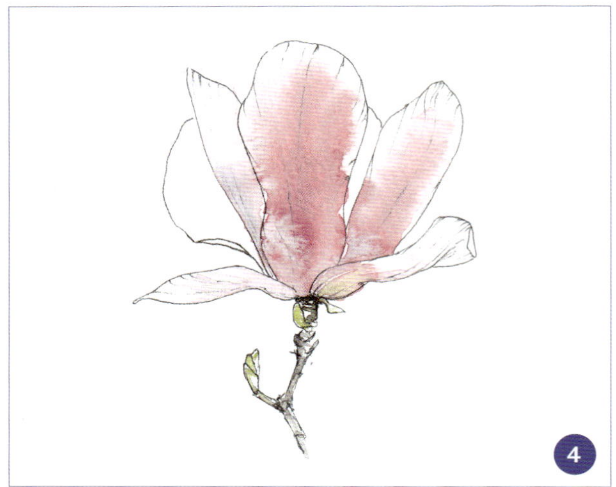

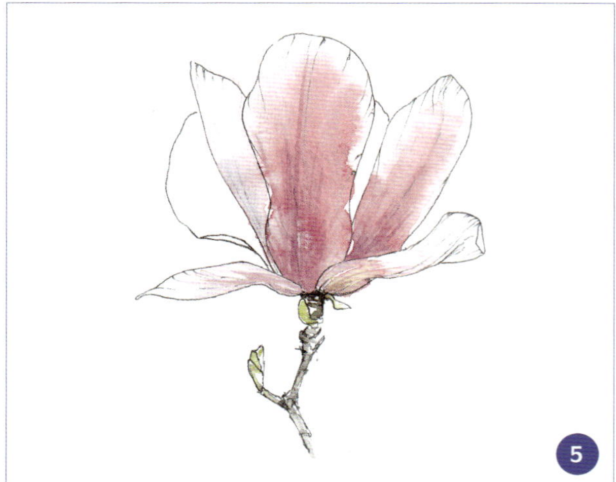

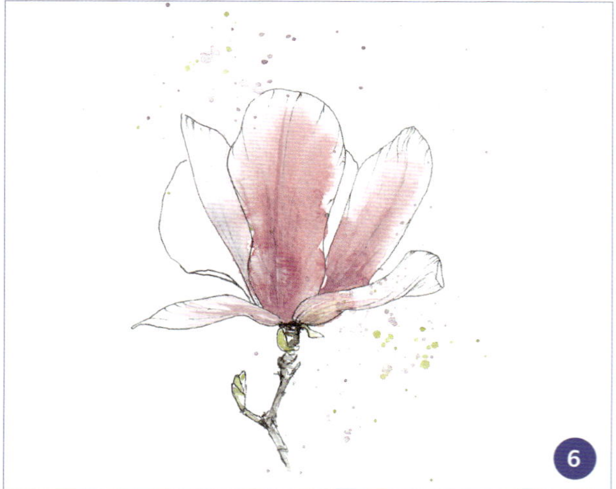

Step 4: Now you can get out your palette and mix a batch of quinacridone rose with a little French ultramarine. Wet the petals one at a time with a medium brush (I use size 7) and just drip in the mix. Try to keep the paint close to the bottom of the flower and not overdo it. It's very easy to go overboard and yes, I talk from experience. Use the wet-on-dry technique to paint the branch with your smaller brush (here I use size 4). Use Van Dyke brown on the branch and bit of green gold for the buds. If the green or brown bleeds into the rosy petals, don't worry—it will be beautiful, I promise. You are now free to take a well-deserved break while it dries.

Step 5: I hope you enjoyed your break and you are ready for some painted details. Grab your size 4 brush again and add a few detail lines to the petals with the same mix of colors, but with less water this time. Start from the center of the flower and paint following the curve of the petal. If the lines get too heavy or too sharp, then soften them with a bit of water.

Step 6: And now it's time for the thing we've all been waiting for: the cool paint splatters. So, remove your phone, your cat and your snacks, and then load your brush with a not-too-wet version of the quinacridone rose first. Then, hold your brush parallel to your paper and carefully tap it, either with your hand or another brush for a bit more control. Afterward, you can give it a few green splatters as well for contrast. If you've never done splatters before, try it a few times on a scrap piece of paper first.

sunflower

the flower of lasting happiness

I don't think anyone can look at a bright yellow sunflower and be moody. It's like looking at a cute puppy with a big smile—it just makes you happy. Period. In this project, I show you how to capture the beauty of the sunflower. I'm just throwing out a suggestion here, but maybe you could paint cards with sunflowers on them to gift your mom or mother-in-law? I mean, who wouldn't love a bit of lasting happiness?

Materials

Pencil and eraser

Paper: Canson Montval 300gsm (140lb) cold press

Fineliners: sizes 01, 005 and 02

Watercolor brush: size 7

Water and cloth

Palette

Colors

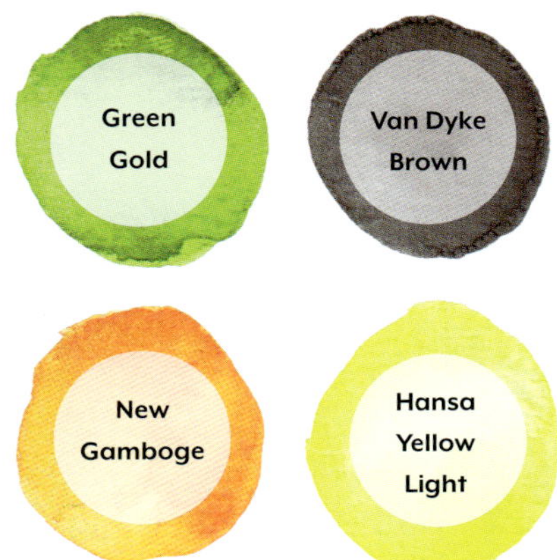

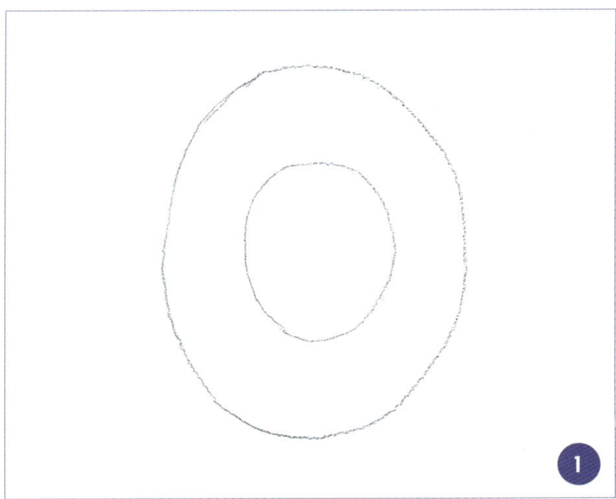

Step 1: Draw two pretty big ovals in pencil to use as your guide. Remember that the center of the sunflower is big compared to the other flowers we've drawn so far.

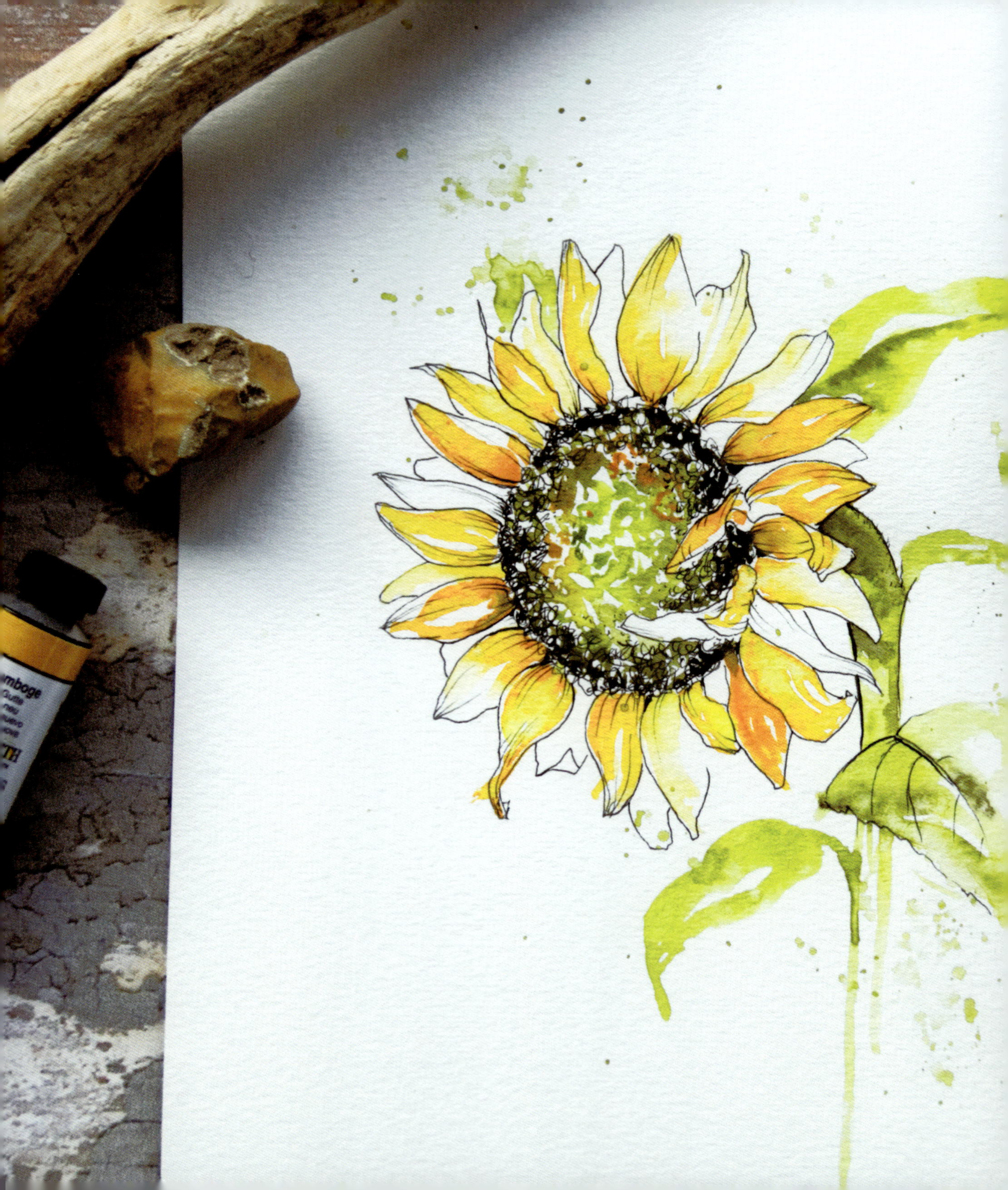

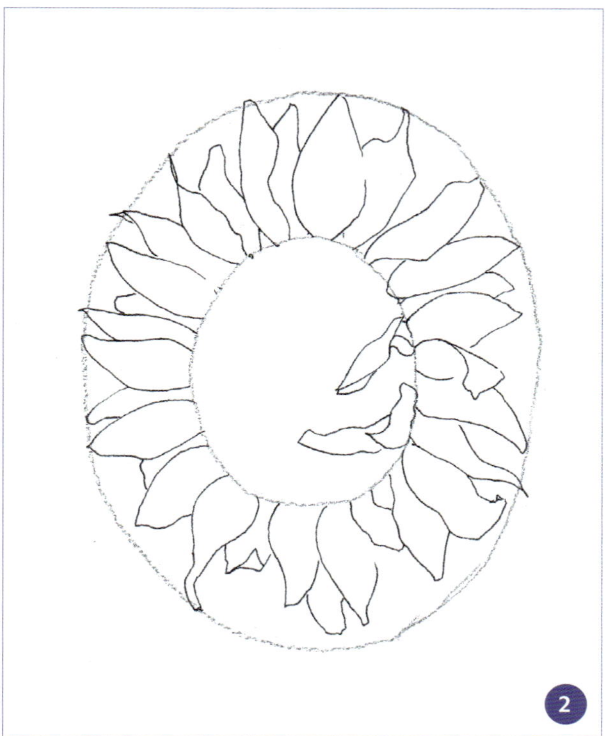

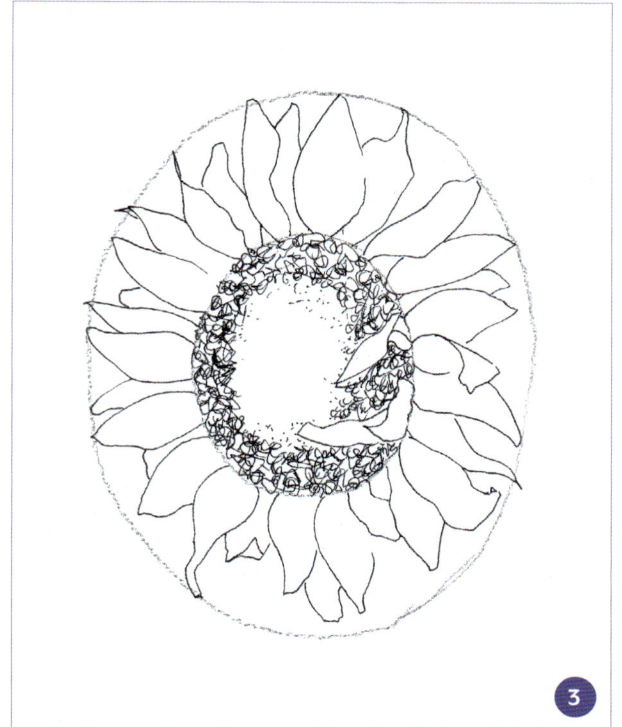

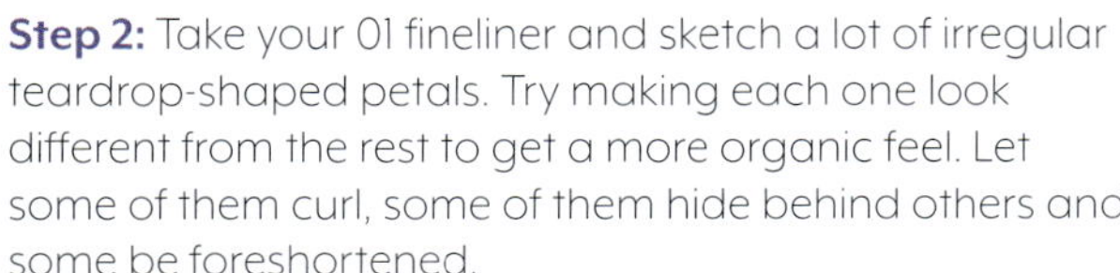

Step 2: Take your 01 fineliner and sketch a lot of irregular teardrop-shaped petals. Try making each one look different from the rest to get a more organic feel. Let some of them curl, some of them hide behind others and some be foreshortened.

Step 3: Doodle around the center to get some texture, but avoid going into the middle. Toward the middle, you can draw small dots to show that the texture has changed.

Step 4: After you gently erase the pencil lines, you are ready for some paint. So, load your brush (size 7) with green gold and, with the tip of the brush, lightly touch down on the center of the flower. Make small dots close to each other, leaving white space, and continue outward, mixing it with Van Dyke brown and a bit of new gamboge. At the edge against the petals, you can use a pure Van Dyke brown to get a nice deep shadow.

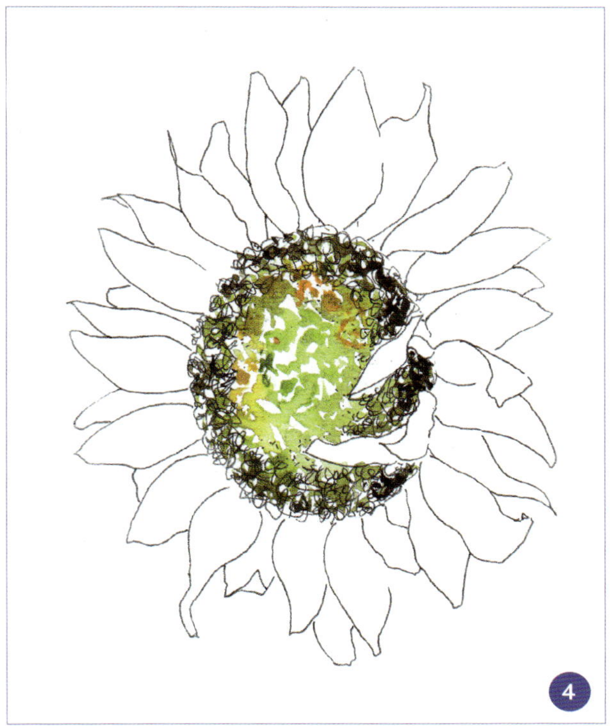

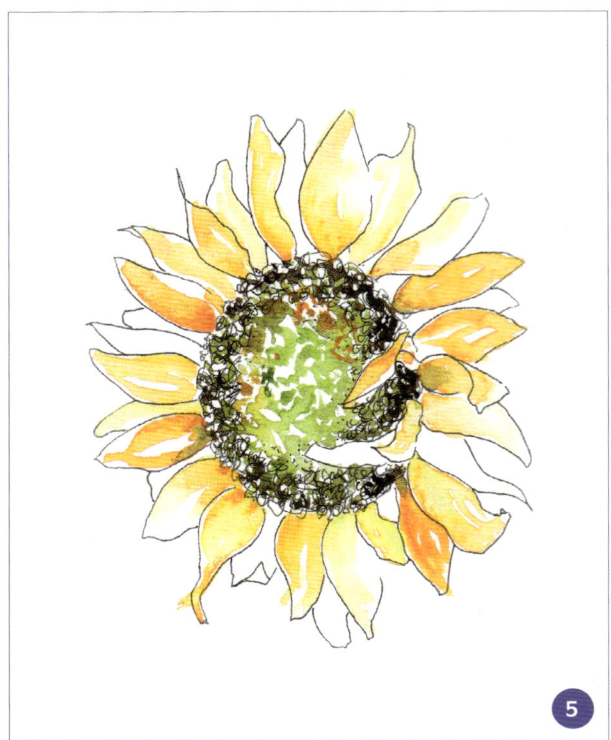

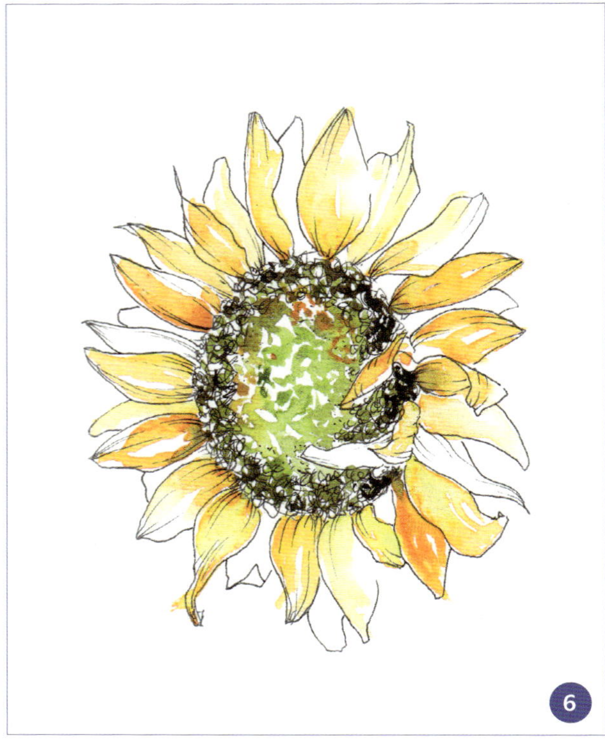

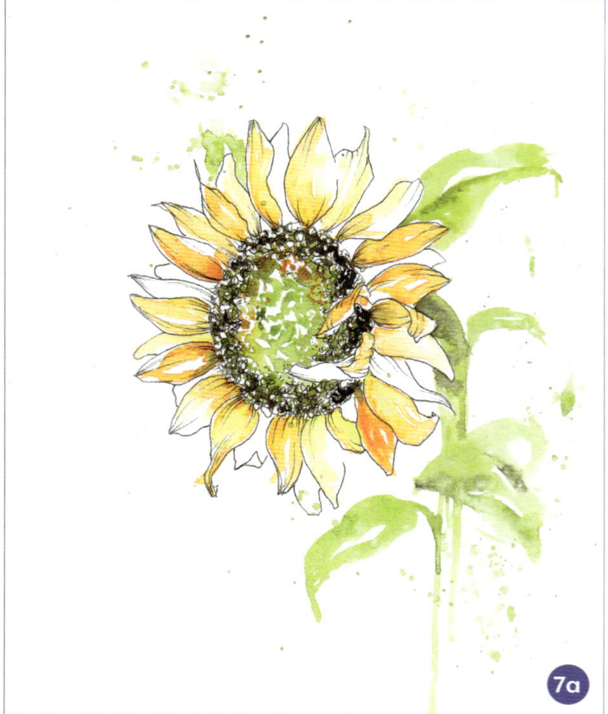

Step 5: The center is feeling a bit lonely, so let's hurry up and get some color on the petals. Use a bit of new gamboge as a start and just begin with one petal. Some of the petals you can paint wet-on-wet and some wet-on-dry. Go with your intuition on this one as you work your way around the flower. Make sure to leave some white space on the petals and also leave some without paint. If you want to mix up the colors, you can add a bit of Hansa yellow light, Van Dyke brown or even green gold while the petals are still wet. Now you can let it dry.

Step 6: We already have some beautiful colors, but we can make this even better with some detail lines. Grab your 005 fineliner and show the curve and direction, as always. You don't have to draw lines on all the petals.

Step 7a: Now you can use the green gold and paint a stem and a few leaves. Keep them super loose and light. I added a bit of Van Dyke brown to the center of the leaves as well for some shadow and color play. Just like I showed you in the magnolia, you can add a nice splatter for an even more painterly and cheerful look.

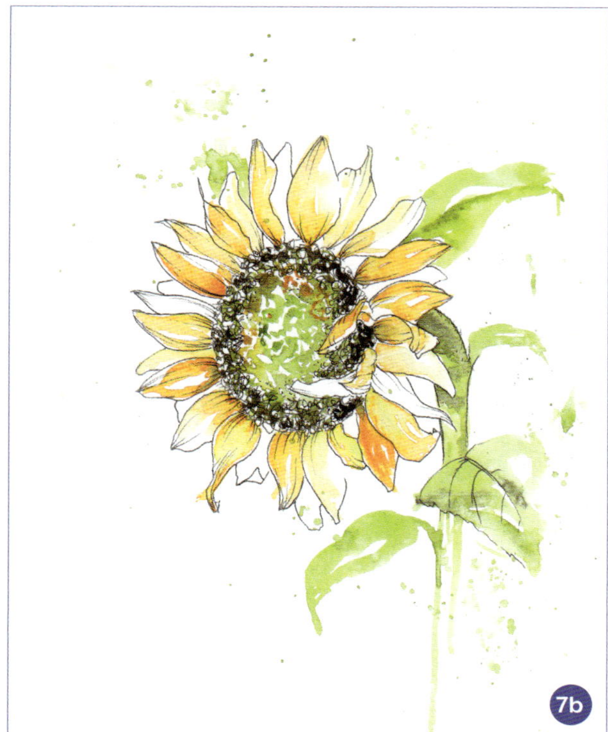

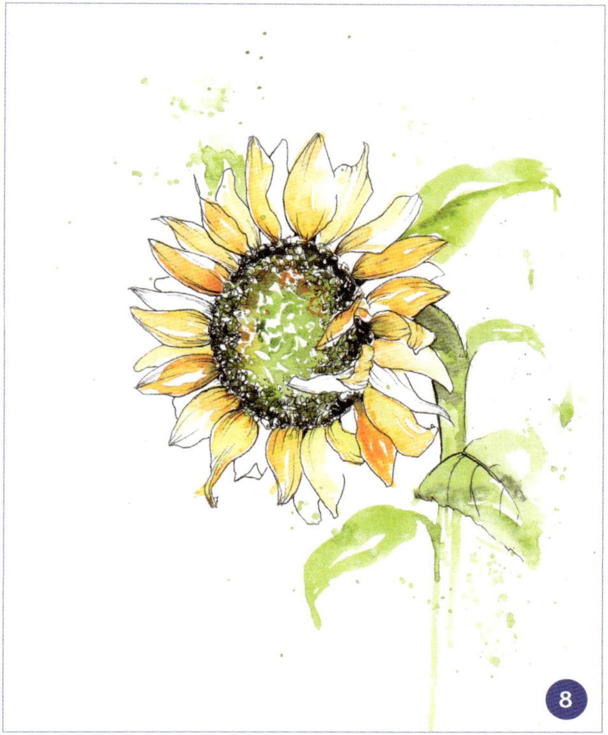

Step 7b: Keep the splatter green gold or add in a bit of yellow as well. Try to keep your splatters around the flower, but not touching the flower too much.

Step 8: Draw the final details with the 02 fineliner. Use this to get a few dark spots between the petals, darkening the outer edge of the center of the flower, and also adding a few details to the leaves and stem. Make sure to keep the leaves super simple, or they will draw the attention away from the flower.

And now, you just need to write a message on your card and you can gift it to someone special.

snowdrop

the flower of hope, innocence and purity

Here in Denmark, the snowdrop is the very first flower to peek out of the ground, making it one of the first signs of spring. Often the days are still short and the weather is still dark and moody, and I've got to be honest with you—those things make the first snowdrop sighting feel like a heaven-sent miracle! In this tutorial, I introduce you to a way of creating a background that can represent the moody winter days. It's flowy and filled with texture, and painting it is more than a little addictive (I warned you).

Materials

Pencil and eraser

Paper: Canson Montval 300gsm (140lb) cold press

Fineliners: sizes 005, 01 and 02

Watercolor brushes: sizes 9 and 4

Water and cloth

Palette

Colors

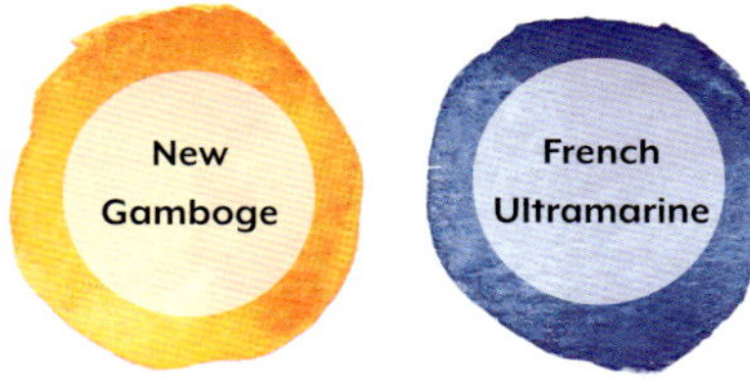

Note: The French ultramarine is a granulating color. I love the texture it brings, but it's not for everybody, especially in this project, because we're aiming for a smooth sky texture. If you don't like that, then go with a different blue.

Mixes

For the background wash, I used an uneven mix of French ultramarine and new gamboge. Some areas have more and some have less. For the stem and grasses, I used a mix with about 70 percent of the blue.

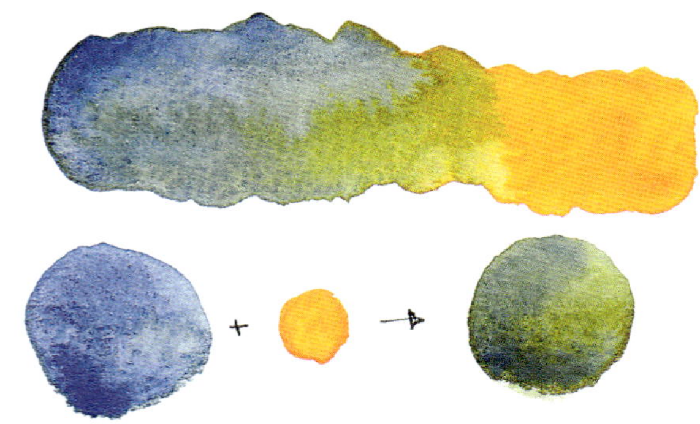

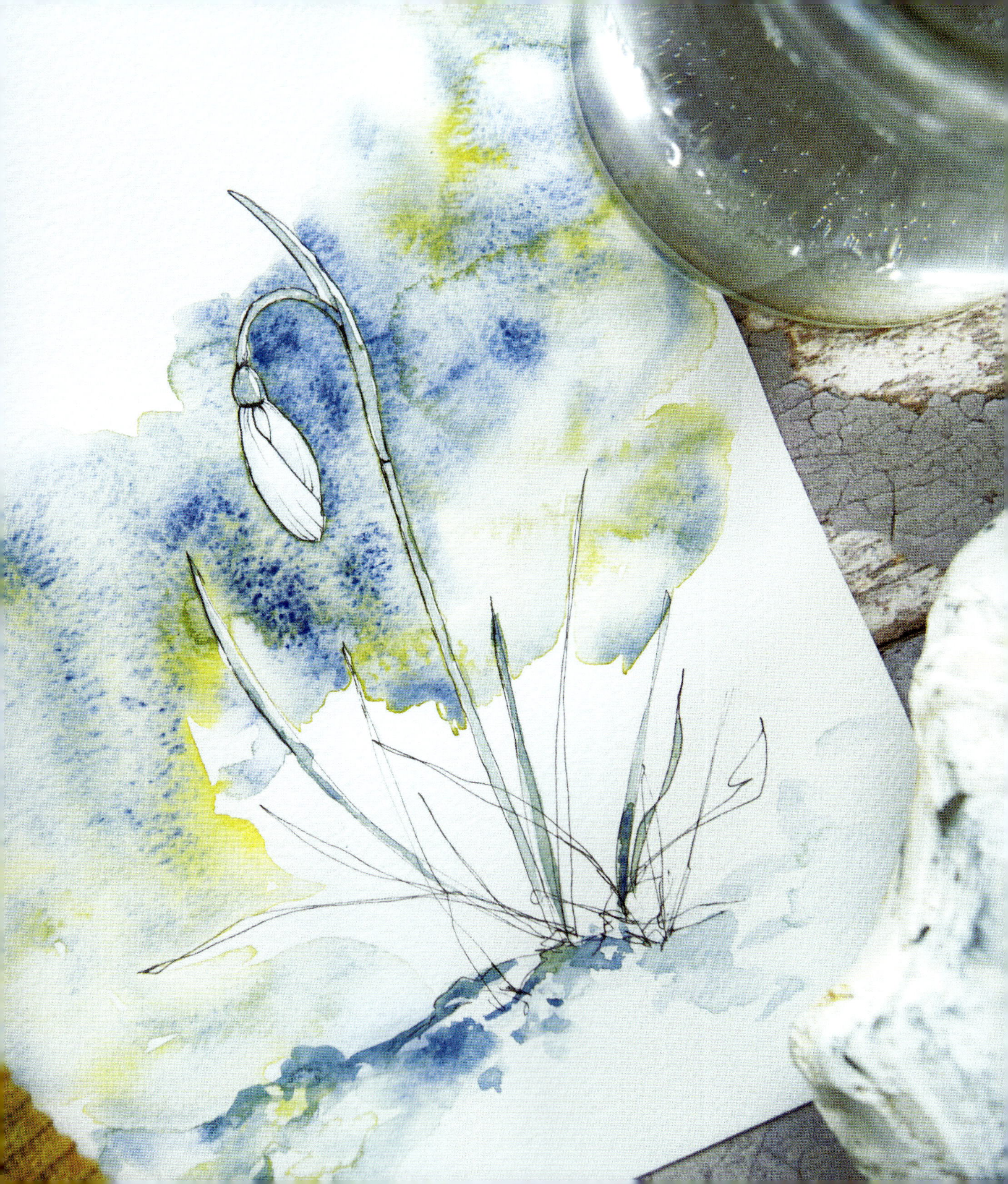

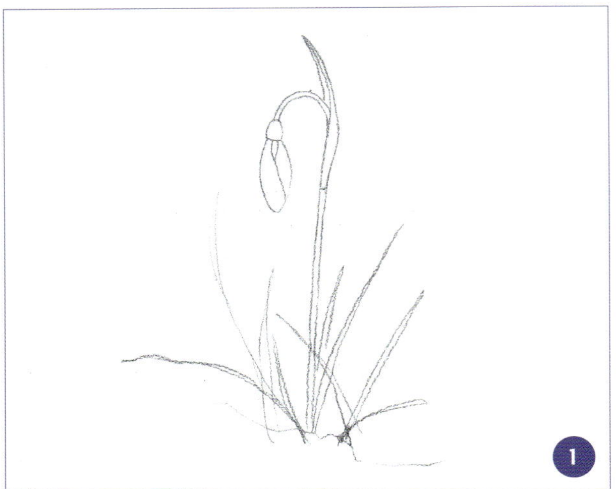

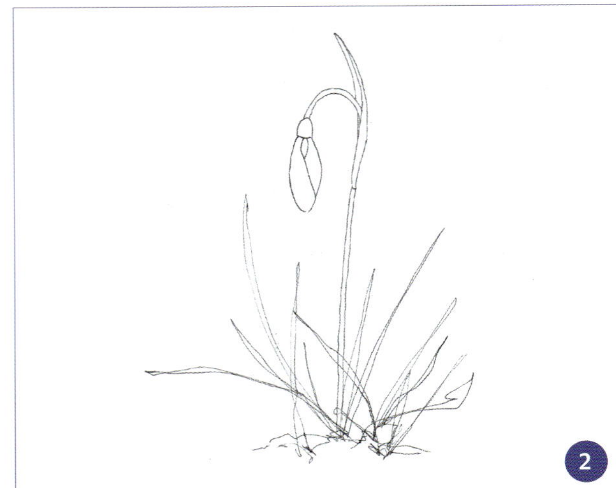

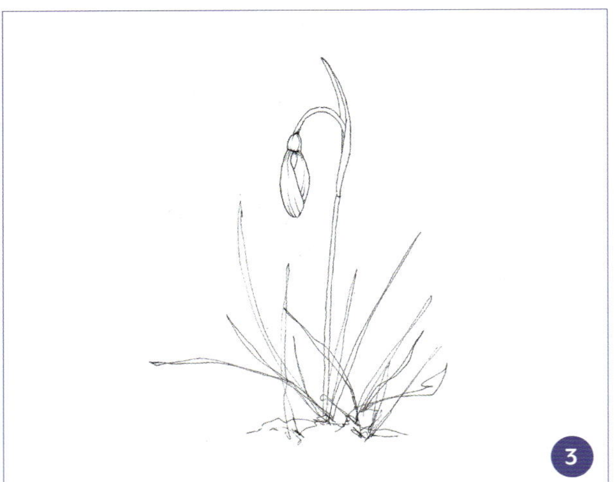

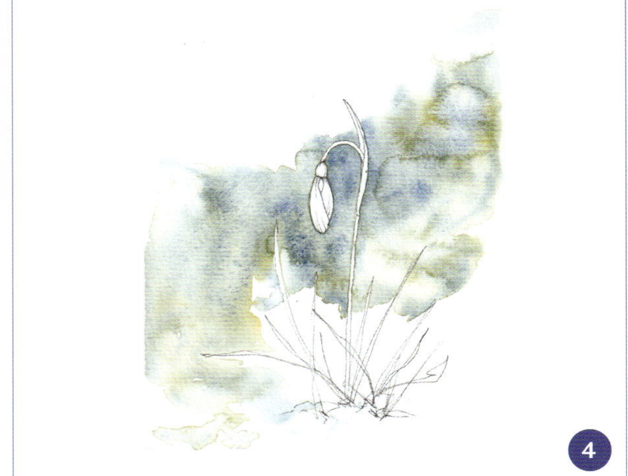

Step 1: Sketch a single snowdrop in pencil. The flower petals are long, teardrop shapes connected to a half oval. This oval is attached to a stem that is bending the head down toward the ground. You can also add a leaf that will go toward the sky instead of bending like the flower head. They can look a little lonely in the snow, so add a bit of grass in different lengths to keep them company.

Step 2: Take your 01 fineliner and follow the pencil line around the flower. Work quickly around the grasses so that they are not overworked.

Step 3: Add some fine details in the flower head with your 005 fineliner. You don't need much here, since it's such a small and delicate bloom (you can erase your pencil marks at this stage).

Step 4: Now, we are all set for the background. Wet a rather big area around the flower with your big brush (I use a size 9) and drip in the background colors. I use a mix of new gamboge and French ultramarine. Be careful not to get color on the flower—we want it to stay crisp white. While the background is still wet, you can play around with it. Drip in clean water to make blooms and drip in more paint for a stronger value. This will take a fair amount of time to dry, so while you wait for that, you can always take a break.

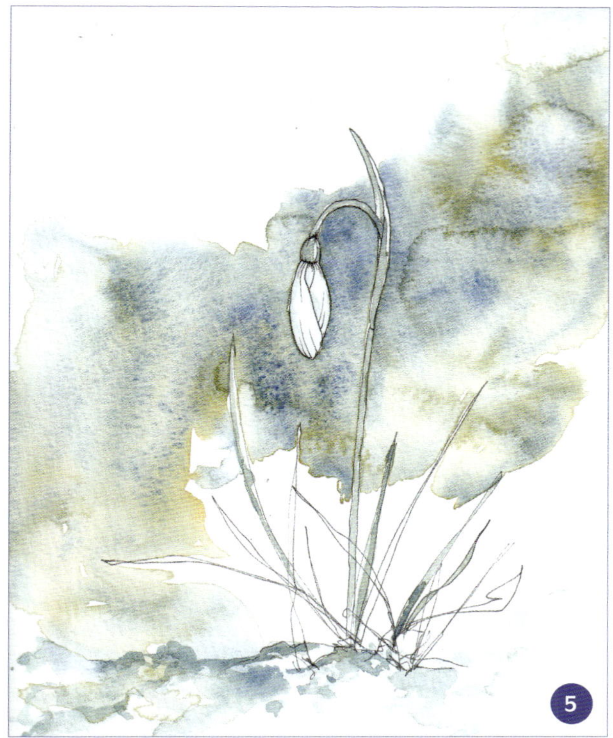

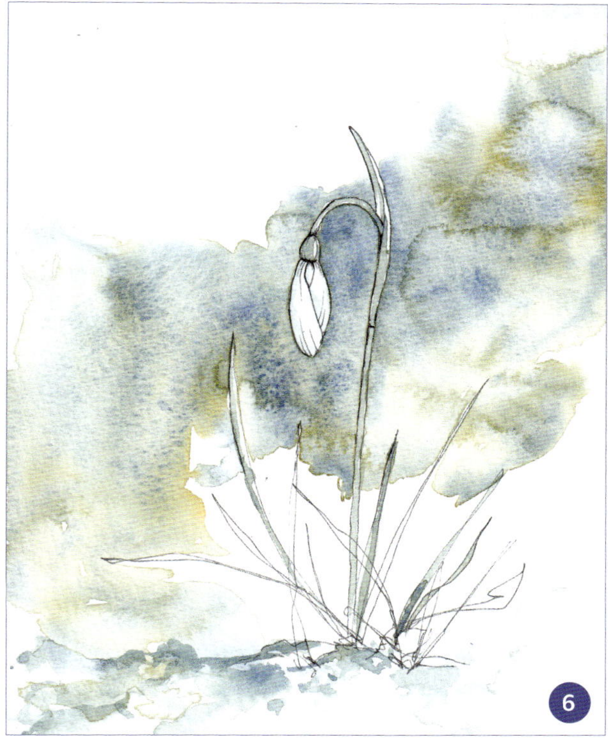

Step 5: I hope you put your break to good use so that you are ready to paint the snowdrop. Mix the colors again now, using more blue and less water. Take a smaller brush with a fine tip (I use a size 4) and add the color to the stem, a few grasses and a bit of color below the grasses to indicate a snowy ground. Finally, take a very watered-down mix on your brush and add it very carefully to the flower head for a small shadow. You want to add just a tad of paint close to the stem and where the small petals overlap. But you know, it's a white flower, so less is most definitely more here.

Step 6: Draw some shadows on the left side of the stem with the 02 fineliner, a bit in the flower head where the petals overlap and also on the left side of the petal.

Well done! You are now free to admire the first sign of spring right there on your paper.

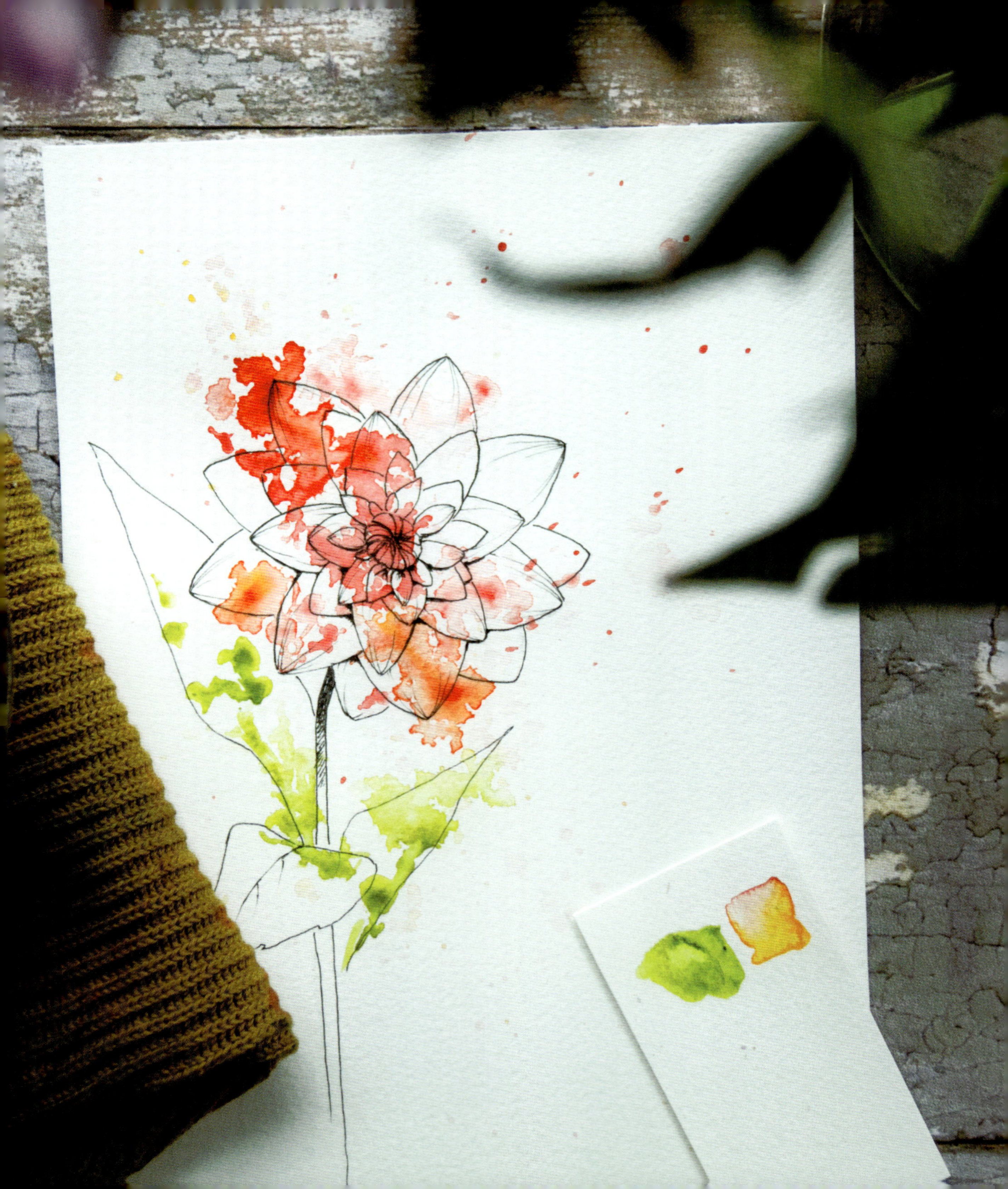

dahlia

the flower of . . . well, almost everything

The dahlia has so much symbolism to pick and choose from, like wealth, elegance, love and inner strength. I chose a red dahlia, which stands for power and strength, two things I think are a little overlooked when it comes to flowers. So, why not celebrate these two strong values by trying something completely new in this tutorial—something powerful, but also a little wild?

Materials

Pencil and eraser

Paper: Canson Montval 300gsm (140lb) cold press

Fineliners: sizes 01, 005 and 02

Watercolor brush: size 9

Water and cloth

Palette

Colors

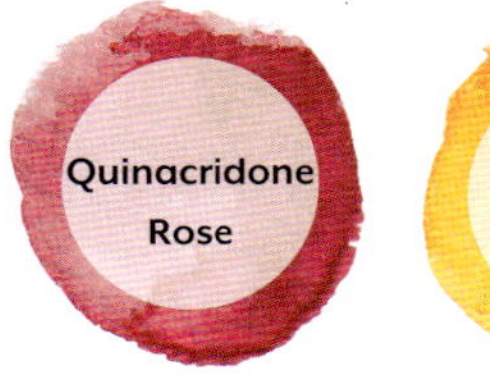

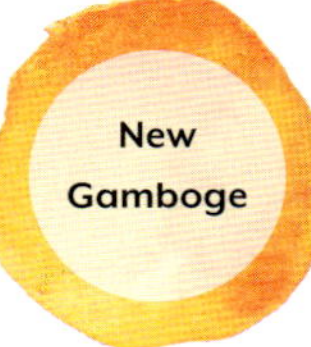

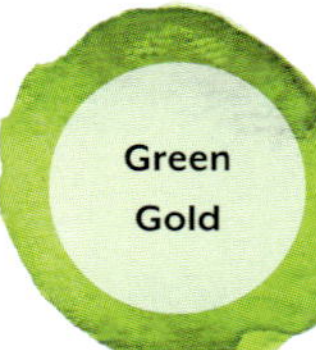

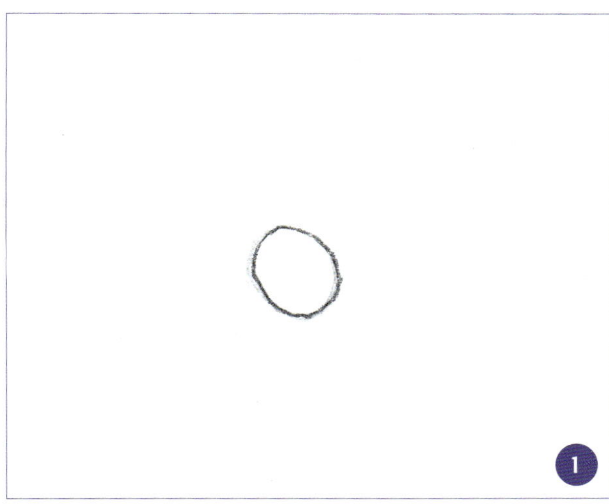

Step 1: Take your beloved pencil and draw a small oval that is a bit askew. This indicates the direction the flower is turning.

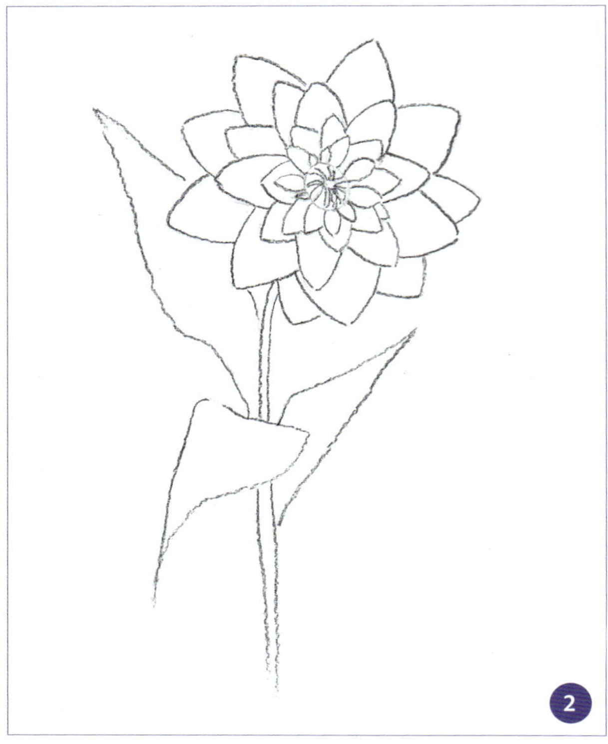

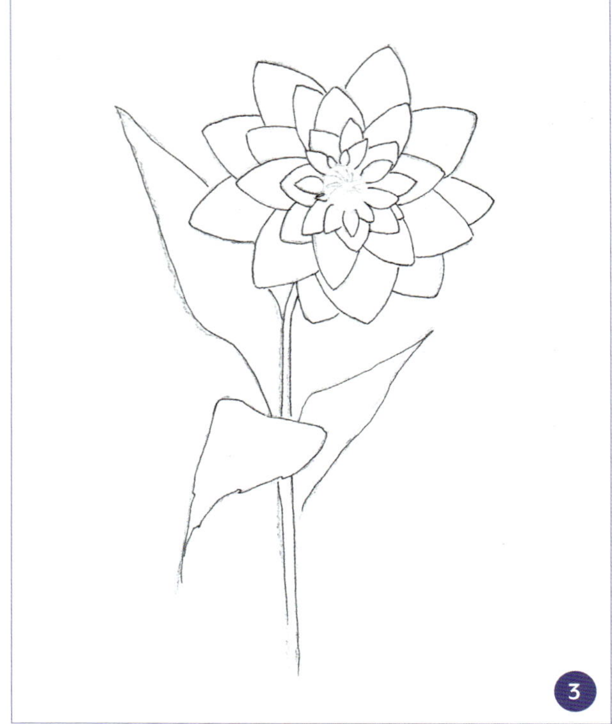

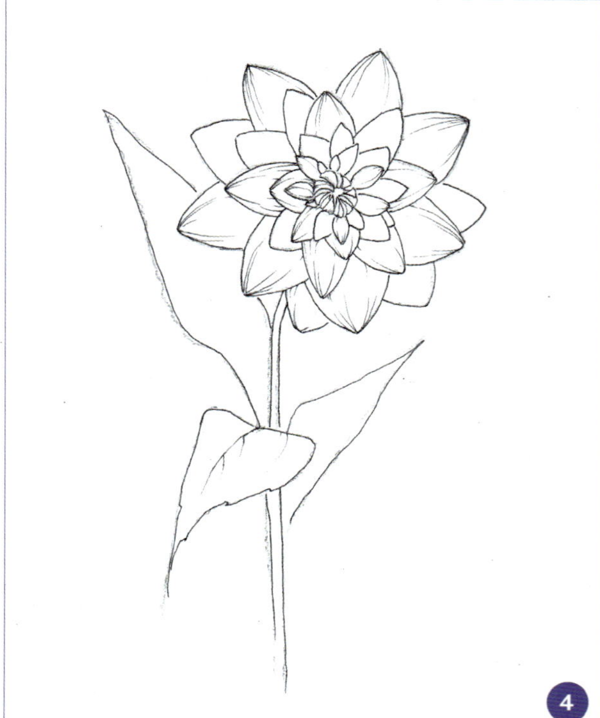

Step 2: Sketch the flower. Start with the small petals close to the center and work your way outward. Close to the center, the petals are almost teardrop-shaped, and when moving closer to the edge, you can think of them as rounded triangles. Let the petals get bigger and bigger, overlapping a bit and also varying in size. Give your flower a stem and a few quick leaves.

Step 3: Make the outline of the petals by using the 01 fineliner. Avoid adding ink to the small oval in the center just yet.

Step 4: Use your 005 fineliner to add details to the petals as well as the center of the flower. The petals will need a few lines going from the tip of the petals and in toward the center. In the oval, you can draw small C-shaped lines that all meet up in the middle. Now you can erase your pencil lines.

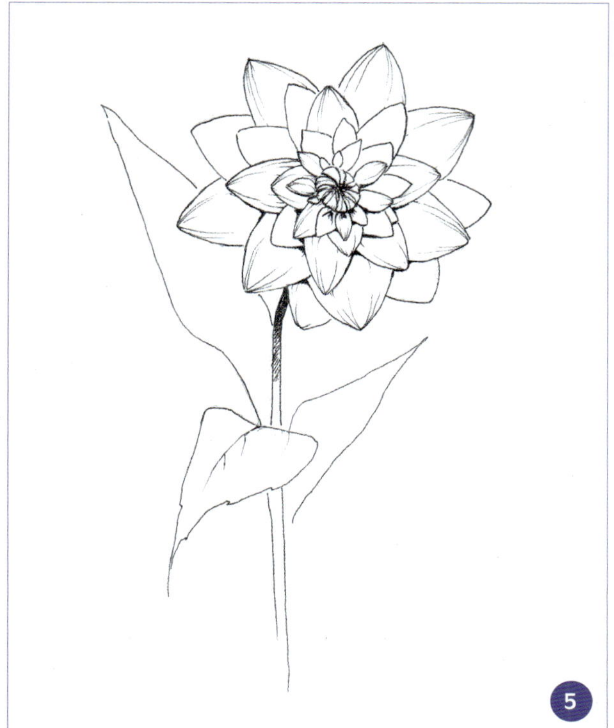

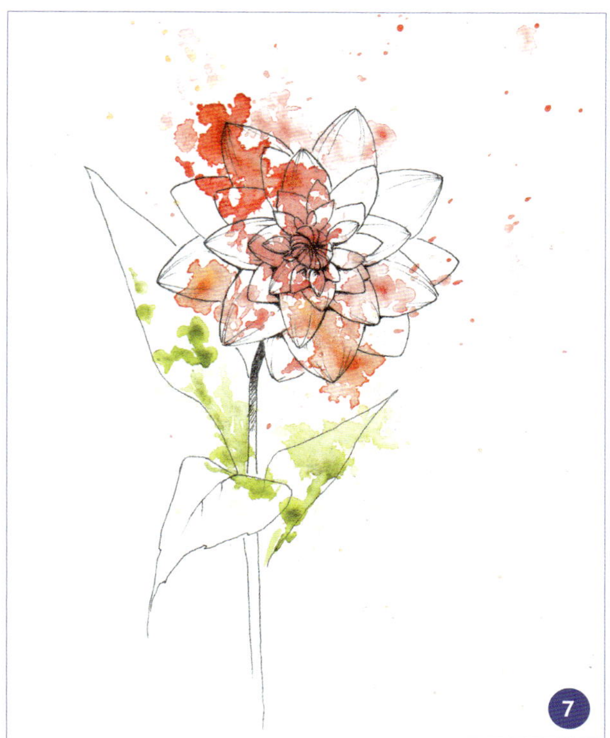

Step 5: Draw dark areas with your 02 fineliner below the petals, on the lower part of the flower. Also add a shadow to the top part of the stem. Here you can use the crosshatching technique (see page 25).

Step 6: Do you remember the crazy new technique I teased earlier? Well, we are here now! First load your big brush (size 9) with clean water and just splatter it on the flower and the leaves. Don't overdo it—you can always add more.

Step 7: Then, load your brush with quinacridone rose and drip it into the water on the paper so it flows around in the petals all by itself. You can also splatter it by tapping the brush (see page 64). Now, drip in a bit of new gamboge in places as well. You decide where it needs more. Make sure to take the time to enjoy watching the paint flow in the water—it's magical. Finally, do the same with the leaves. The page is still wet, so just drip in a little green gold in the water on the leaves and let it spread. This takes some time to dry, so be patient.

If you managed to do this technique without any fear at all, then very well done! But if you found this a bit intimidating, that is totally okay too. In this technique, you really give up control and just let the water and paint do the work, and giving up control takes practice. I promise you'll get there and have fun while doing it!

poppy
the flower of remembrance

To many, the poppy symbolizes remembrance and is used around the globe to honor lost soldiers. But what does the poppy mean to you? It might be completely different. To me, the poppy brings back memories of my childhood vacations. When we traveled around Southern France as kids, my mom's face always lit up when we drove past the glowing poppy fields, and that has made me love the dancing poppies even more. In this step-by-step project, I'll introduce you to another approach to line and wash, which is to wash first. Let's dive in.

Materials

Pencil and eraser

Paper: Canson Montval 300gsm (140lb) cold press

Watercolor brushes: sizes 6 and 4

Fineliners: sizes 005 and 01

Water and cloth

Palette

Colors

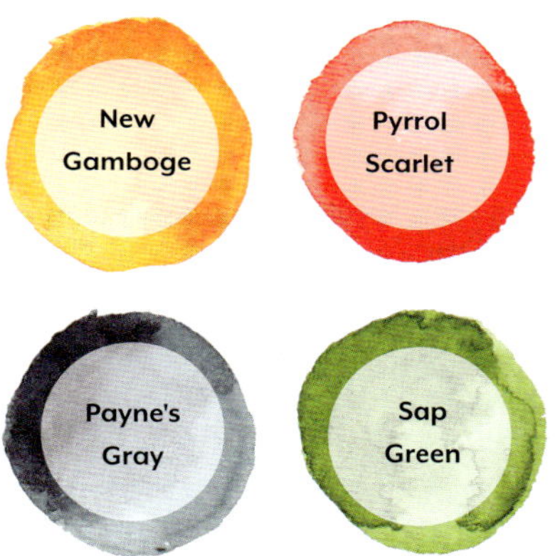

Mixes

To get the red/orange color, mix new gamboge with pyrrol scarlet. You decide how much of each color to use—more yellow will give you a brighter and warmer color, while less yellow will give you a purer red.

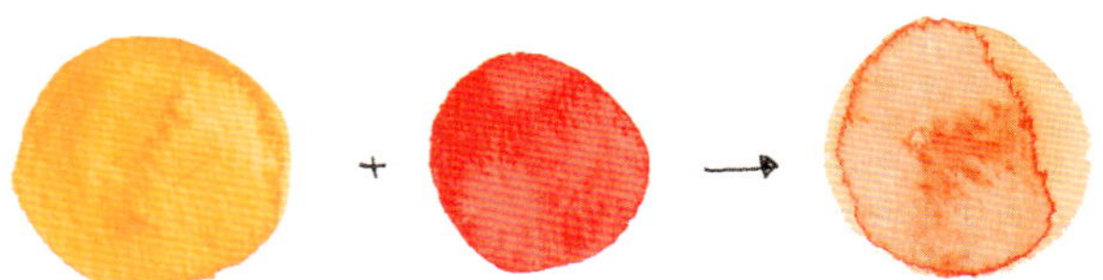

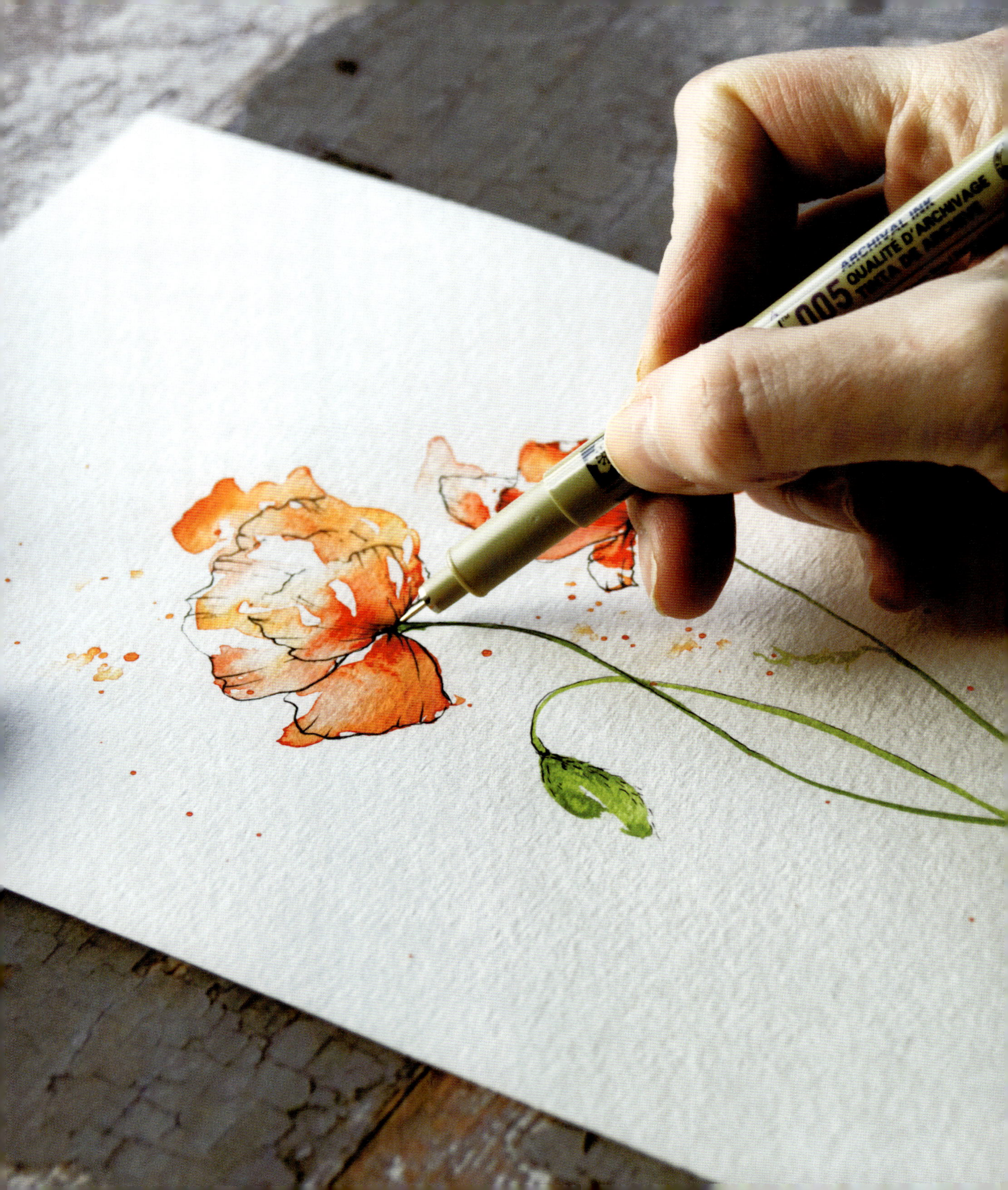
005
ARCHIVAL INK
QUALITÉ D'ARCHIVAGE

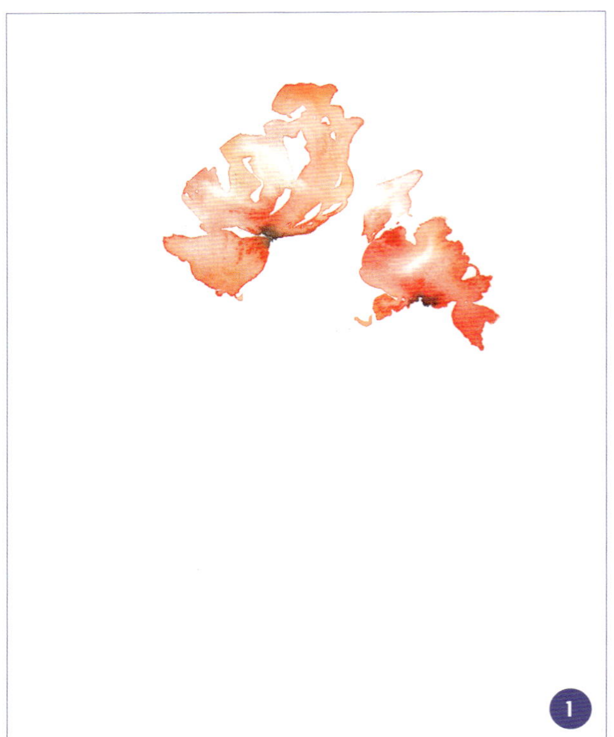

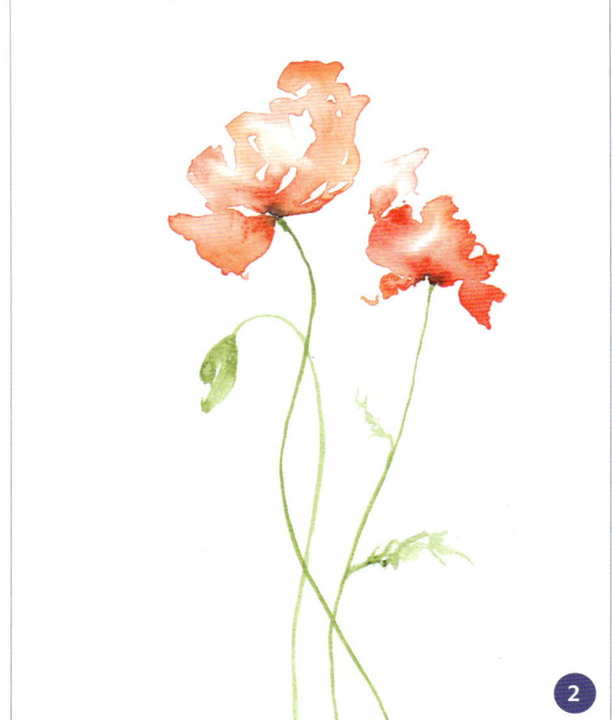

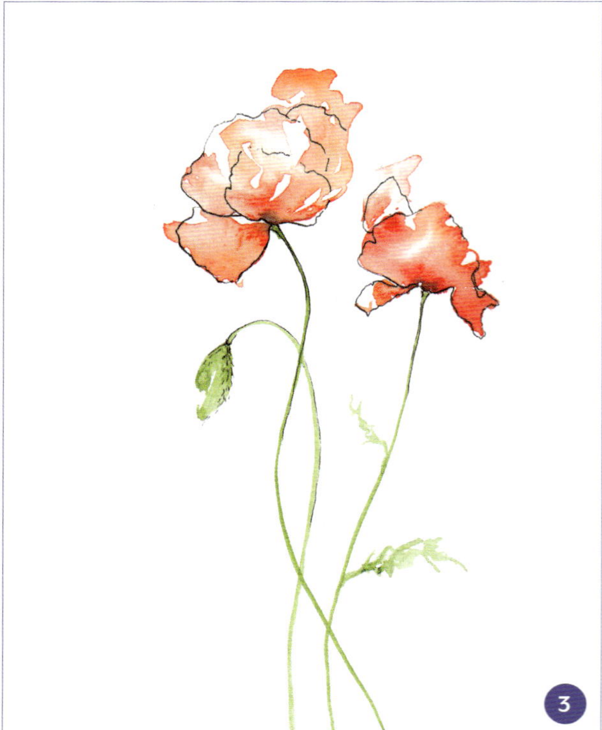

Step 1: Observe how the poppy head is looking and paint the flower heads with clean water and a medium brush (size 6). You can't be super precise and that is exactly the point, because you don't have to be. Just make sure to leave random white spaces (see page 22) and you are good. Tilt your head a bit so the light catches the water surface. That way, it is easier to see what you are doing. Now drip in a mix of new gamboge and pyrrol scarlet and let it flow freely in the water. When it starts to dry (but is not completely dry), drip in a small amount of Payne's gray at the bottom of the flower. Let it flow into the flower head and then dry. I know this seems annoying because you just got started, but good things are worth the wait. So, paint another one or two in the meantime.

Step 2: When the flowers are almost dry, you can paint the stem wet-on-dry with the tip of your small brush (size 4). Use sap green and keep it light and flowing. Let the stems overlap to give a bit of perspective. Then, add a small pointy oval for a bud.

Step 3: Take your 01 fineliner and draw a rough outline to the flower heads. Try being super loose and don't aim to follow the lines of the paint. This will make it look free and flowy.

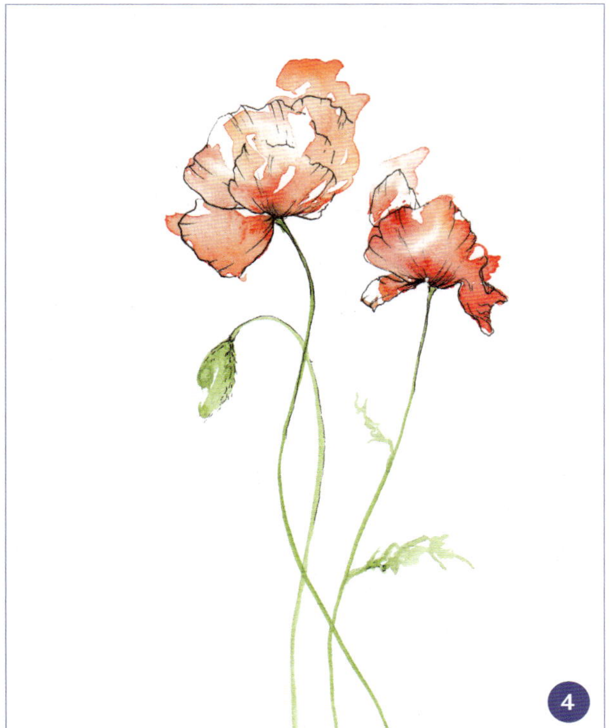

Step 4: Now, take your 005 fineliner and add some pretty details to the petals. Less is more, so just add enough to show the delicate folds and textures.

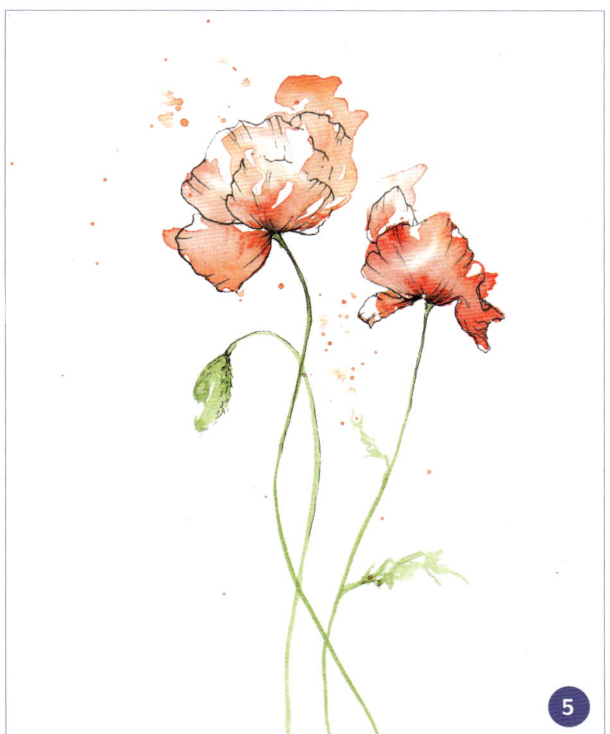

Step 5: If you feel it needs a little more of something, then load your brush with the red mix. Make some wonderful splatters with your brush of choice. Then, load your brush with clean water and do a few splatters on top of the paint splatters to turn them into small explosions.

And that was your first "wash first" flower. Yay you!

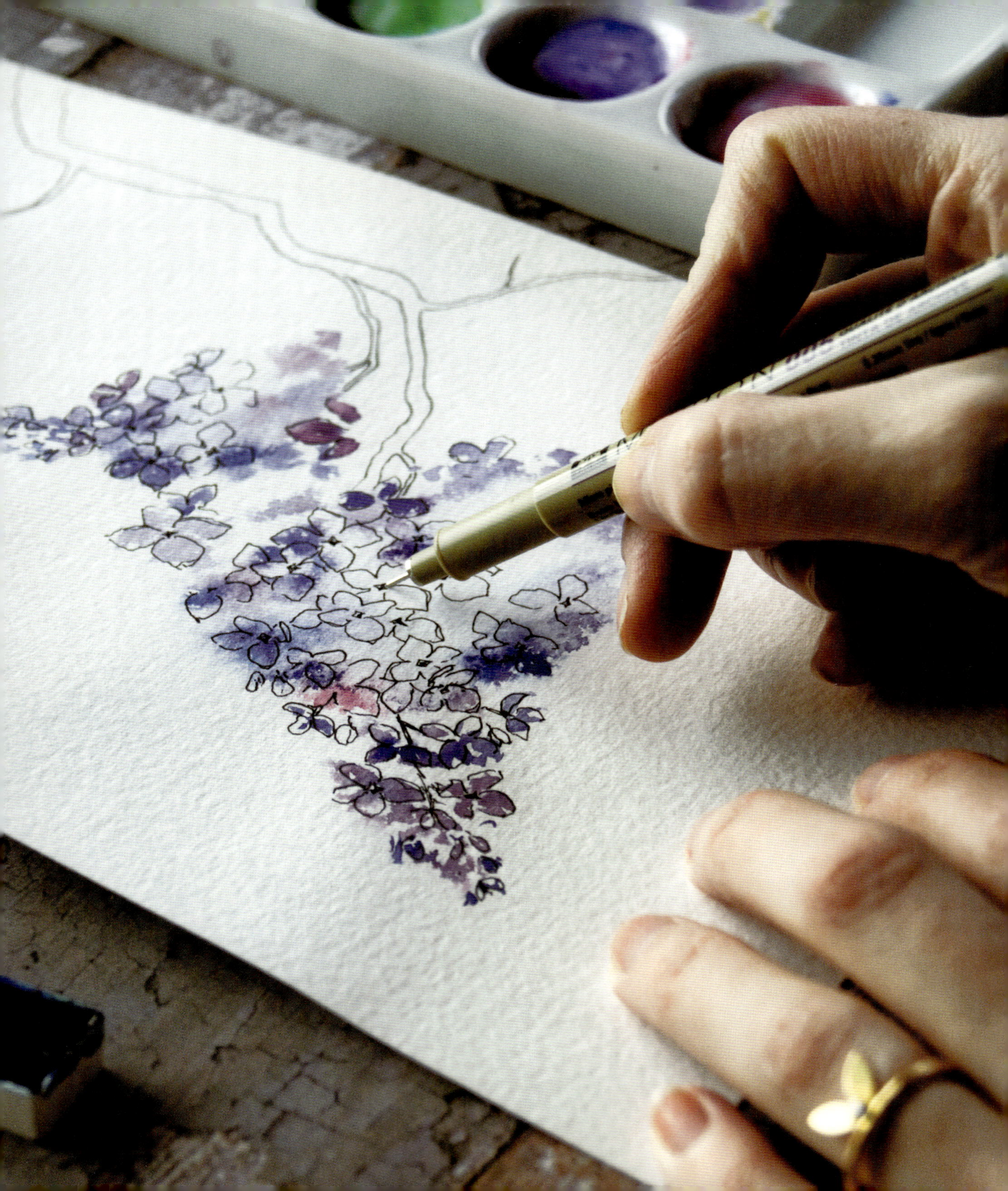

lilac

the flower of renewal

Can you imagine standing below a lilac shrub, feeling the sun on your arms, closing your eyes and just breathing in the floral scent? There is a reason why lilacs are found in so many perfumes–the scent is divine. And to honor that, I decided to show you a technique with inspiration from perfumes. Think about pressing down on the top of the flask of scented water, spraying it lightly on your wrists. Hold that thought and then move down to step 1, where I'll tell you why that is a thing in line and wash.

Materials

Small water mister

Paper: Canson Montval 300gsm (140lb) cold press

Watercolor brush: size 7

Water and cloth

Palette

Fineliners: sizes 005 and 01

Pencil and eraser

Colors

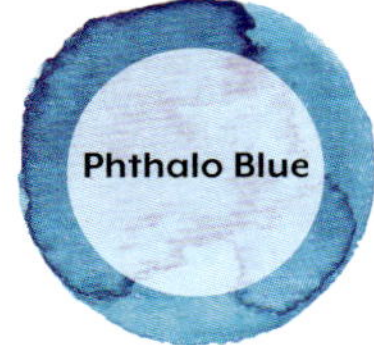

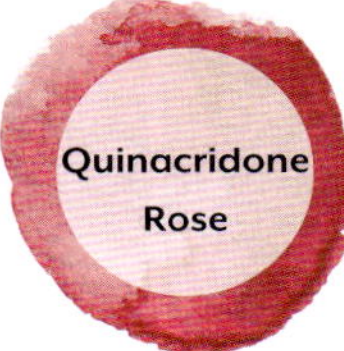

Mixes

Use an uneven mix of the phthalo blue and quinacridone rose to get the violet in different shades.

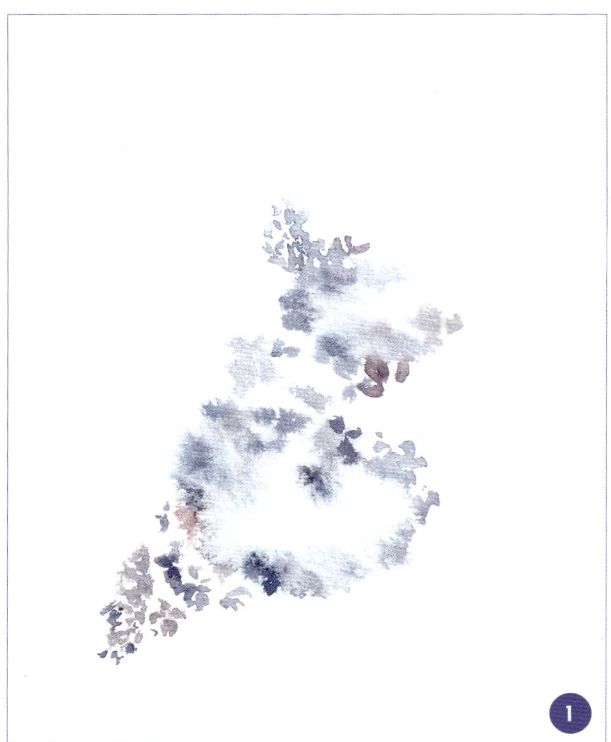

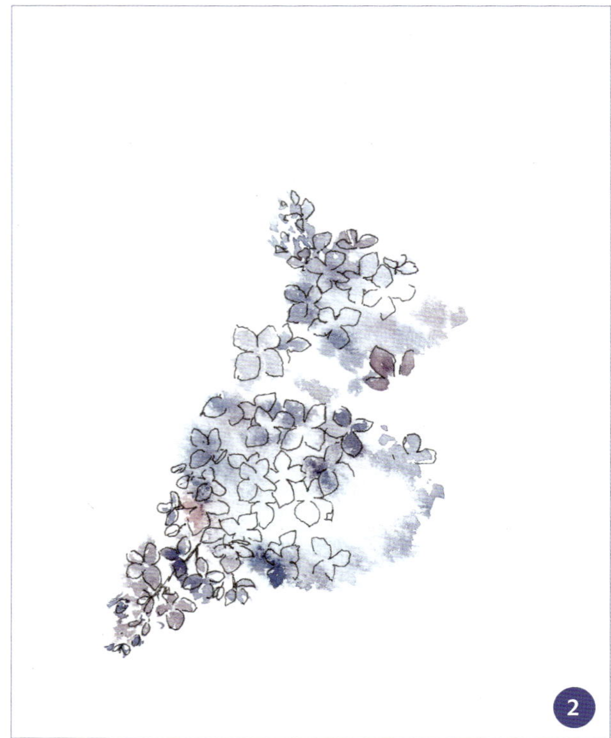

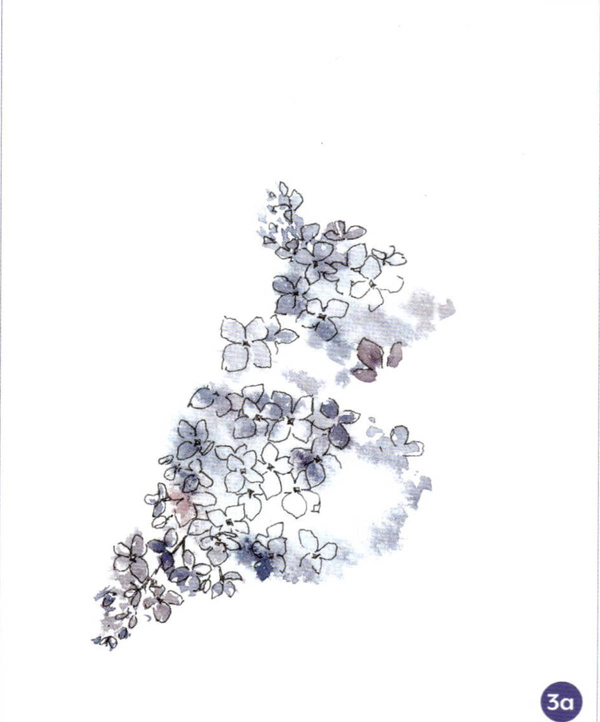

Step 1: Start by spritzing your paper lightly, not with perfume, but with clean water from a water mister. Spritz where you imagine you want your flower. Think of the lilacs as a lot of small flowers with four teardrop-shaped petals. Now, just paint with your lilac mix directly in the water. Some areas will bleed, and some will be on drier land. Work on the shape of your flowers in and out of the water and trust the process. Toward the bottom of the panicles (the cluster of flowers), use more paint and less water. Here, you can add a few ovals for buds. Let the painting dry completely before moving on.

Step 2: Take your 01 fineliner and draw out single blooms. Again, think of them as just four-petaled small blooms and then a few ovals at the bottom for buds. The important thing here is that you don't sketch out every single bloom. Add just enough to show that this is a lilac. You don't need more than that.

Step 3: Take your 005 fineliner to draw small star-shaped squares in the center of the blooms. The corners of the star should point to the middle of each small petal.

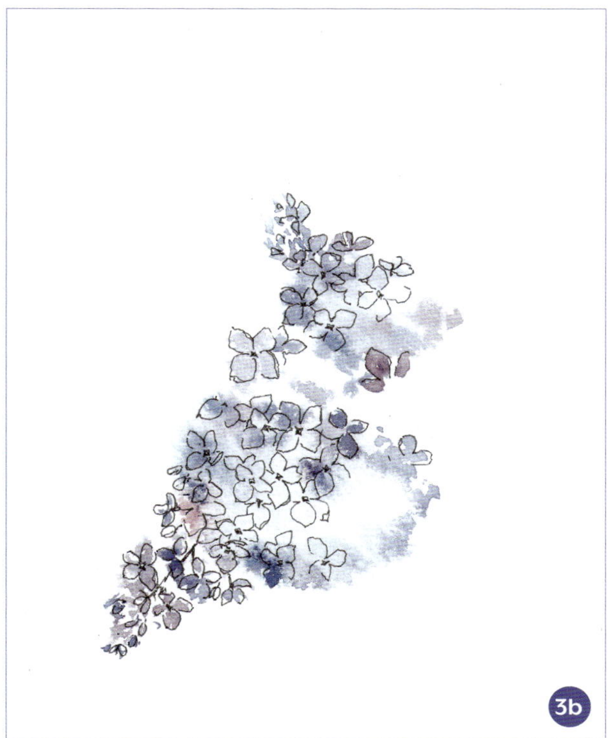

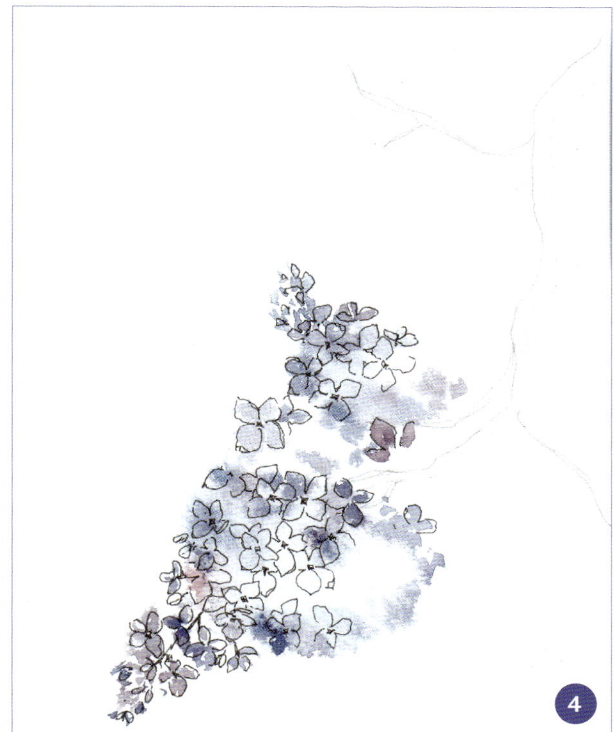

Continue adding detail by drawing small bends on some of the petals. This gives it a bit more life and variation.

Step 4: The lilac is actually in the same family as the olive tree, and if you can imagine how an old olive tree looks, then that's what we are going for. So, grab your pencil and draw a curvy, old-looking branch.

Step 5: Now you are almost there. Take your 01 fineliner and do a quick outline of the branch and erase the pencil line. Keep it simple and without too much detail, so that all the focus will go to the lilac.

How fun was that to spray water and just paint? If you want to take the technique even further next time, you can also spray a bit after you put down your paint and then tilt the paper. The water will let the paint flow softly down over the page. Then just let it dry and paint it again, and it will be super pretty.

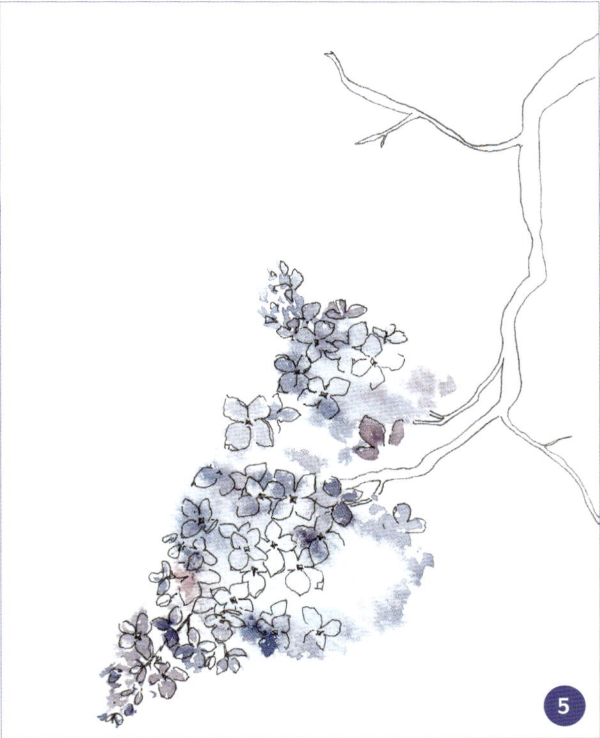

rose

the flower of love, energy and admiration

This might be the flower most people know the meaning of because everywhere we look in movies and books, the guy always shows up with a bunch of red roses. And to be honest, I am a romantic and have kept the first rose my husband gifted me. But for this step-by-step, I didn't choose to paint a completely red rose. I wanted to make the colors a bit more unique, so I included a bunch for you. I hope you are ready to paint the flower of love with me.

Materials

Pencil and eraser

Paper: Canson Montval 300gsm (140lb) cold press

Watercolor brushes: sizes 7 and 4

Water and cloth

Palette

Fineliners: sizes 005, 01 and 02

Colors

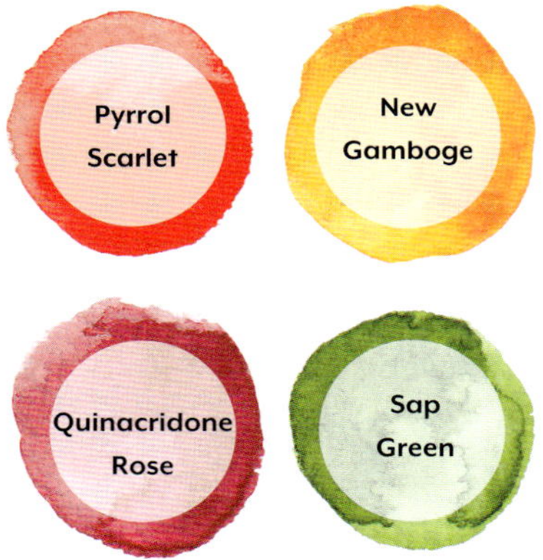

Mixes

The stem and leaves are a mix of sap green and a bit of pyrrol scarlet.

The flower head is a good mix of pyrrol scarlet, new gamboge and quinacridone rose at the edges. All the colors are dripped into the clean water and mix naturally on the paper.

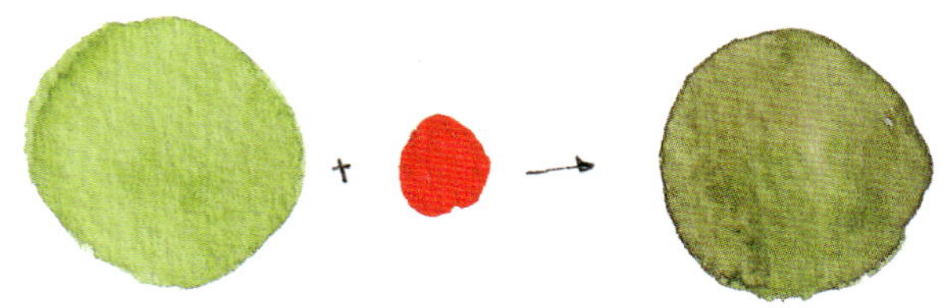

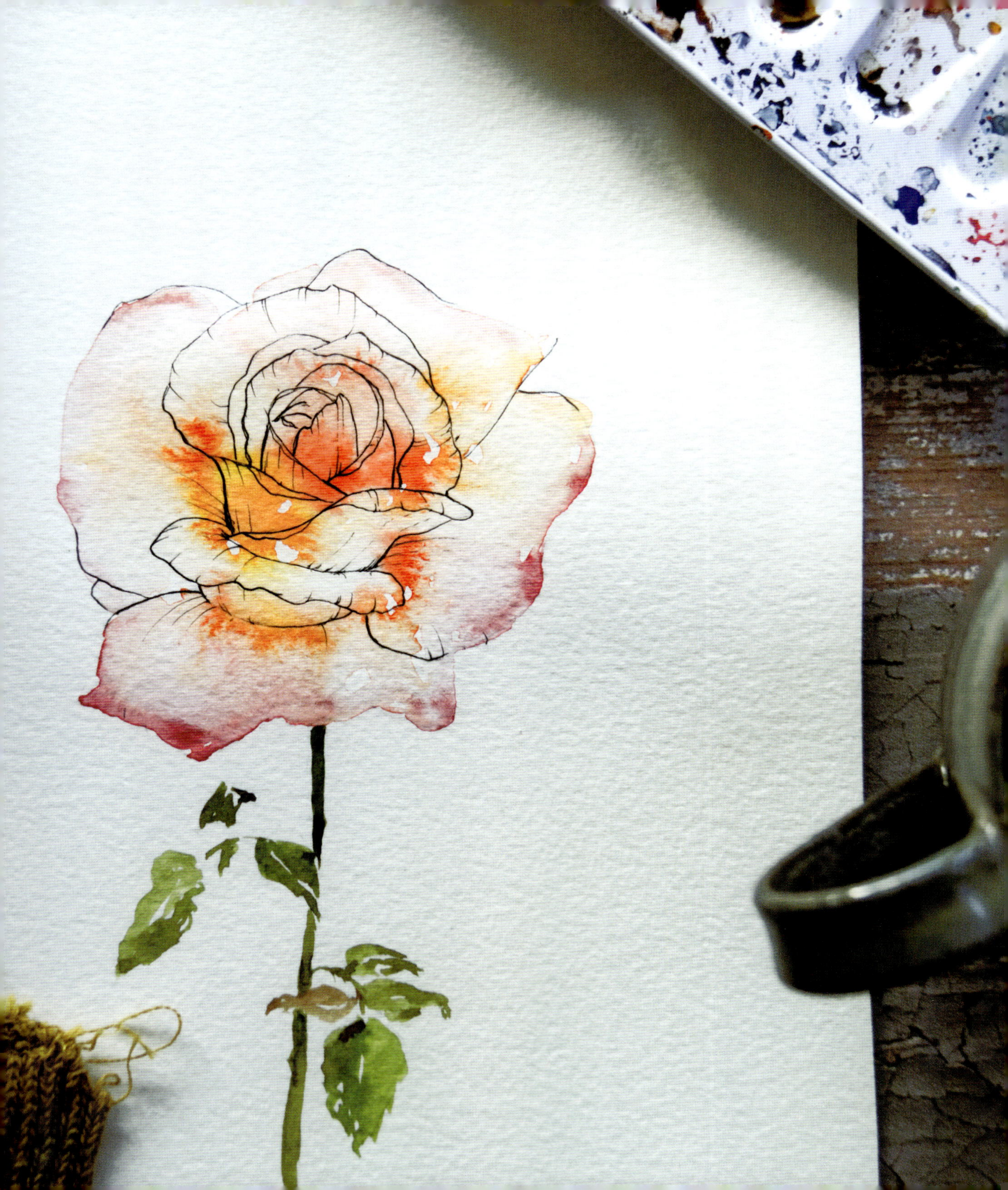

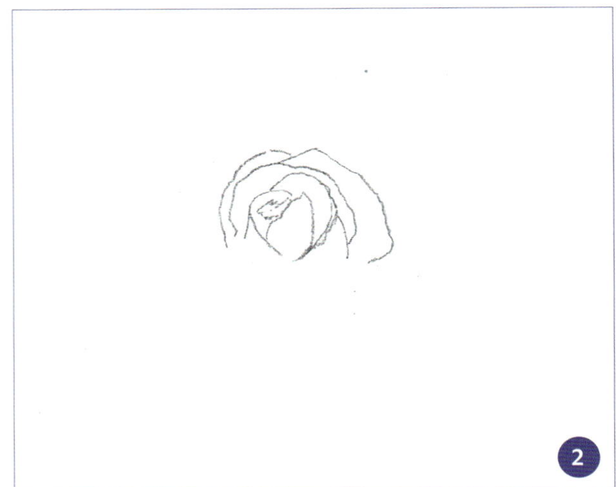

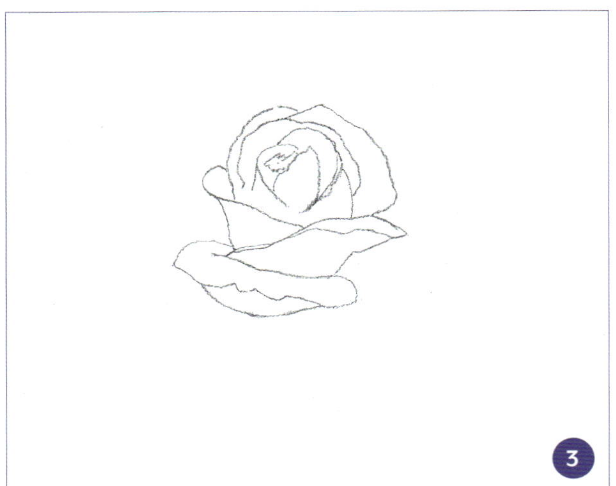

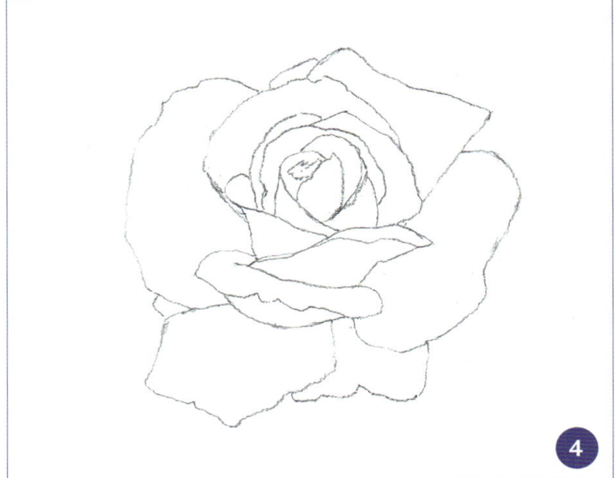

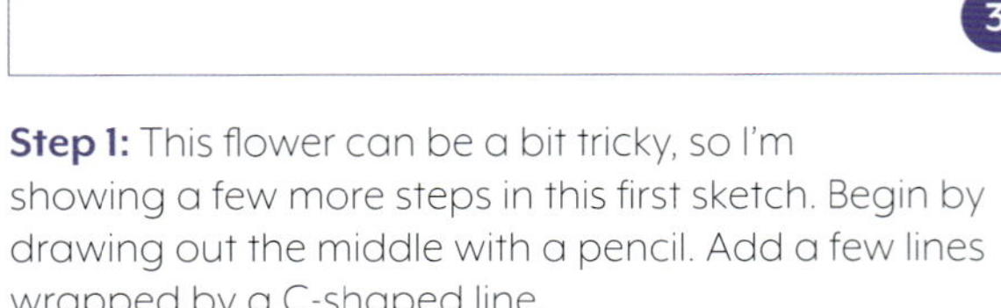

Step 1: This flower can be a bit tricky, so I'm showing a few more steps in this first sketch. Begin by drawing out the middle with a pencil. Add a few lines wrapped by a C-shaped line.

Step 2: Draw a few C-shaped lines behind the center. You can almost let them frame the middle of the flower.

Step 3: Now, draw the petals in the front. These are foreshortened and curved. I know it looks weird right now, but stay with me.

Step 4: Now you can draw all the big petals surrounding the flower. Make these nice and organic. Remember, no flowers are perfect, especially not the outer petals that are withstanding wind and rain.

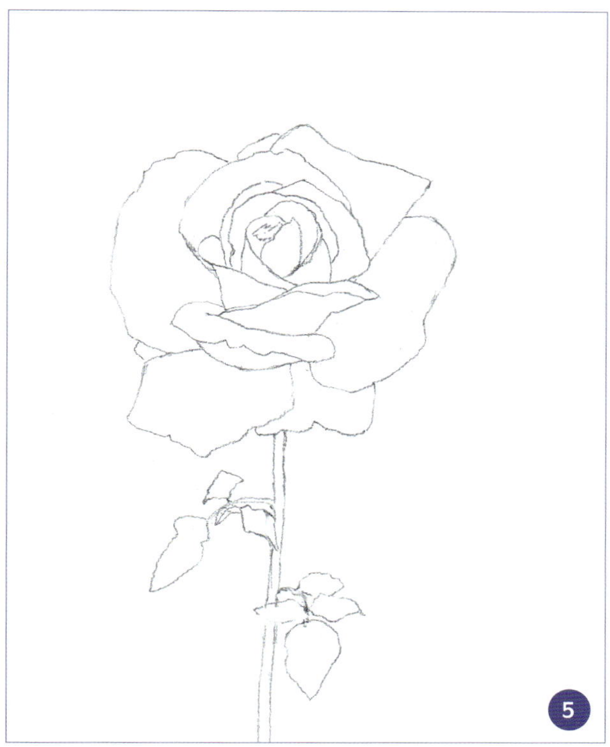

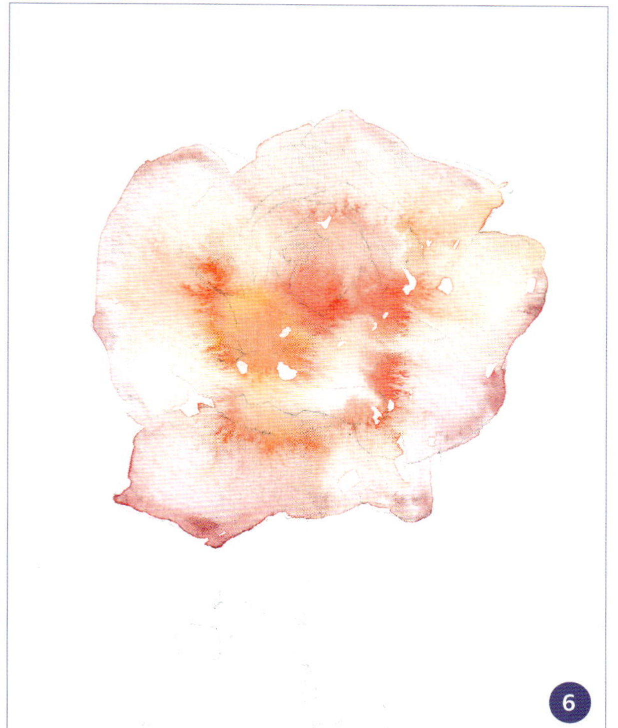

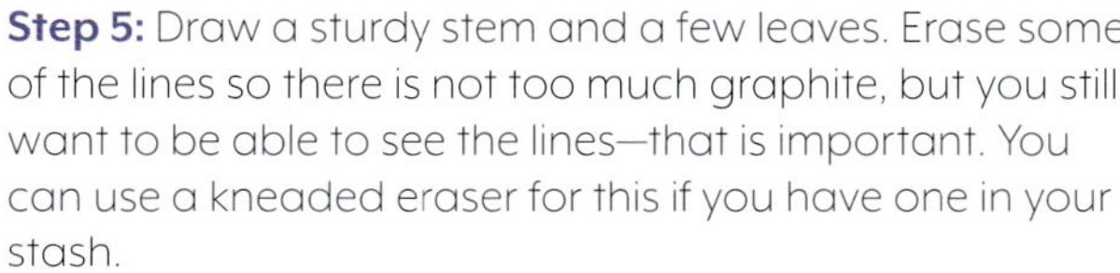

Step 5: Draw a sturdy stem and a few leaves. Erase some of the lines so there is not too much graphite, but you still want to be able to see the lines—that is important. You can use a kneaded eraser for this if you have one in your stash.

Step 6: Now wet the entire rose head with a big brush (size 7) and drip in pyrrol scarlet and new gamboge close to the center. At the edge you can use a cool red like quinacridone rose. Let it all mix and mingle. Don't be scared of water and color bleeds—they will be the magic of this flower. After it has dried a bit, you can drip in a little more color to areas that might be in shadow. Wait patiently for it to dry. Since it is the flower of love, maybe spend the break by sending your partner a kissing emoji.

Step 7: After it's dried, you can paint the stem with the tip of your smaller brush (size 4) using the wet-on-dry technique. Use a mix of sap green and a bit of pyrrol scarlet for a nice neutral green. Try painting the leaves so there are hints of a white line in the middle. This will define the shape of the leaves.

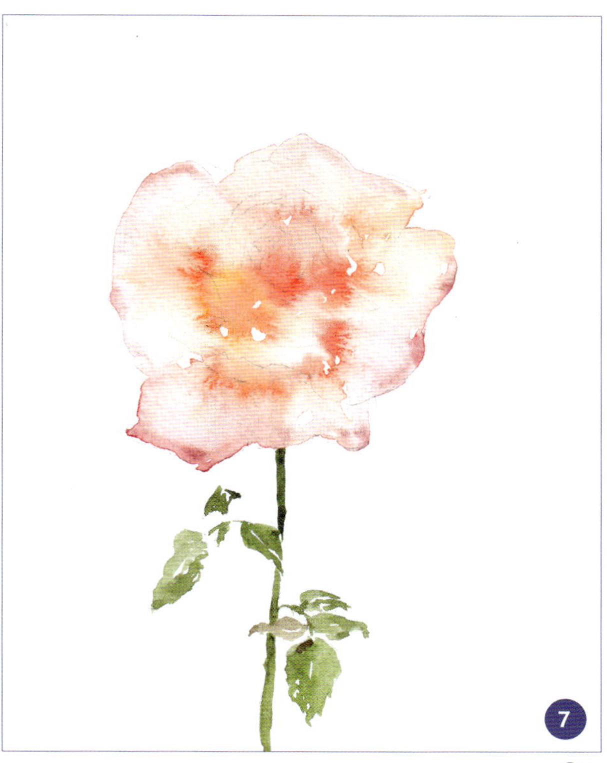

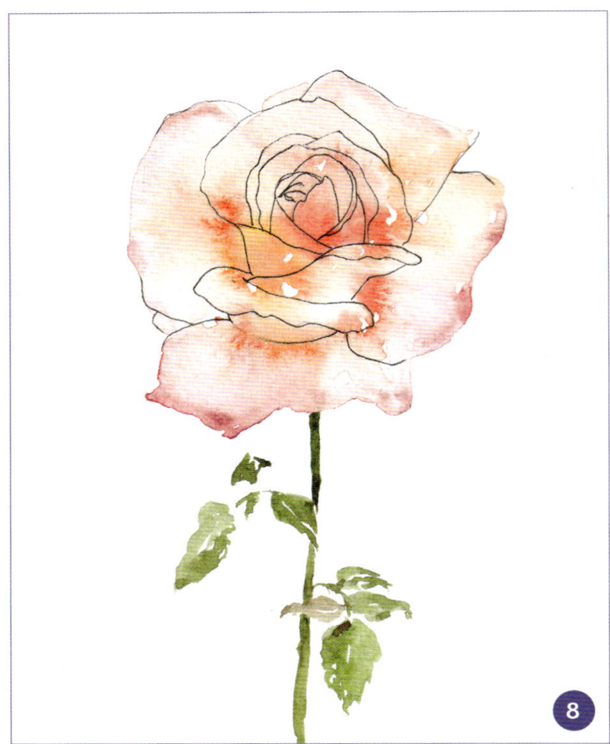

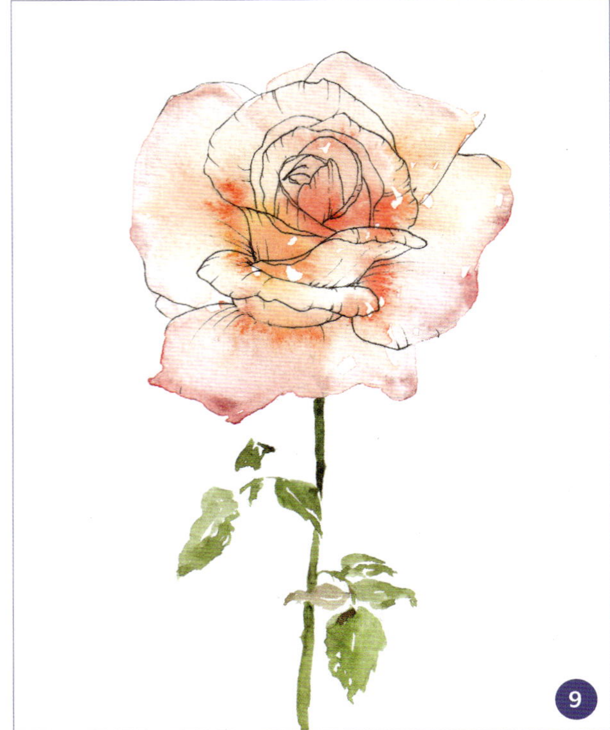

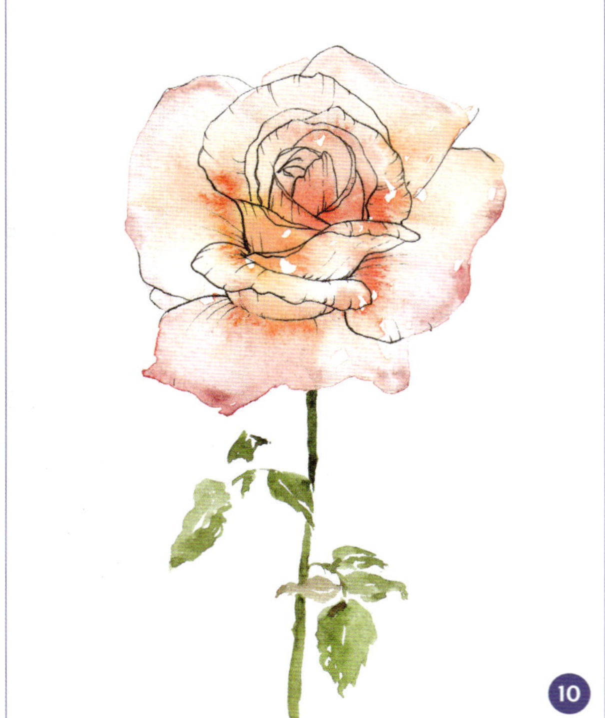

Step 8: Take the 01 fineliner and draw a rough outline following the pencil lines beneath. Leave the outer edge of the petals, the stem and leaves without ink.

Step 9: Add fine details with the 005 fineliner. This is where you will really shape your rose. The part of the petal that is hugging the center of the flower will mostly be straight lines going down toward the bottom of the flower. The curled petals will have more C-shaped lines following the direction of the curl.

Step 10: Finally, add some darker details where you feel like it needs it with the 02 fineliner.

Pop the champagne—you did it! Go celebrate with someone special!

hydrangea

the flower of gratitude and beauty

Hydrangeas are such generous flowers in their blooms. They start early in the season with graceful green buds, continuing into a full bloom and then they just keep going, changing colors with the seasons. One of the characteristics of the hydrangea is the abundance of flowers in a flower head in full bloom, which can seem a bit crazy to start drawing. So, in this tutorial I want to show you that you don't have to draw the individual flowers—at all.

Materials

Watercolor brush: size 7

Paper: Canson Montval 300gsm (140lb) cold press

Pencil and eraser

Water and cloth

Palette

Fineliners: sizes 005 and 01

Colors

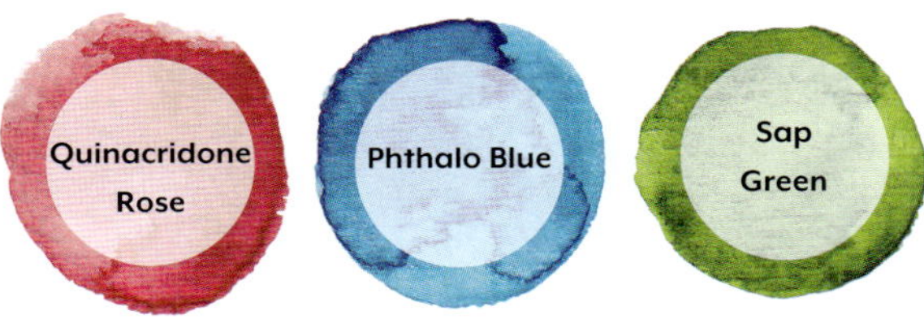

Mixes

The beautiful violet is a mix of quinacridone rose and the bright phthalo blue. Don't mix them too well on the palette; instead, mix a little and then use the many shades of violet that it brings.

The green leaves are a mix of sap green and phthalo blue.

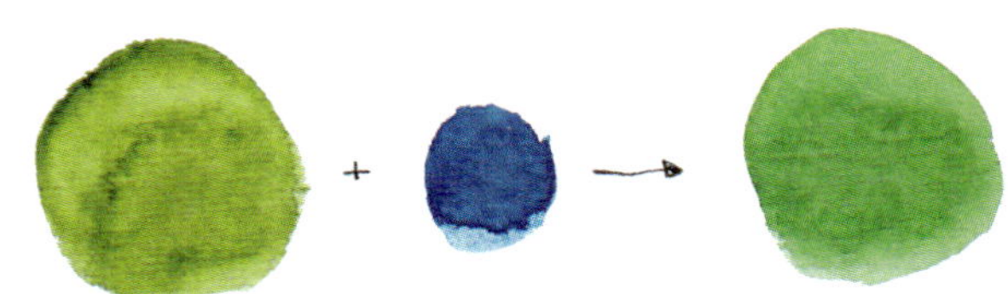

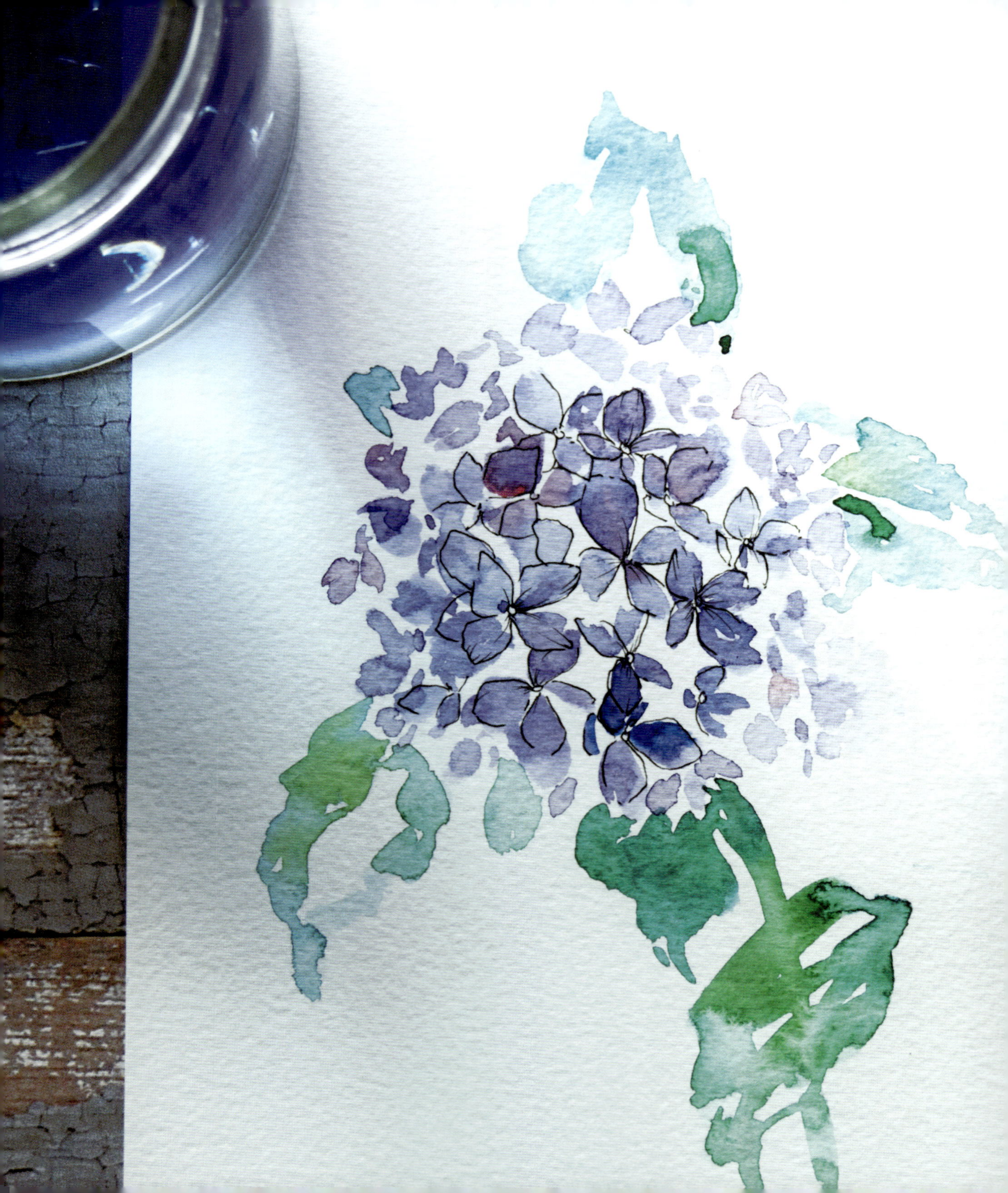

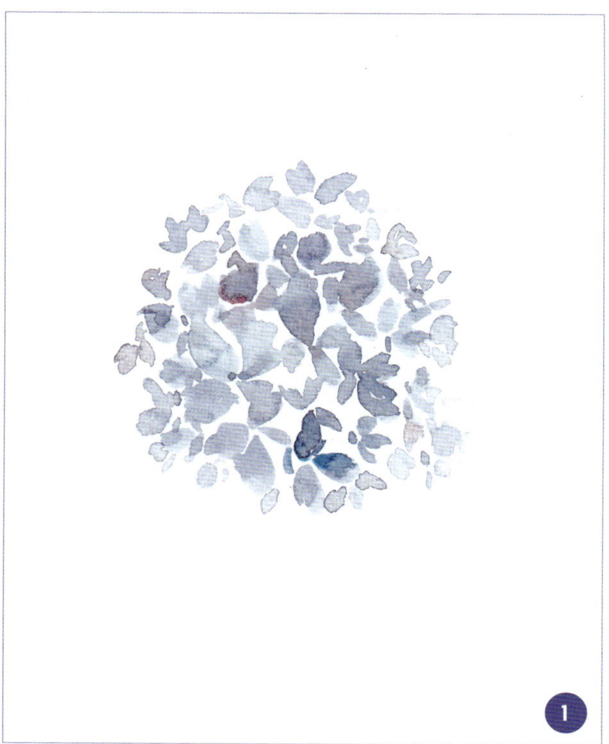

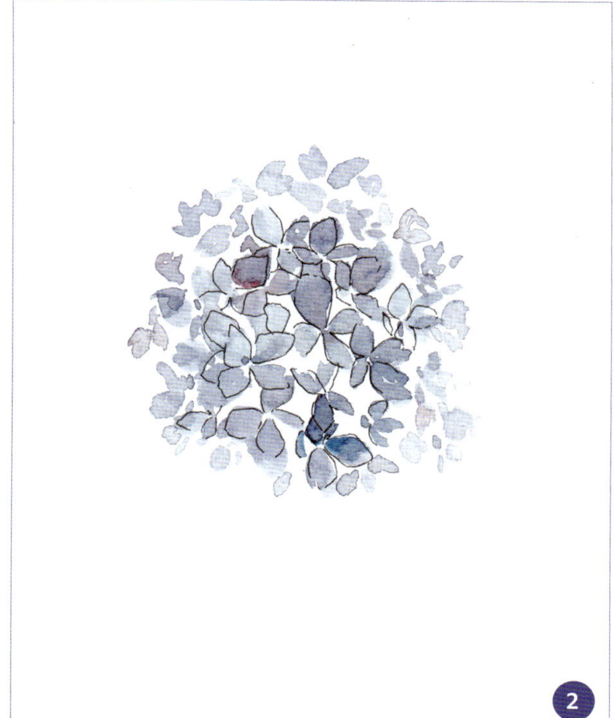

Step 1: Take your medium-sized brush (I use a size 7) and start by using your violet mix to loosely paint small blooms wet-on-dry. Think of the hydrangea head as a ball, where you begin in the middle with pretty big blooms and go smaller as you work your way toward the edge, using less paint and more water as you go. Don't think too much about the single blooms. After all, the single bloom is just a cluster of four teardrop-shaped petals. To help you paint loose, hold high on your brush handle and put on some relaxing tunes.

Go make yourself a cup of tea while it dries.

Step 2: Now, grab your 01 fineliner and sketch out the single four-petaled blooms, loosely and one at a time, starting from the center. Look for patterns where you see flowers. What kind of brush mark looks like a flower? You probably don't need to draw your way to the outer edge for people to see that this is a hydrangea. Changing the detail level like this, so that a part of the flower has ink lines and another doesn't, helps guide the viewer into your drawing.

Step 3: Add a small oval in the center of the blooms with your 005 fineliner.

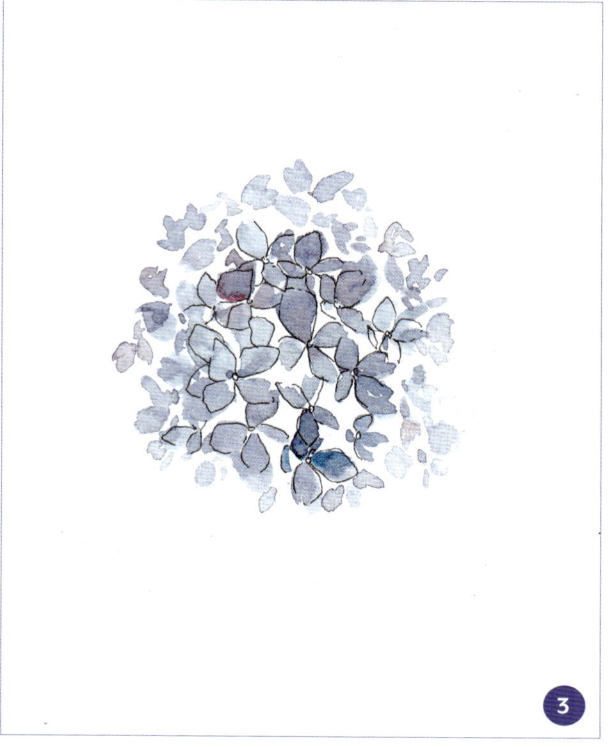

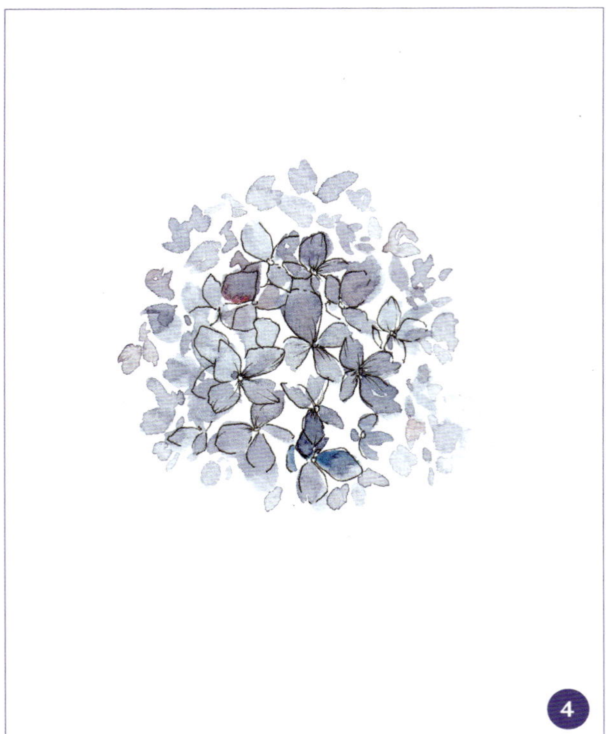

Step 4: Still using the same pen, draw the small lines showing the direction of the petals. Keep these lines to a few of the blooms so you switch up the detail level once again.

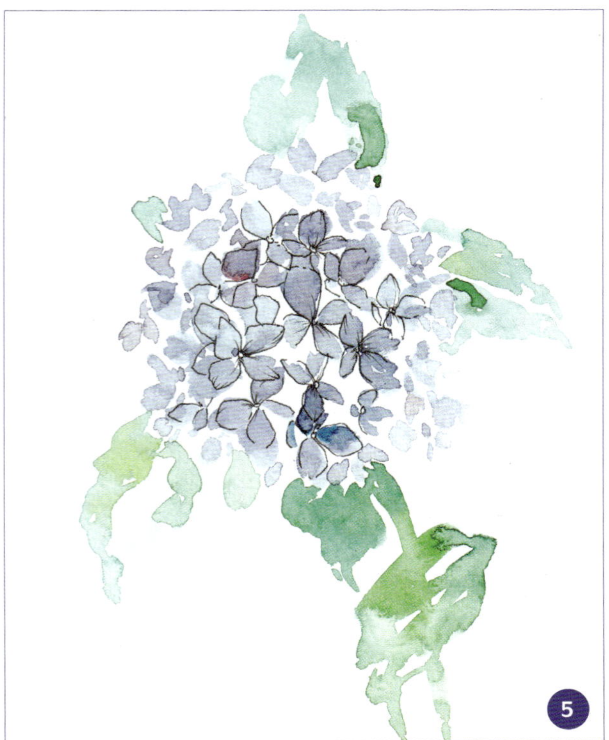

Step 5: Even though I want to keep this simple, I do want to give the hydrangea a few leaves to frame the flower head. Paint these leaves loosely in a mix of phthalo blue and sap green. That way, the colors tie together beautifully with the rest of the flower.

And that's that! Easy, right? Painting complex flowers does not have to be hard at all. Just be loose and relaxed, and have fun with it.

peony

the flower of romance and luck

Can I tell you a secret? I didn't always love peonies. Yes, true story! I found them way too big and overrated. But then, I got one. And then just one more. And suddenly, I kind of loved them for their extravagance and superiority. However, the extravagance in the number of petals on this bloom can also make a peony rather terrifying for those new to painting. So in this tutorial, I'll show you how the technique you learned while painting the hydrangea (page 91) can really help simplify the peony as well.

Materials

Watercolor brush: size 7

Paper: Canson Montval 300gsm (140lb) cold press

Water and cloth

Palette

Fineliners: sizes 005, 01 and 02

Pencil and eraser

Colors

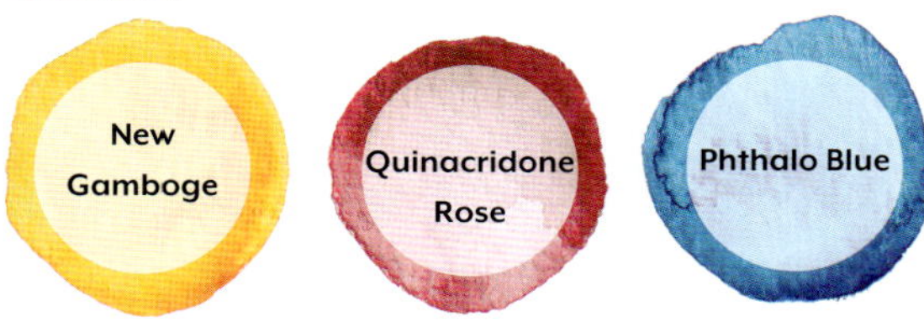

Mixes

To get the red, mix quinacridone rose and new gamboge.

The shadow color is a mix of the rose and phthalo blue, but be careful not to use too much blue or it'll turn purple.

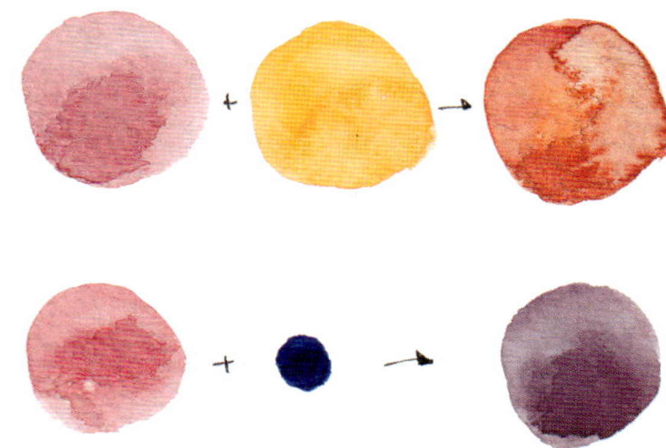

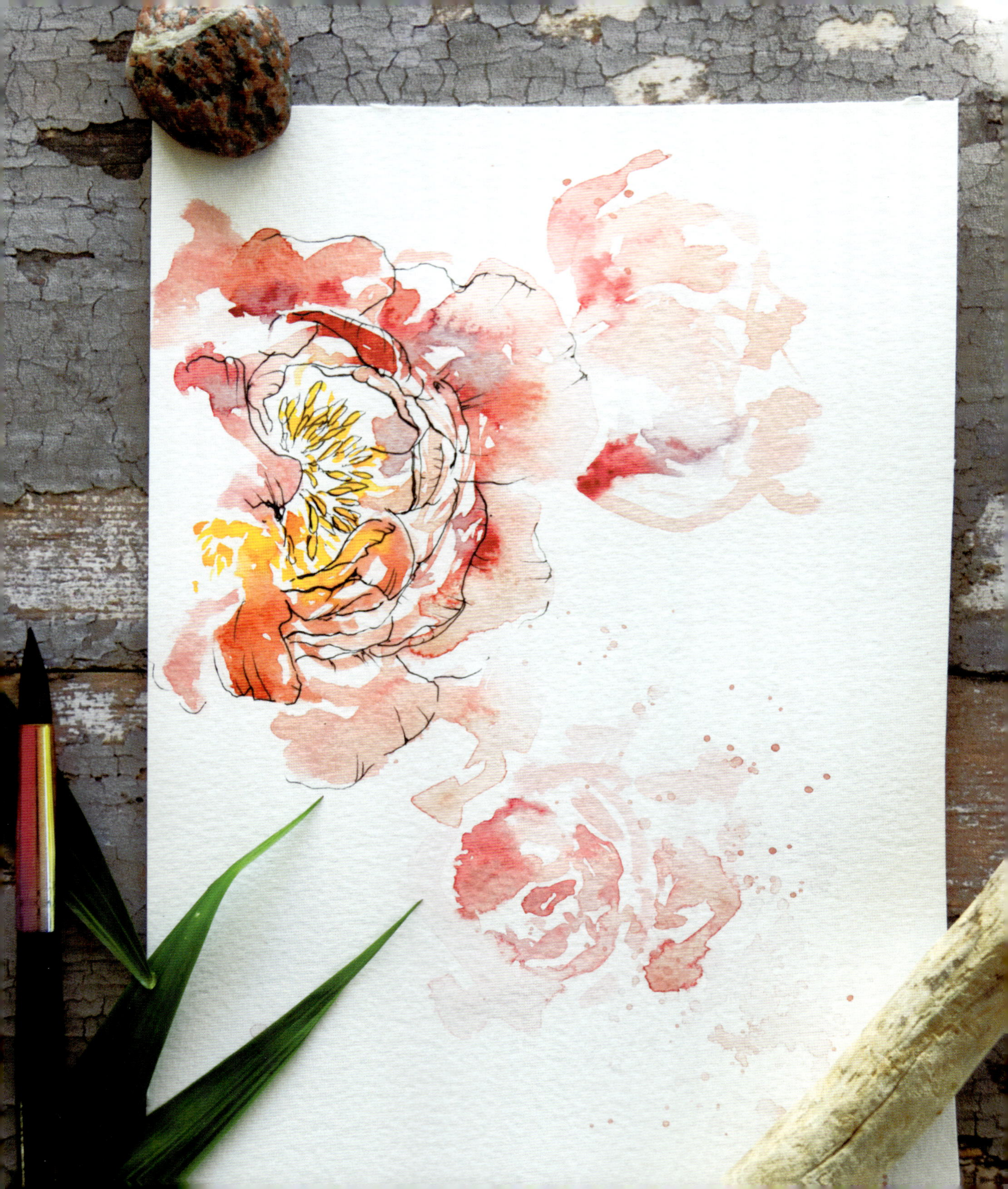

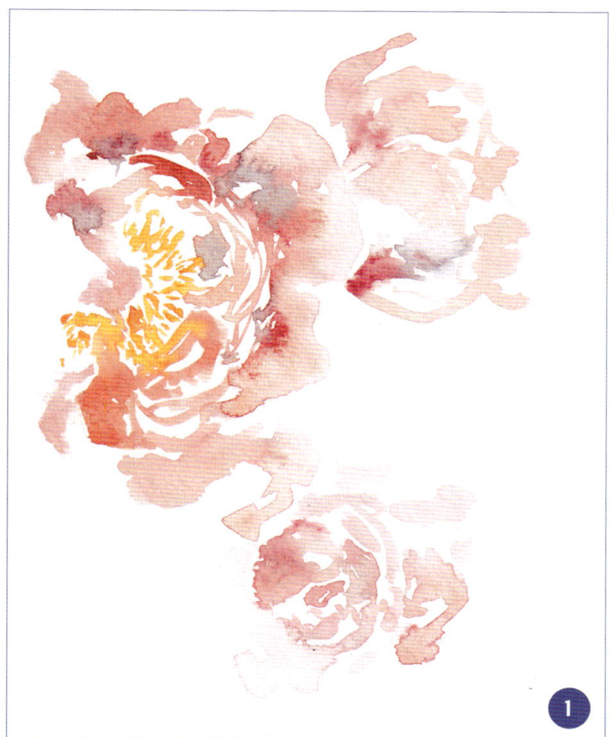

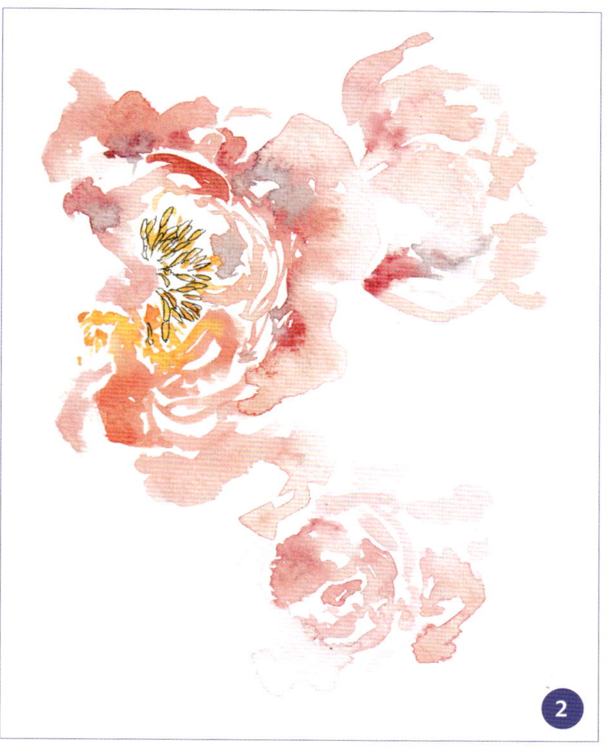

Step 1: Choose a big brush that also has a fine tip so you can paint big and small. I used a size 7 all the way through, but if you don't have that, just go with a small and big brush instead like a size 2 and 9. Load the brush with the warm yellow and paint small, long ovals in the center of the big bloom with the tip of your brush. Make sure to leave plenty of white space. While it's still wet, you can paint the petals around the center with the red mix of quinacridone rose and new gamboge. Keep them narrow and close to the center and bigger as you go outward. If you can paint a petal that is kind of overlapping the center, it will give a great sense of depth. Don't think too much about this process, hold your brush high on the handle and go with the flow. While it's still wet, you can drip in pure paint and the shadow color made from quinacridone rose and phthalo blue. Add a few more blooms with more water.

Step 2: Now this looks pretty good already. But after you let it dry, grab your 005 fineliner, because we want to make it even better. Roughly outline the stamens with the pen by drawing small, long ovals.

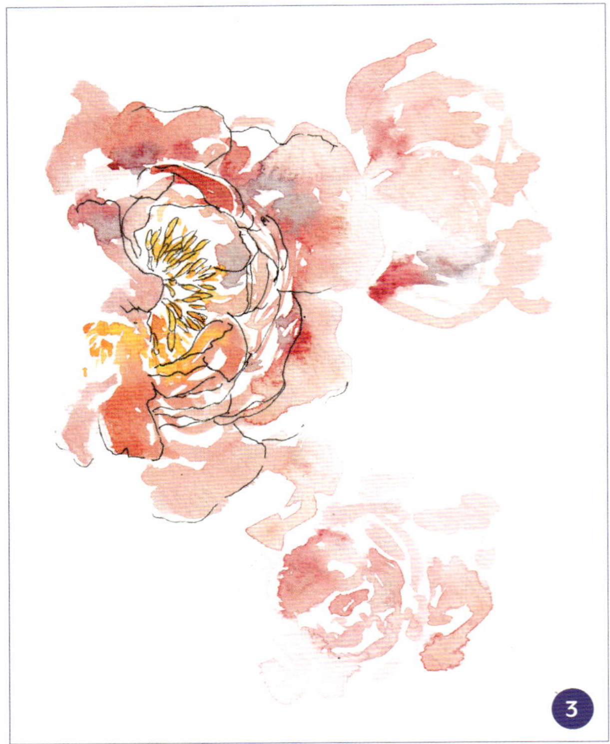

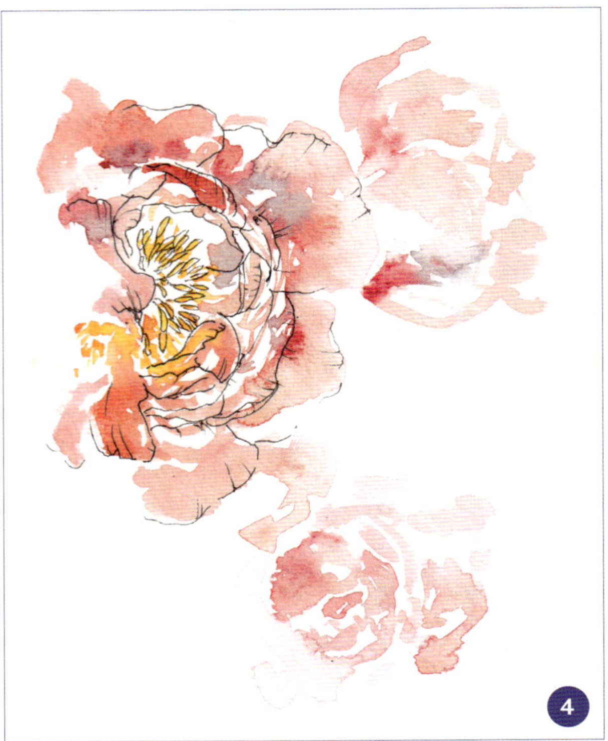

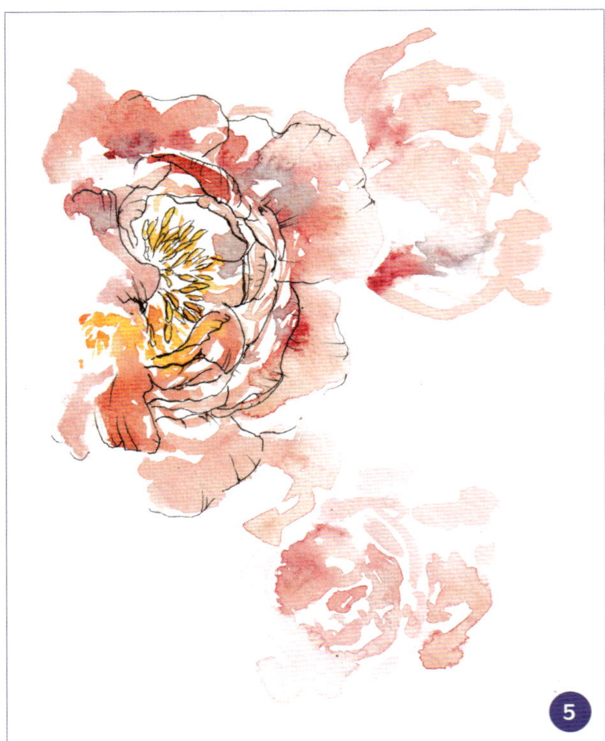

Step 3: And now, we can get started on the petals. Grab your 01 fineliner to loosely draw petals surrounding the middle. If you painted more than one flower, then just add ink to the big one.

The petals close to the center are curled toward the stamens like protecting hands. Draw the outer edge of them and add the curl afterward. The outer petals are big and point away from the flower. You can imagine they are almost like a nest for the flower to rest on. I know this can be tricky to draw, so you might want to use a pencil first.

Step 4: When you've got your petals down, you can add the details with your 005 fineliner to show the curves of the petals. Remember the nest and the protecting hands, which will help you with the direction of the petal lines.

Step 5: If you want to give your flower a bit more dimension, you can add some line variation with the 02 fineliner. Use it closest to the center to increase the detail level there and to guide the viewer.

hibiscus

the flower of romantic love and the perfect woman

If you want a symbol of tropical beauty, this is the perfect flower. It's colorful, vibrant and apparently, it symbolizes the perfect woman. I am not kidding when I say that I laughed so much that I fell out of my chair when reading that. Of course I could be wrong, but I don't think there has ever been a perfect woman. To me, beauty lies in the imperfections, and this book celebrates just that—imperfections in nature and in paintings—so that is how I want to approach this project too.

Materials

Pencil and eraser

Paper: Canson Montval 300gsm (140lb) cold press

Fineliners: sizes 005, 01 and 02

Watercolor brush: size 7

Water and cloth

Palette

Colors

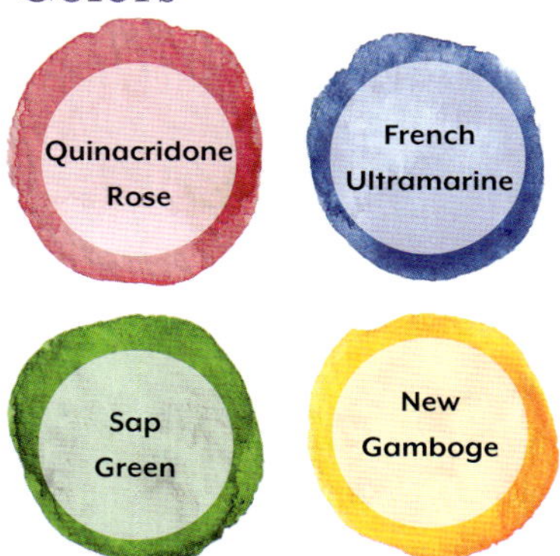

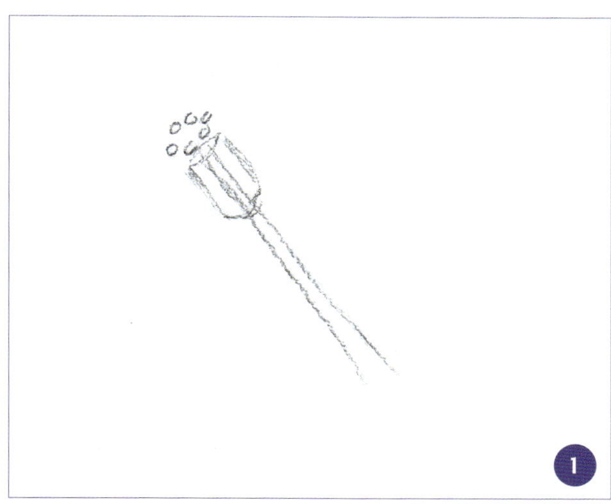

Step 1: Start by grabbing your pencil and sketching out the tall, stalked center. Just draw two parallel long lines, and then you can indicate the placement of the stamens with a rounded box. Add a flat circle of six small ovals, which shows the top part of the stamens.

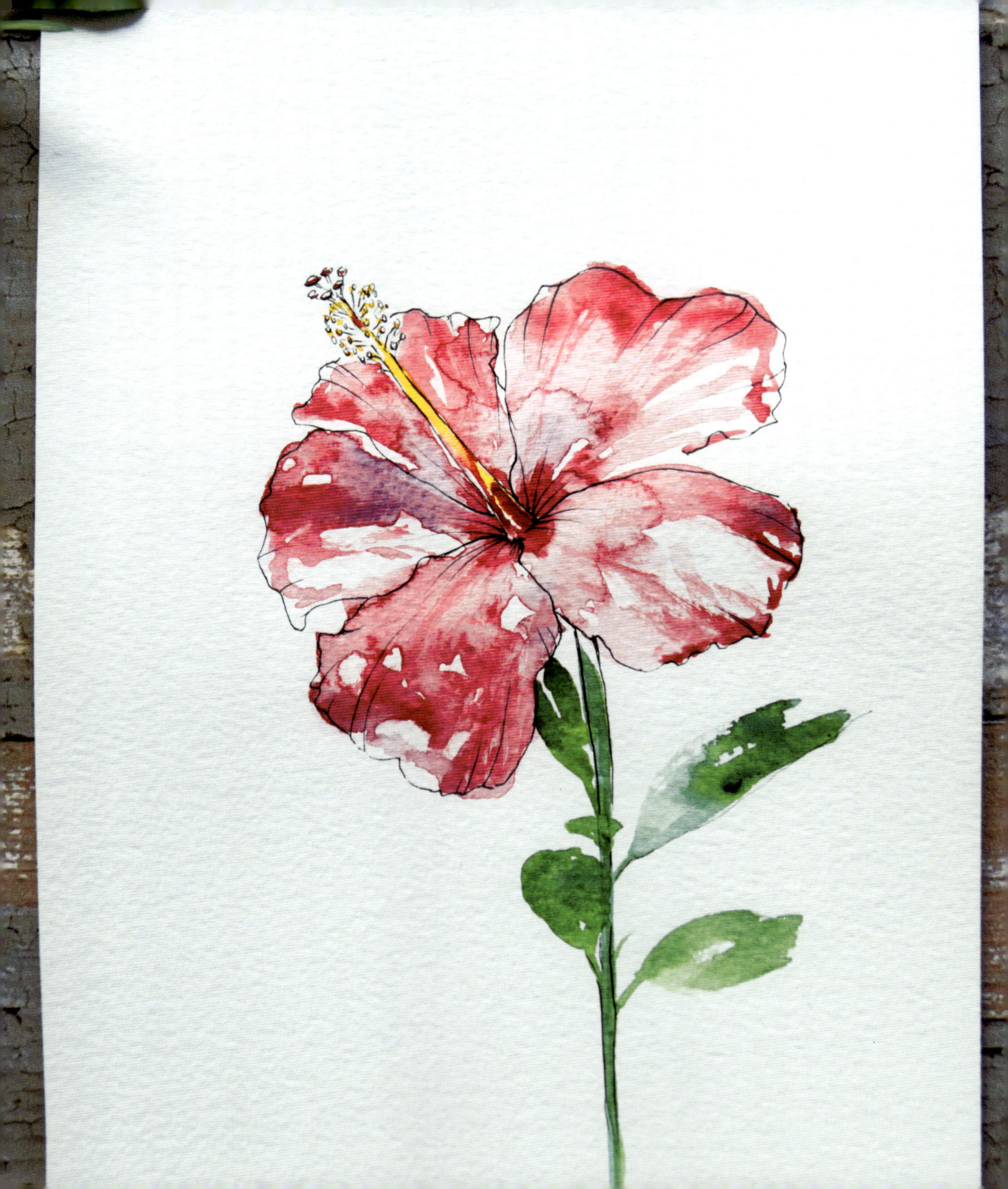

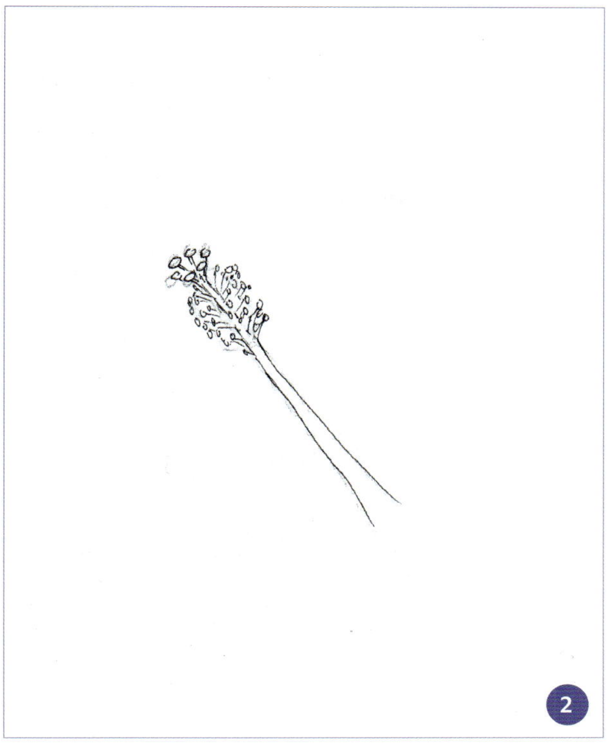

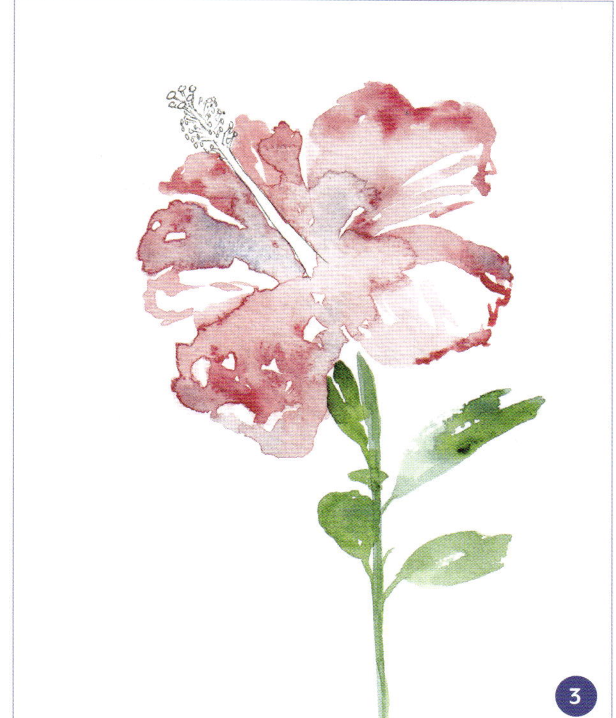

Step 2: Before going any further, you want to outline the important details in the stalk. So, take the thin 005 fineliner and draw the stamens and stalk in detail. Start with the small round circles around the stalk and the lines connecting them to it. Then, finish up by drawing the two lines for the stalk. Remember we can always make the lines thicker later (you can erase your pencil lines at this stage).

Step 3: Grab a nice big brush (I use a size 7) and paint the petals loosely from the center outward. Paint one at a time wet-on-dry, using a watery quinacridone rose and leaving plenty of white space. When you finish a petal, drip in a thicker paint at the outer edge. Here and there, you can also drip in a bit of blue on the petals for a nice color play. To give the flower some texture, drip in clean water in the middle and let it dry. Paint the stem with a mix of sap green and French ultramarine by also using the wet-on-dry technique. Then, add leaves as you work your way down the stem. Now put your painting away for a little bit while you wait for it to dry.

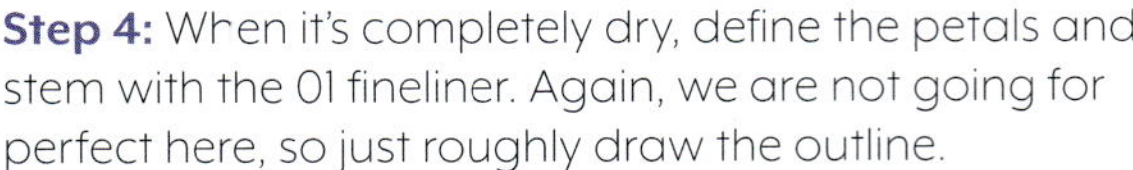

Step 4: When it's completely dry, define the petals and stem with the 01 fineliner. Again, we are not going for perfect here, so just roughly draw the outline.

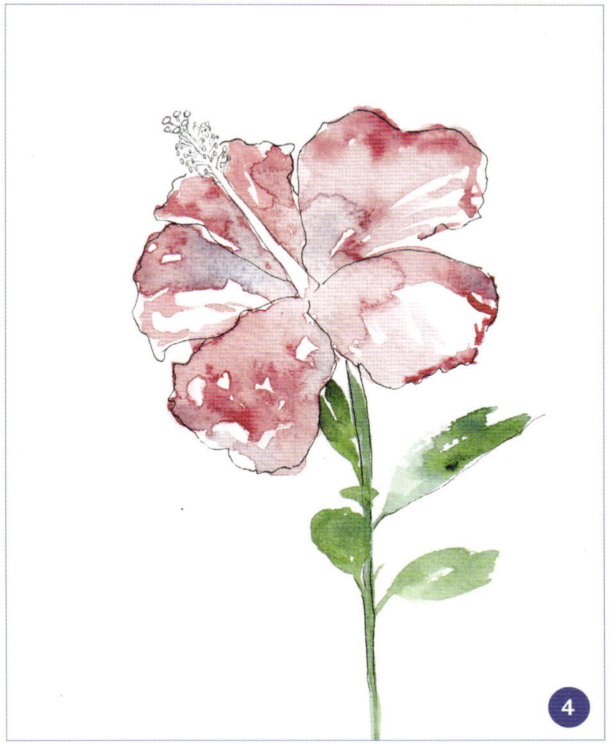

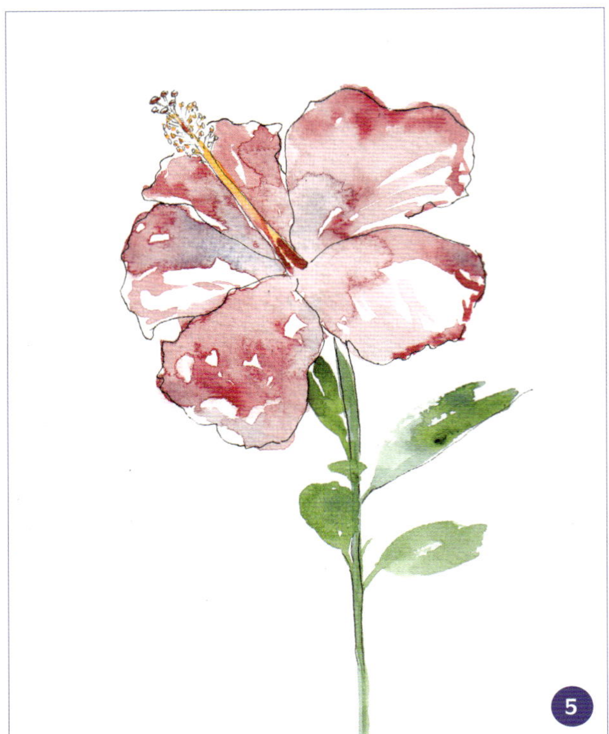

Step 5: Paint the stalk with new gamboge. While it's still wet, you can drip in a bit of quinacridone rose at the bottom of the stalk to connect it to the petals and beneath the stamens for a shadow.

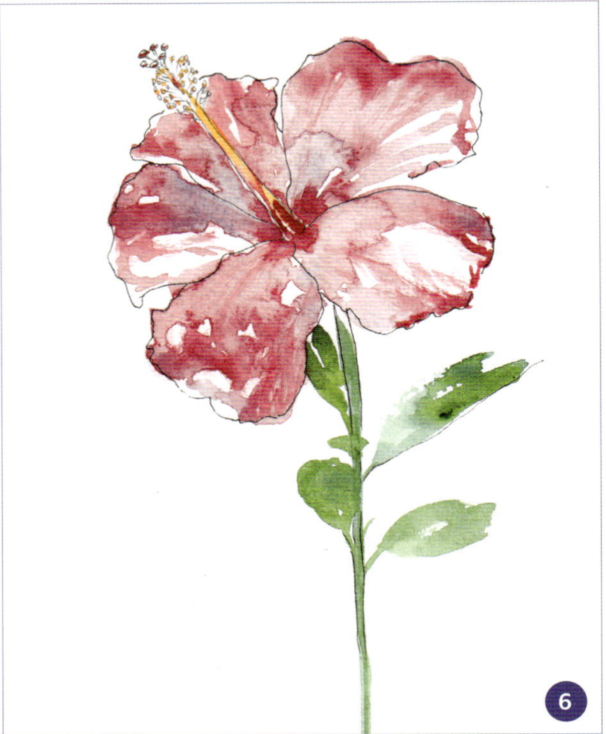

Step 6: While the stalk dries, you can carefully paint around the center with a thicker amount of quinacridone rose. You can soften it at the outer edge like we do with soft shadows (see page 25). Now, drybrush the quinacridone rose on the petals in the direction of their curve for texture and color (see page 21).

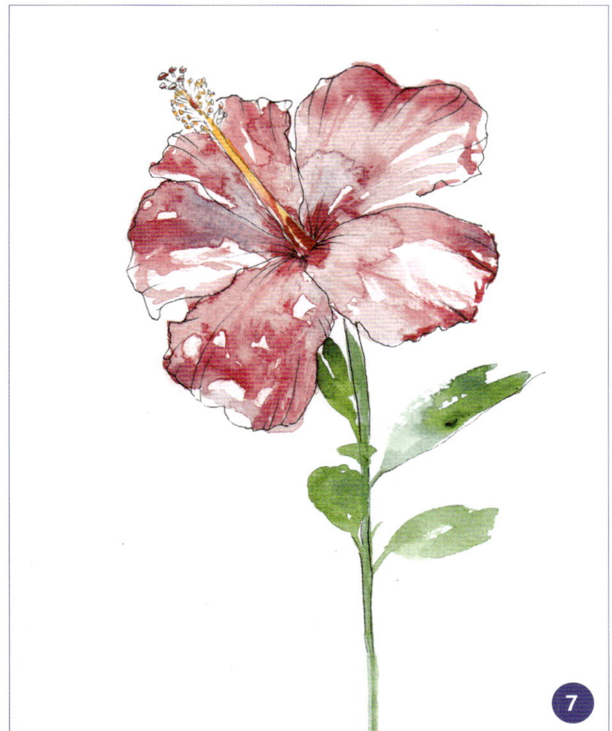

Step 7: When that has dried, go in and finally add the details with your 005 fineliner. The drybrushing did a lot of the work for you, so you don't need many lines here.

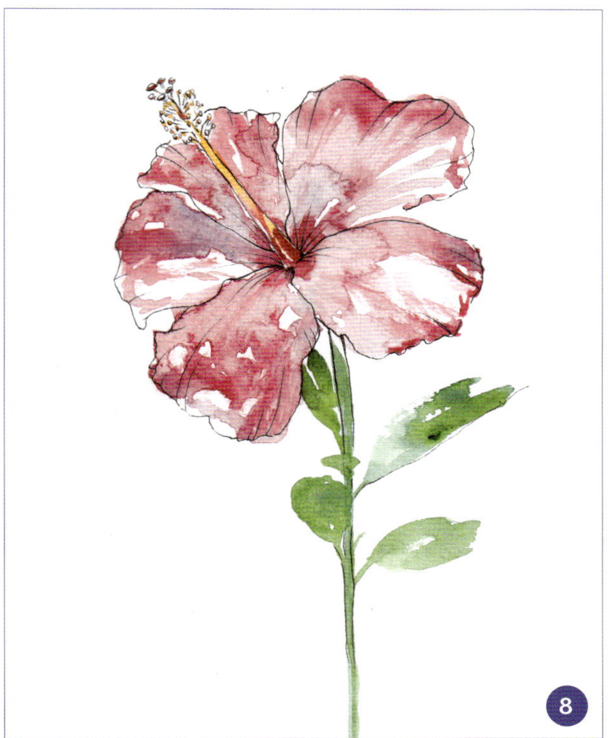

Step 8: In the end, you can add line variation with your 02 fineliner. Strengthen the lines toward the center a bit and add a few edges here and there.

Wow! Not only have you just painted a tropical beauty, but you also finished the part of the book with all the single flowers! I'm so proud of you! Go mix yourself a margarita, put out all your flowers on your table and enjoy admiring your progress.

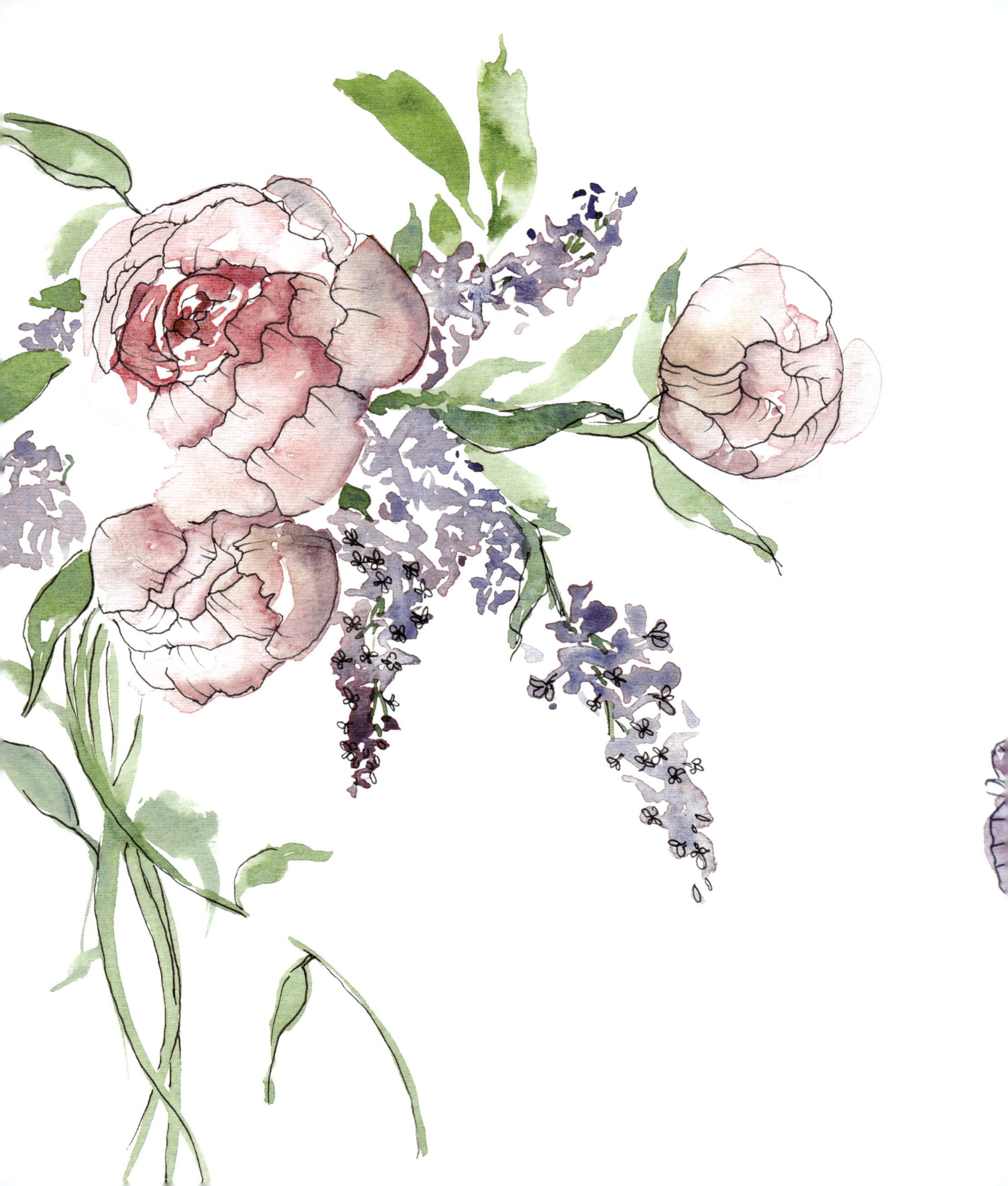

part III: drawing a harmonious composition

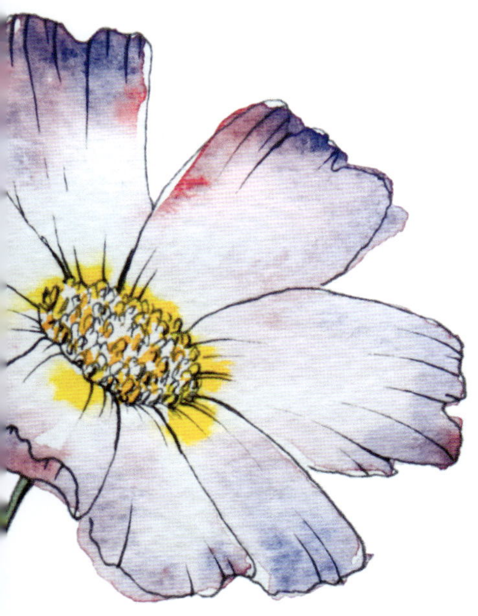

Now that you've completed the individual flower projects in the book, you are well equipped to start creating floral compositions, and that is exactly what you will be learning in this section. When we start a painting, the worst fear is just taking out that paper and having that white page staring back at you. How are you going to approach it? It's always a good idea to start out with a sketch on a different paper. Cheap copy paper will do. Then, you just sketch the ideas you have in your head. In this case, I want to paint a posy (see the artwork on the left). The sketch will help me position the flowers next to each other and I will be able to catch the flaws before they happen on the good paper. I have a few tips for when you sketch bouquets. Let's have a look at them.

exercises for experimenting and honing your personal style

Just like the step-by-step projects in the last section, I made all of the floral compositions slightly different. Some start with line first, some with watercolor, some have a background and some don't; some are super loose and some are tidy. Again, these variations are to help you hone your own creative style. A couple of things before you start:

Honor the Flower in All Stages of Life

When sketching flowers, we are so lucky to be able to show them to the world, thereby making them immortal. With that in mind, we have to think about the complexity of the bloom. Most people just draw flowers in full bloom, but they are actually just as beautiful in their early stages and as a withered flower. By thinking about including different stages of growth, you benefit in more than one way. You respect the flower and you get a sketch that is a lot more interesting to look at.

Vary the Angle

Be sure to show off your flowers from different angles. It's the combination of a subtle sideview and a full-on open portrait that creates a beautiful combination.

Mixing Flowers for a Harmonious Composition

When you choose your flowers, you want to make sure you have three sizes of flowers.

Statement Flowers: These flowers are the focal point of your composition. You want to keep these to just a few so that they don't overpower each other. Examples of focal flowers could be roses, hydrangeas or peonies.

Secondary Flowers: Have flowers in the medium range to fill up the space and give the posy character. These could be daisies, tulips and a ton of other flowers.

Detail Flowers: In between the statement and secondary flowers, you want to add details. This will give your bouquet some texture and give it that extra pop of interest. Choose small flowers or flowers with a lot of texture like Queen Anne's lace, forget-me-nots or maybe even berries when we get closer to fall.

If you only want one or two types of flowers, think about how to switch up the size in a different way. Maybe you can add smaller flower heads, buds, leaves or small details of some kind.

placement of the flowers

When deciding where to sketch your flowers in a composition, you want to consider a few things.

Draw Thumbnails

A thumbnail is a small sketch of how you imagine your drawing will look. Before working with your watercolor paper, it's great to sketch out a few versions of your flowers on a piece of copy paper. You can do as many as you like because they only take a few seconds to draw. Experiment with this and make as many thumbnails as you need before you love the way it looks.

Start Big

Start out with the biggest flowers, and then add the medium-sized ones and fill up the empty space with detail flowers for texture.

Odd Numbers Are Your Friends

When it comes to compositions, I always choose to have one, three or five of one type of flower in my bouquet. For some reason, two or four flowers just ruin everything. So let's not go there.

Make Your Florals Dance

Put on some sweet tunes while drawing your flowers. The music will get into your pencil and help you sketch with music in mind. All beautiful art has a rhythm that you can almost see in the brushstrokes and in the lines. Think about this when drawing stems, petals and leaves. And it is totally up to you if it is Mozart or Beyoncé.

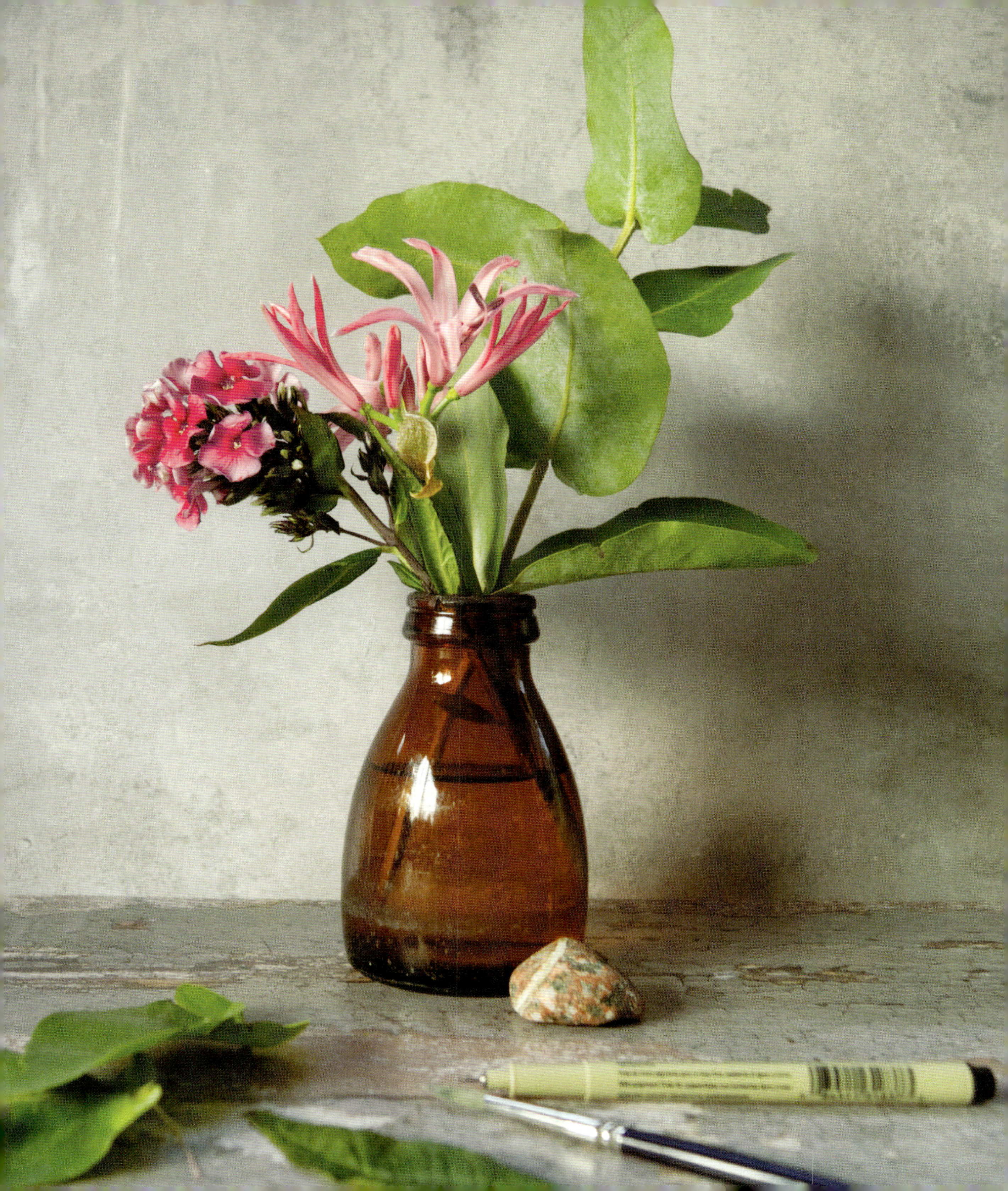

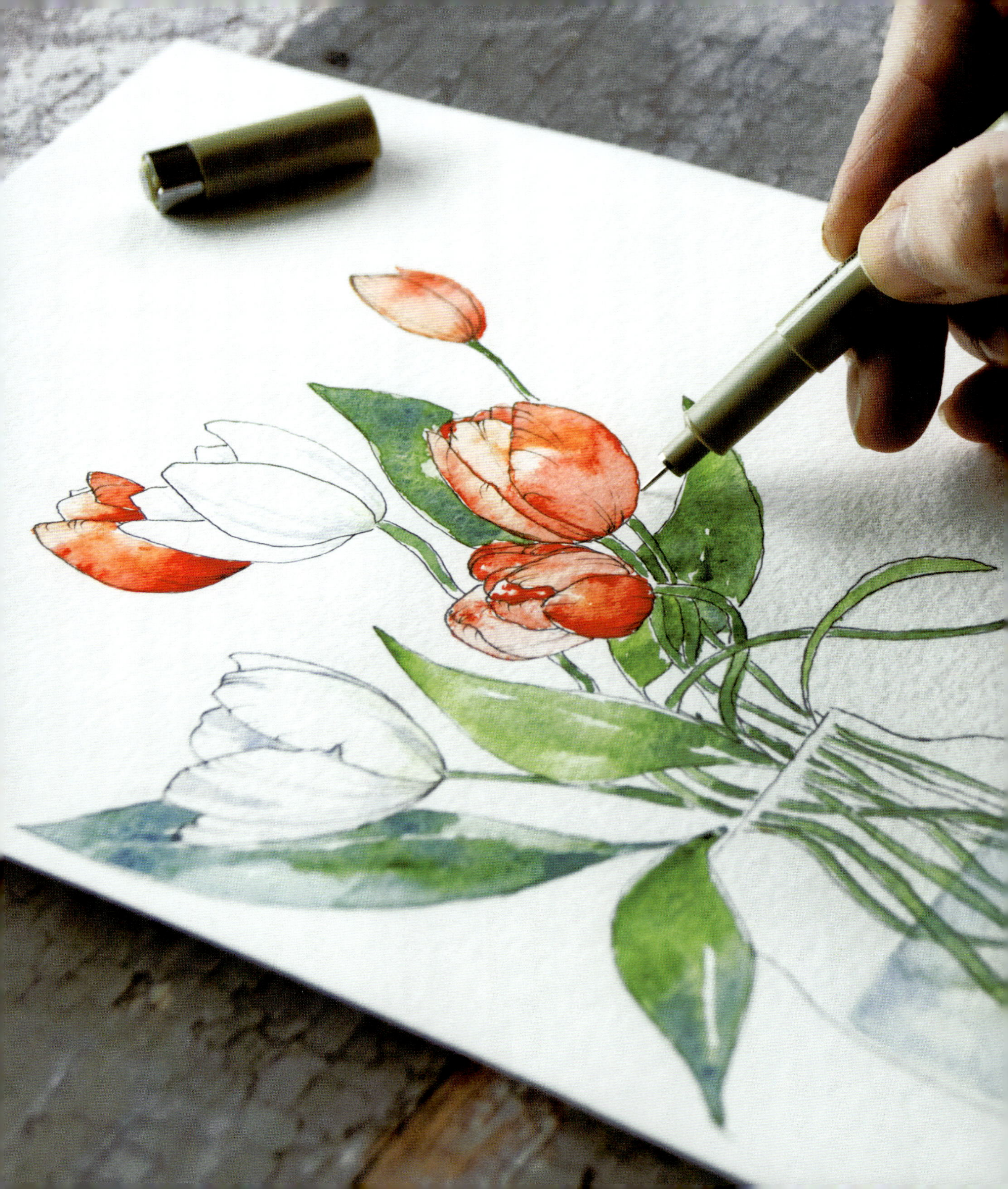

red and white tulips

in a glass vase

This step-by-step project is the first in the section of compositions, and it's all about tulips. Tulips are a great flower to start with because their stems tend to bend and dance, which makes them a lot of fun to play with in a drawing like this. You can easily create a composition with lots of life, like I talk about above (page 106). Here, I thought I'd challenge you, as always, with something new—painting white flowers. You did it a little bit with the snowdrop (page 70), but here you really experiment with it. You are going to love it, I promise.

Materials

Pencil and eraser

Paper: Canson Montval 300gsm (140lb) cold press

Fineliners: sizes 005 and 01

Watercolor brush: size 7

Water and cloth

Palette

Colors

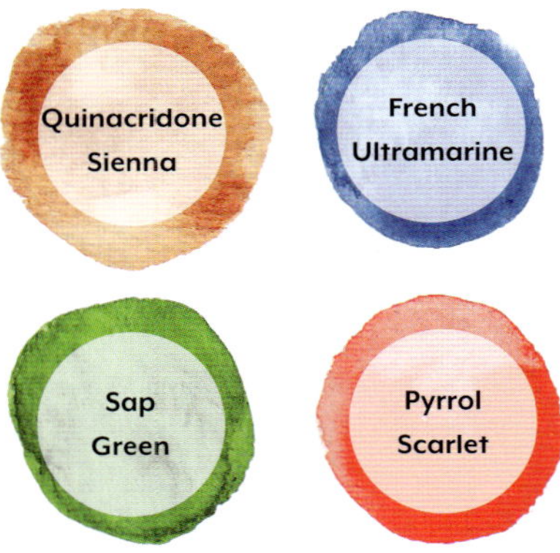

Mixes

The color used in the white tulips is a mix of French ultramarine with quinacridone sienna to get a pretty gray.

The green leaves are a mix of French ultramarine with sap green.

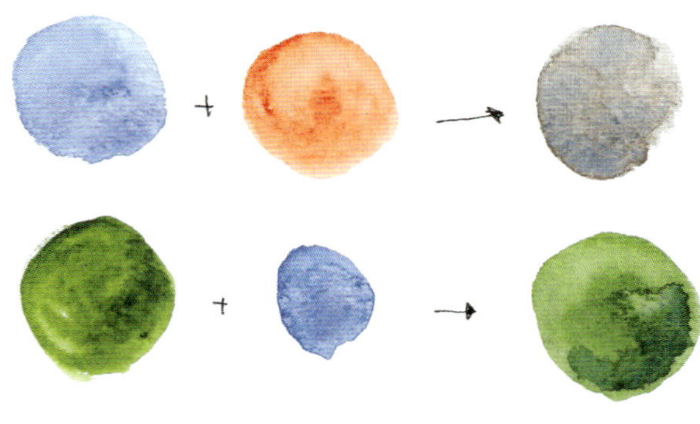

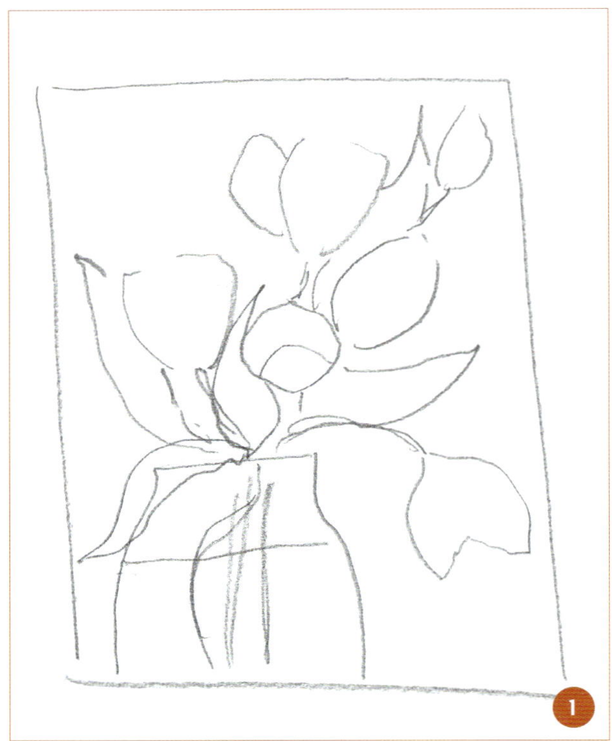

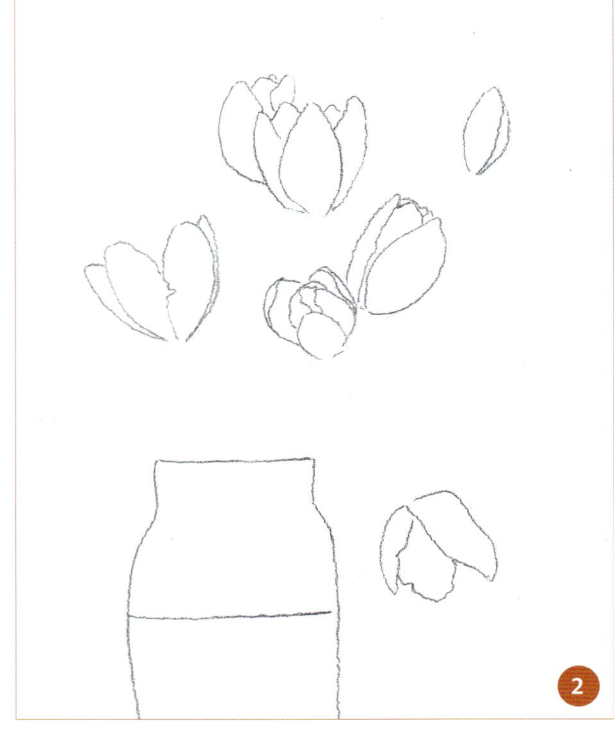

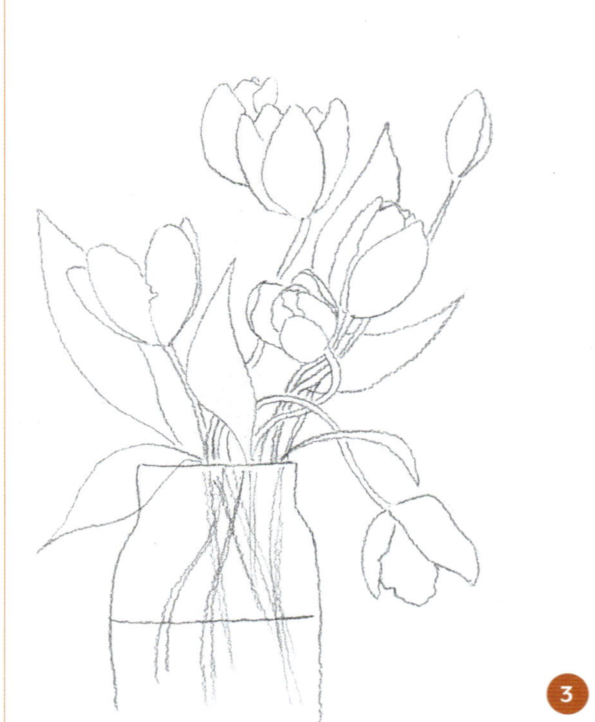

Step 1: Start out by drawing a thumbnail in pencil on a scrap piece of paper to place your flowers. It's totally okay to draw more than one thumbnail—it's all about closing in on a pretty composition. Remember we already did tulips on page 49, so if you want an in-depth guide, you can use that as a reference.

Step 2: Now, get out your watercolor paper and your pencil. Begin by placing the vase and the flower heads. Start with the biggest flower heads and work your way down to the smaller blooms afterward.

Step 3: Then, still with your pencil in your hand, draw out your leaves and stems. Be careful to follow them through. Some will overlap and hide behind others, so try to make sure that if you start a stem, it also ends somewhere that make sense. Also remember what I talked about on page 106 and try to keep your stems dancing to give your bouquet life and movement.

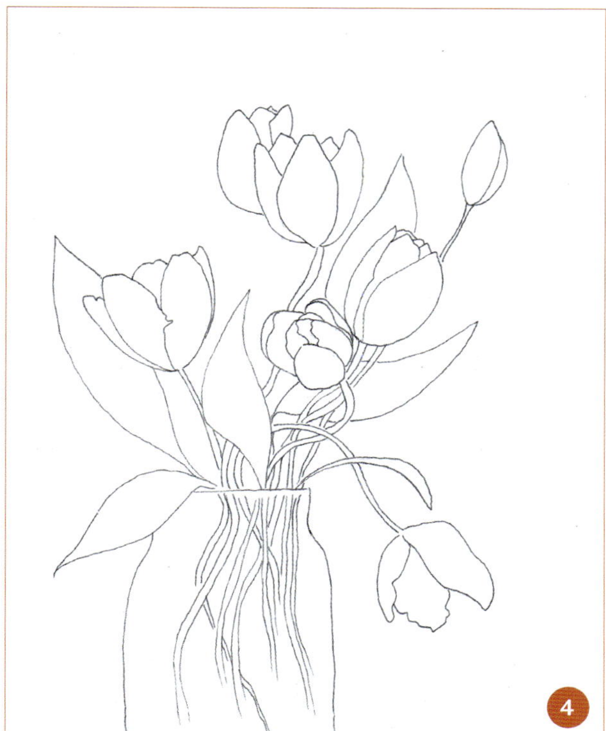

Step 4: When you are happy with your sketch, you can grab your 01 fineliner and, just like we did with the single flowers, sketch out a rough outline. Afterward, you can erase your pencil lines so that you are ready to start painting.

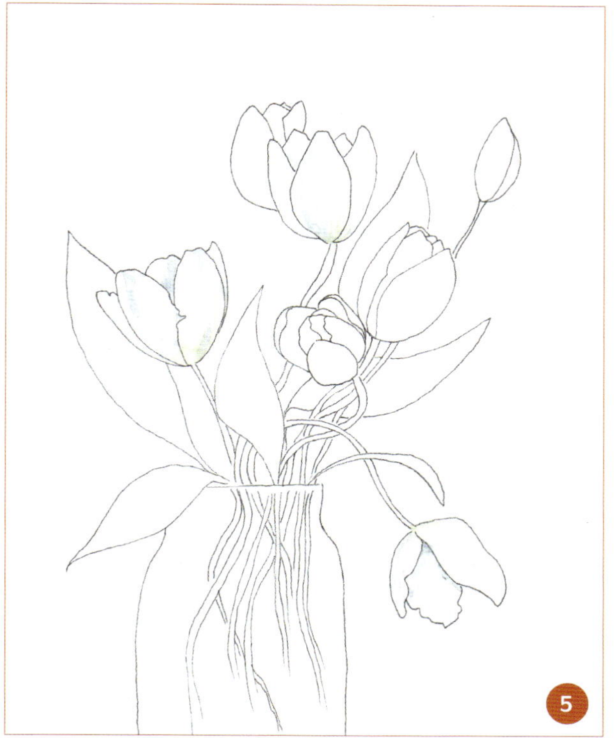

Step 5: Let's start with the hardest flowers first, the white flowers. White flowers are actually not white at all (mind-blowing), but instead reflect what is surrounding them. So, I mixed a very watery mix of quinacridone sienna and French ultramarine to create a neutral out of the colors I also use in the rest of the painting. Carefully paint where you feel there would be shadows and folds from the bottom of the petals and from the top, just like you did with the painted details on the magnolia (page 61). Before it's completely dry, paint a bit of watery sap green at the bottom. This will be the petals reflecting the leaves.

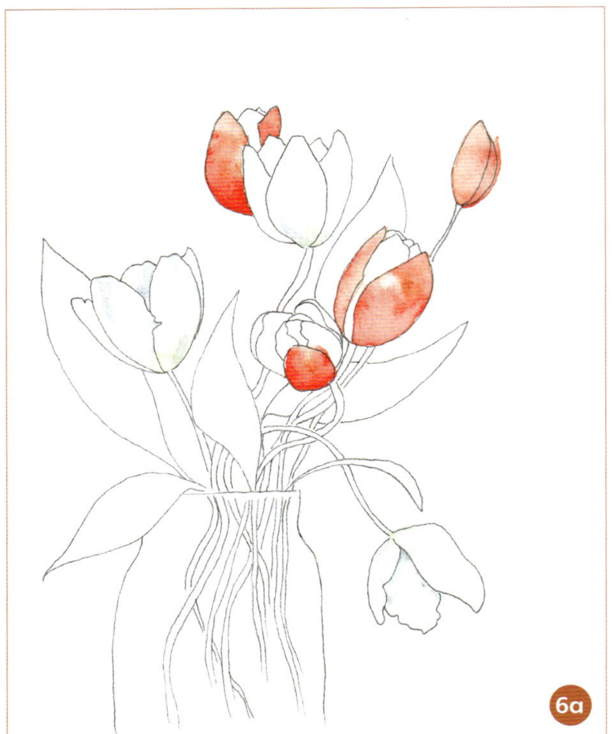

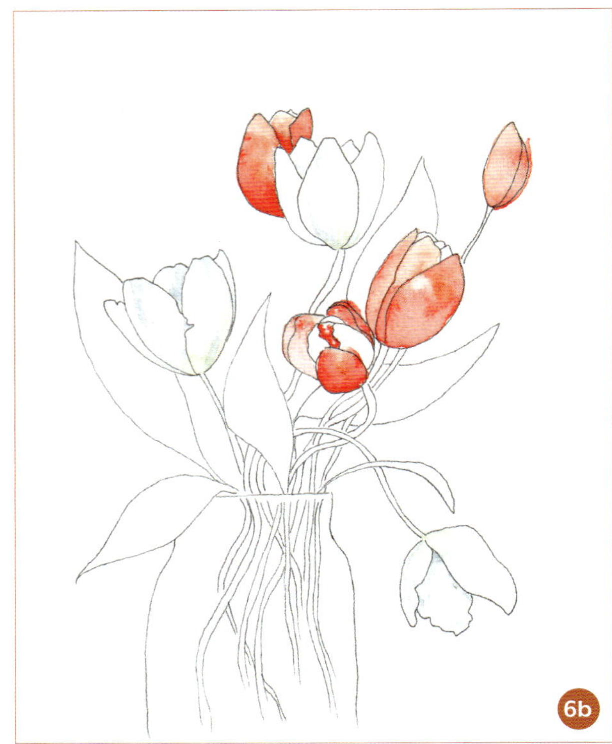

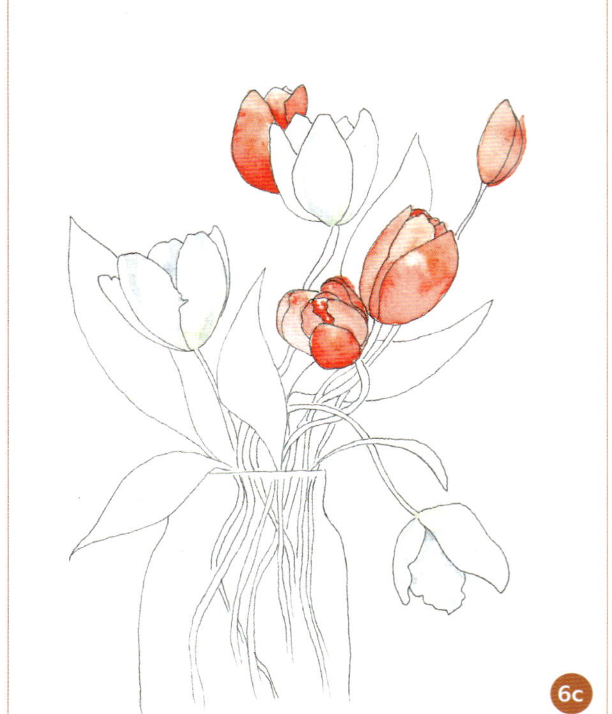

Step 6: The red tulips are painted in three rounds to make sure they don't bleed into each other. Wet one petal at a time with your size 7 brush and drip in pyrrol scarlet and quinacridone sienna. Don't go overboard with the colors, but let them flow freely. While you wait for some to dry, you can add detail lines with your 005 fineliner, just like you did the first time you sketched the tulip on page 49.

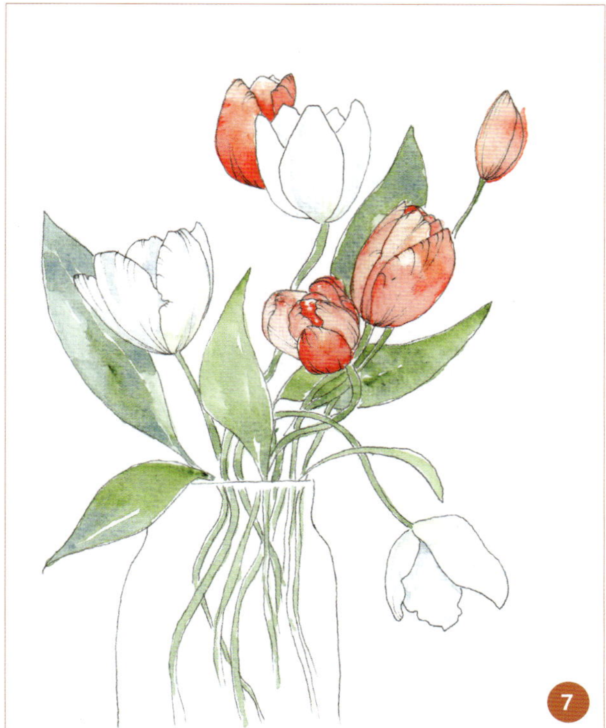

Step 7: When the flower heads are dry, you can paint the stems and leaves. Use an uneven mix of sap green and French ultramarine to get a beautiful color variation. Also, see if you can keep a white space in the center of the leaves to show the vein going through.

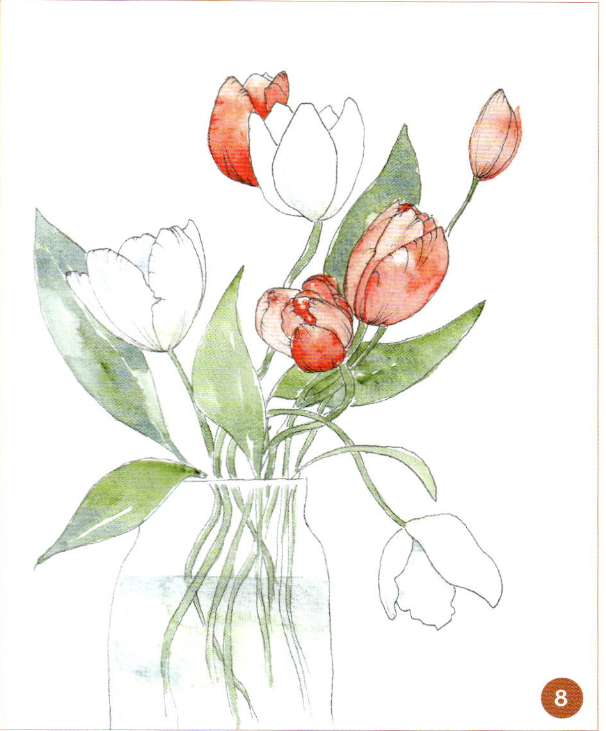

Step 8: Finally, wet the area in the vase where you want water. Make sure you leave some space between the water and the edge of the vase to show the thickness of the glass. Now you can load your brush with a bluer mix of the color you used for the leaves and drip it into the top of the water. Let it flow into the water and mingle all by itself. Don't mess with it too much, but let it dry freely.

And that was a vase of tulips for you! Well done!

a dancing bouquet
of cosmos and daisies

As I talked about on page 106, it's always powerful to combine different sizes of flowers when you are thinking about your composition. So, in this bouquet I chose cosmos for you to draw as your main flower and daisies as the supporting actors. The beauty about the cosmo is that it is stunning from so many angles, so when you draw your thumbnail, think about twisting and turning the flower heads.

Materials

Pencil and eraser

Paper: Canson Montval 300gsm (140lb) cold press

Fineliners: sizes 005, 01 and 02

Watercolor brush: size 4

Water and cloth

Palette

Colors

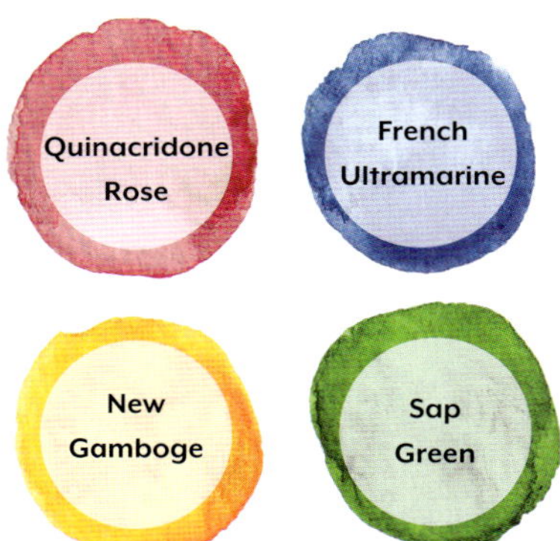

Mixes

Premix a batch of quinacridone rose with French ultramarine for the cosmos. You don't want too much blue, so make sure to use mostly quinacridone rose. You don't need a big batch for this—just a little bit more than you would use for the other paintings in the book—and you can always mix more. That way, your flowers will get different tones depending on your mixes.

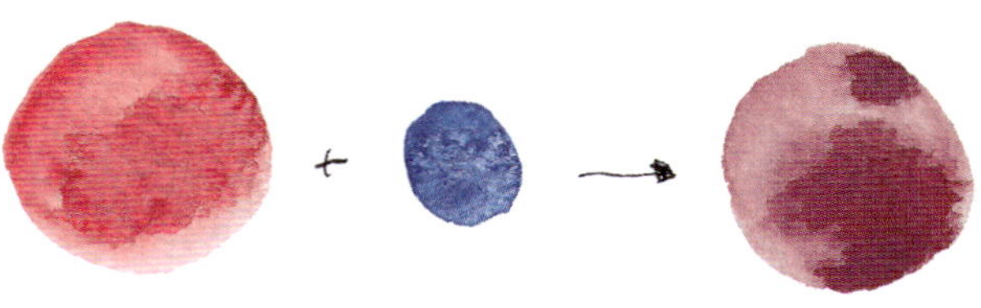

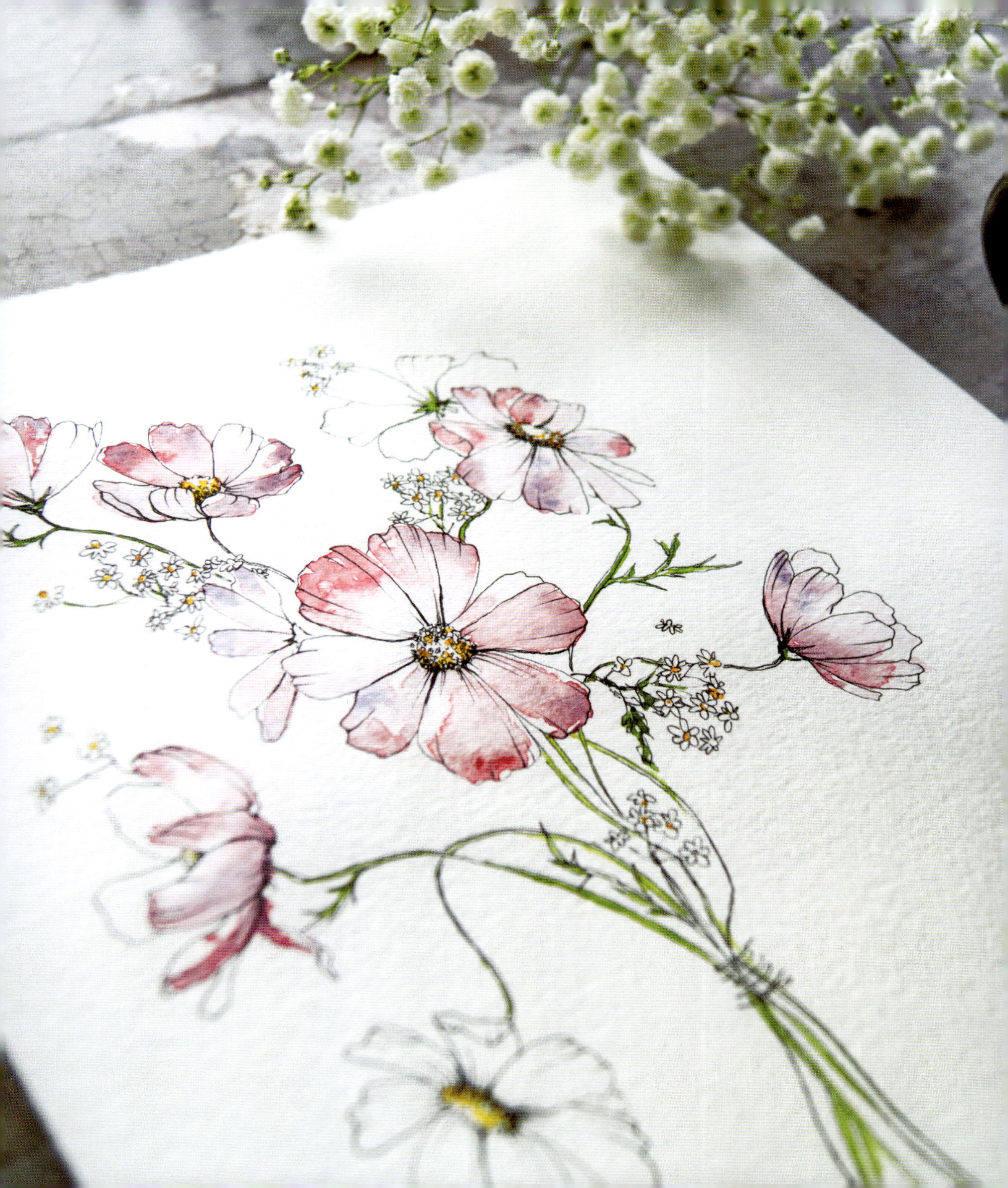

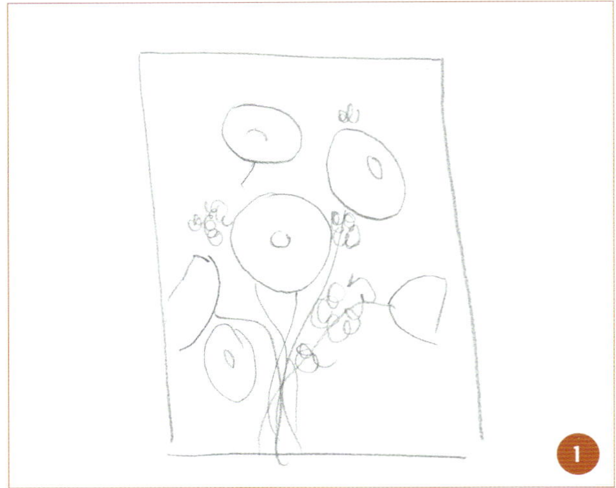

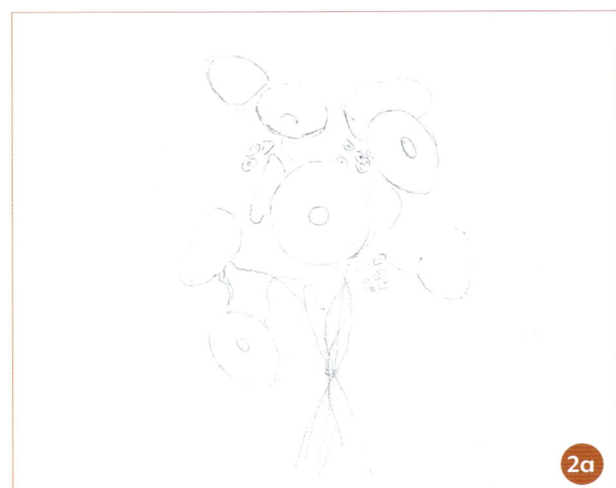

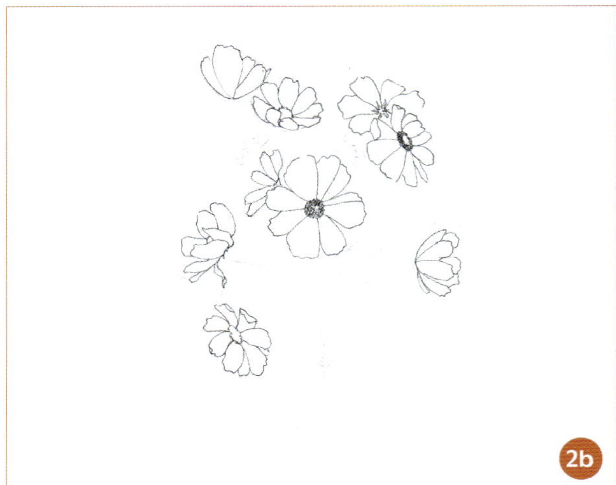

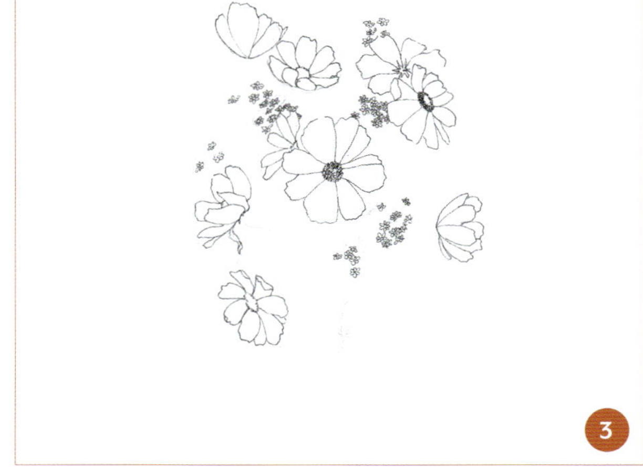

Step 1: Start with a thumbnail (or ten) like before. Try positioning your flowers so you show off their angles as well as giving them an organic, dancing feel. Some are bowing down and others reach for the sky. For a more in-depth guide into drawing daisies and cosmos, see pages 29 and 45.

Step 2: When you feel like you have your dancers ready, you can continue to your watercolor paper. Use the 01 fineliner and follow your pencil guide on the big flower heads to let your dancers come to life.

Step 3: Now, you can fill in some of the areas between the cosmos with small daisies. Keep them very small by using your 005 fineliner to draw them.

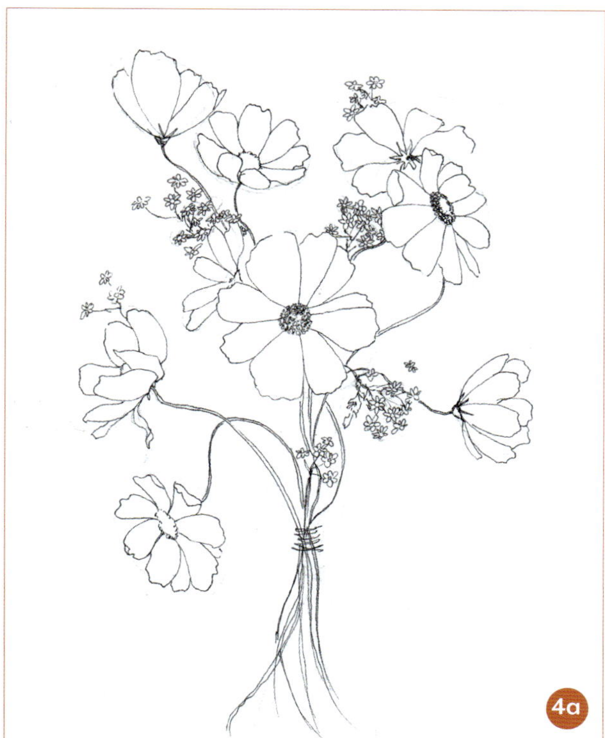

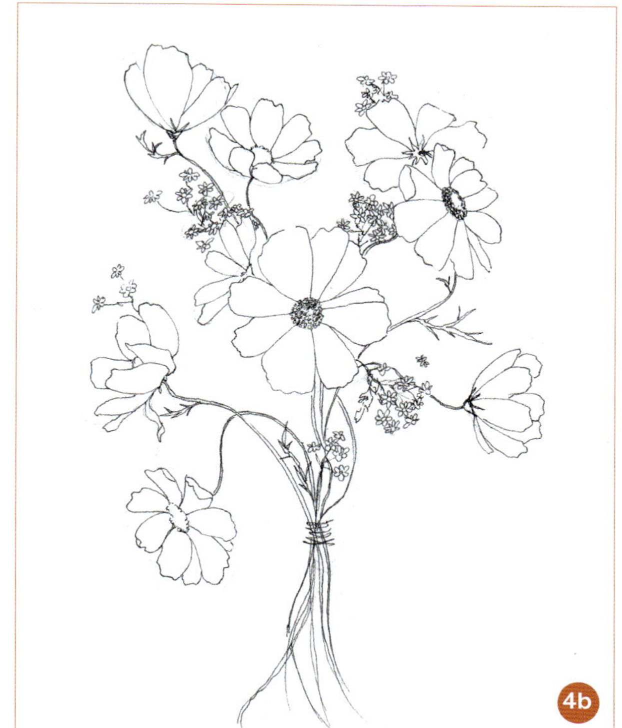

Step 4: Now that you have your blooms all ready, you can draw in your stems and leaves. Think about how the stems hide behind the flowers, and let them meet at some point so you can draw a small thread to tie up the bouquet. Now, you can safely erase your pencil guide.

Step 5: It's time for the first watercolor wash. Start with the cosmos. Here, you can wet the petals and drip in the color you premixed of quinacridone rose and a tad of French ultramarine. While it dries, you can drip in some purer paint. While you are waiting for that to dry, you can work your way through the daisies by giving them a small yellow center with new gamboge. Then, continue to the stems and leaves with a quick wet-on-dry stroke of sap green. You will notice that while you painted that, the cosmos have dried and you can give them a bit of the new gamboge in the center. Yes! You are so good!

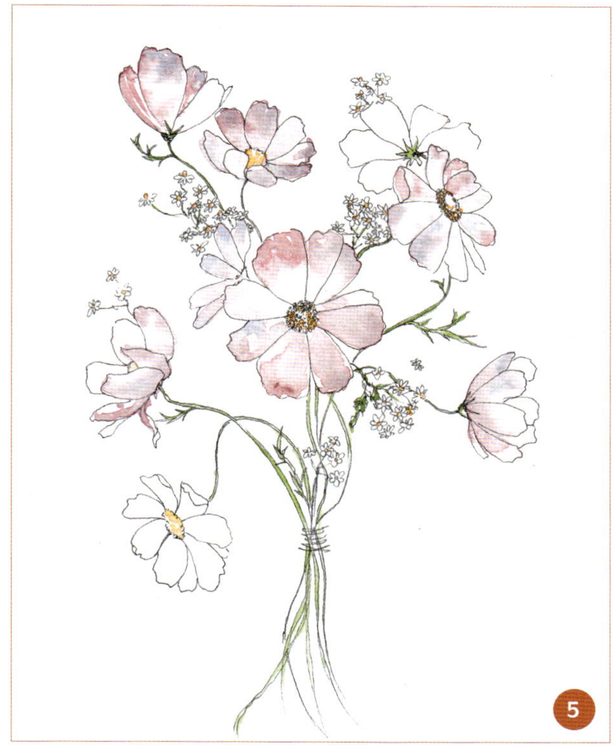

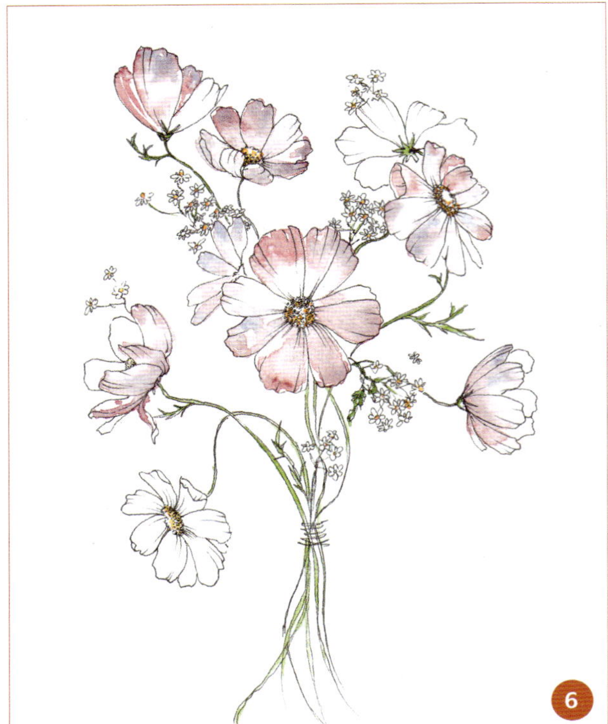

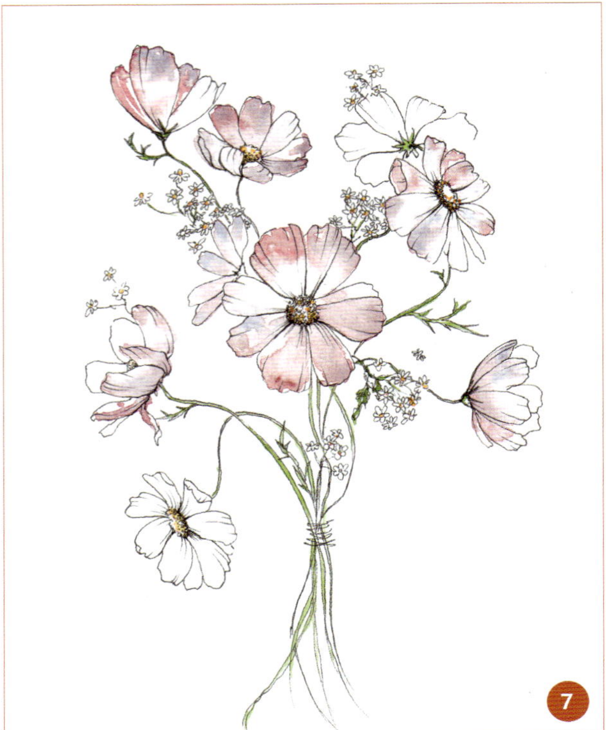

Step 6: When it's completely dry, you can go in again with your 005 fineliner and add a few detail lines to the cosmos, shaping the petals a little.

Step 7: Finally, strengthen the areas around the flower centers with the 02 fineliner. Use it close to the border between the middle and the petals, as well as between some of the petals to indicate an overlapping shadow.

You have just painted my favorite summer cosmos! I love it!

a bouquet of peonies and lilacs

As you know, peonies are big and bulky. So, how can you make them look light and airy in a composition? I like to do this by using a few flowers that are almost still in bud, combining them with a textured and lively sidekick, the lilac. In this tutorial, you can really see the effect of having flowers of varying sizes. The combination of the bulky peony and the very detailed lilac gives us a harmonious look and, combined with flowy stems, we get a super fun and light composition.

Materials

Pencil and eraser

Paper: Canson Montval 300gsm (140lb) cold press

Watercolor brush: size 7

Water and cloth

Palette

Fineliners: sizes 005 and 01

Colors

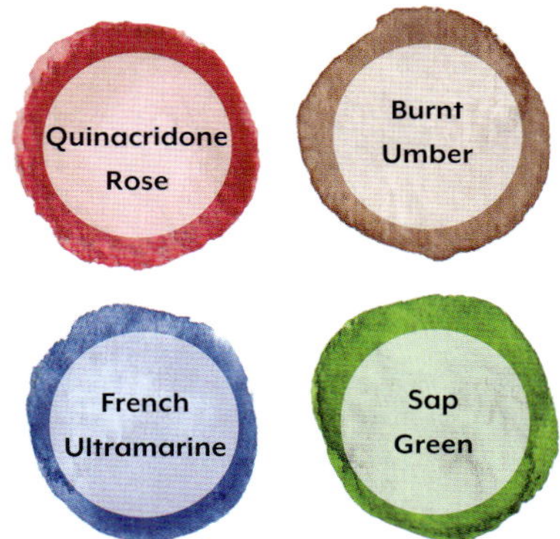

Mixes

The lilacs are painted with a mix of French ultramarine and a bit of quinacridone rose.

The leaves are painted with sap green and a bit of French ultramarine

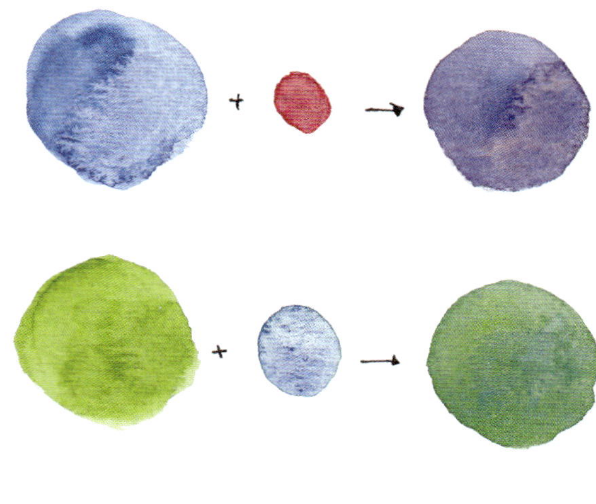

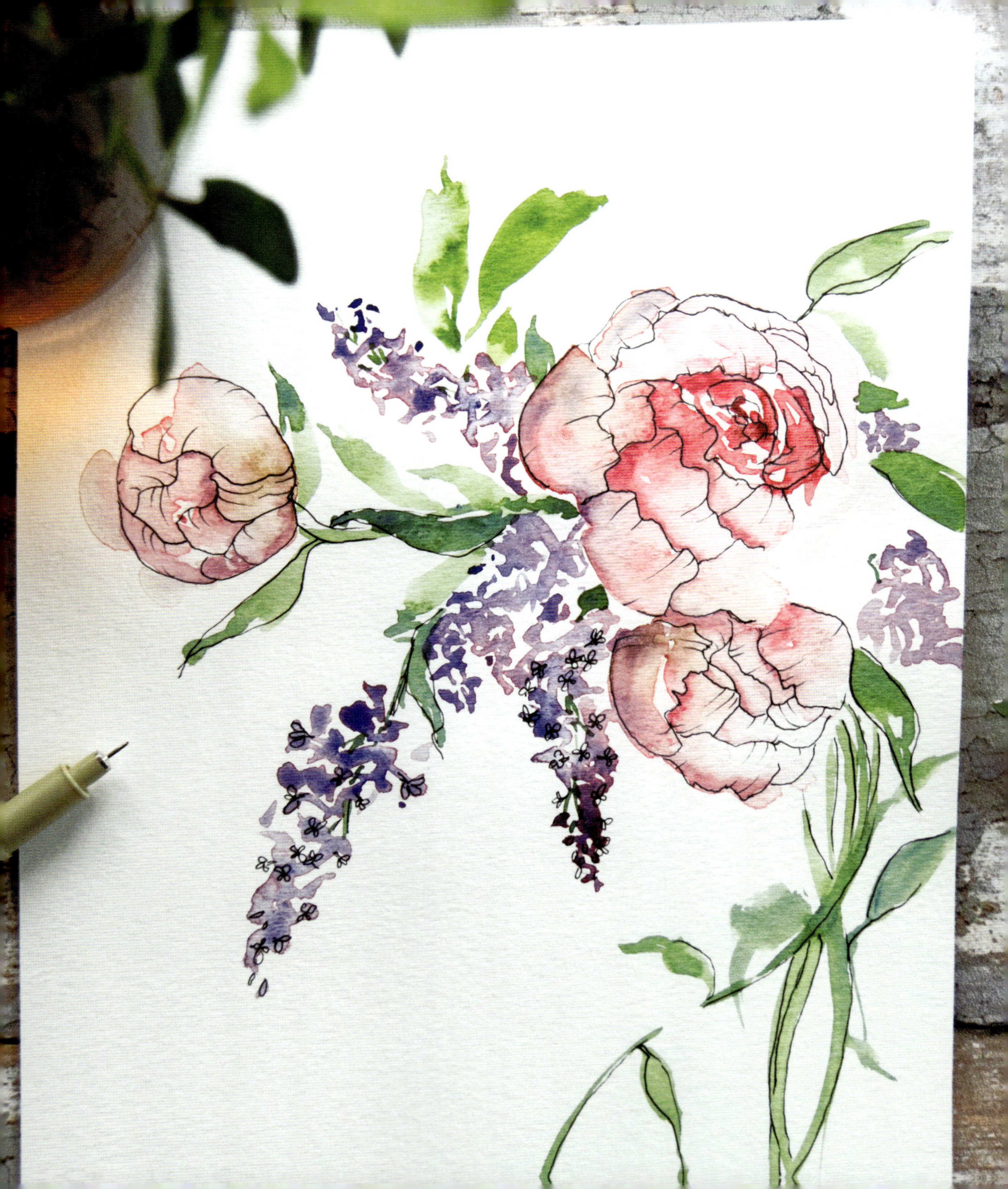

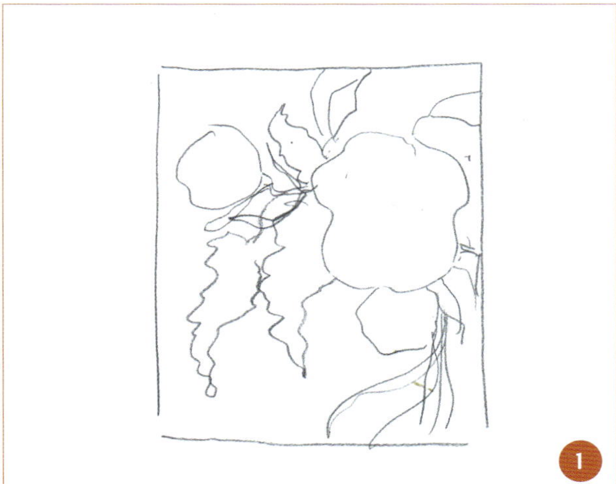

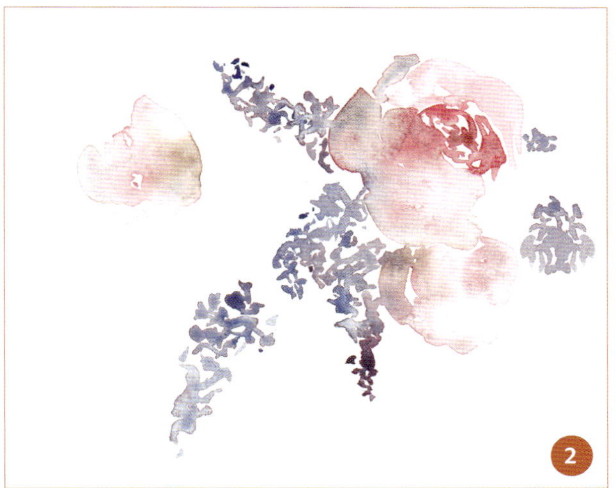

Step 1: Draw a thumbnail again and, this time, think about how you can make the peonies less heavy. Try to see if you can give it a balance with some light stems and leaves against the heavy flower head. If you want to go back to see how to draw peonies and lilacs, you can find that on pages 95 and 83.

Step 2: This time, we start with watercolor first and we are going to begin with the flowers. So, start out by putting some quinacridone rose in your palette and paint the peonies very loosely with a big brush, like a size 7, by making small strokes in the middle and bolder and bigger strokes as you move out. Think about the shape and the white space, not the details of the petals at this point. While the paint is still wet, take some burnt Umber and drip it into the petals in a few places. Then, find your mix of French ultramarine with a bit of the quinacridone rose in it, and use the tip of your brush to very loosely paint lilacs cascading below and over the peonies. Let them end in a tip, almost like an organic-looking cone. That was a lot of brush movement, so stand up and do some yoga while you wait for it to dry.

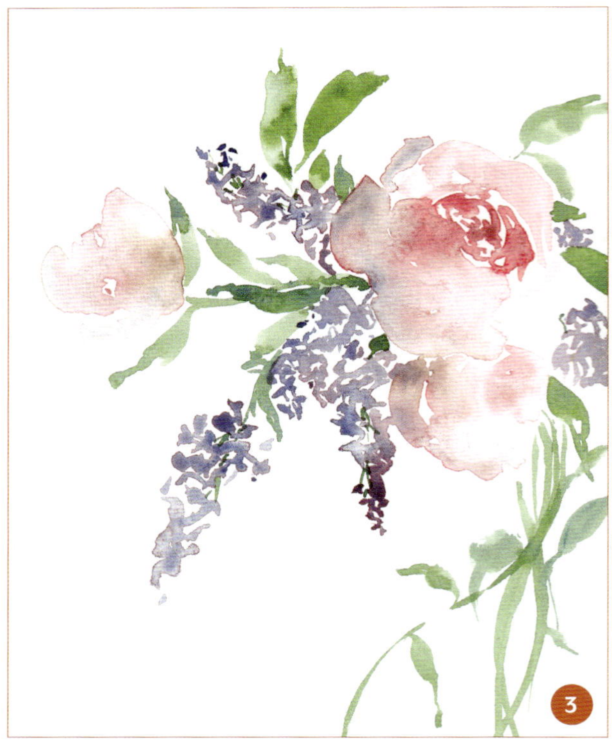

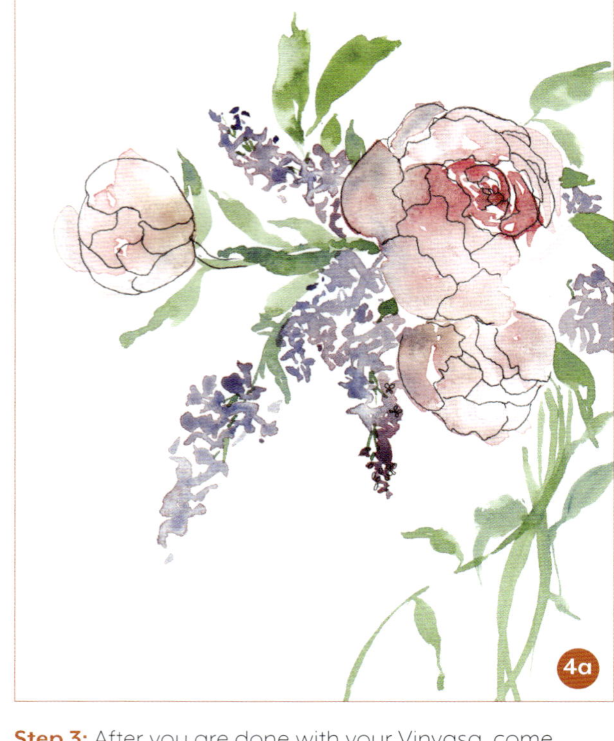

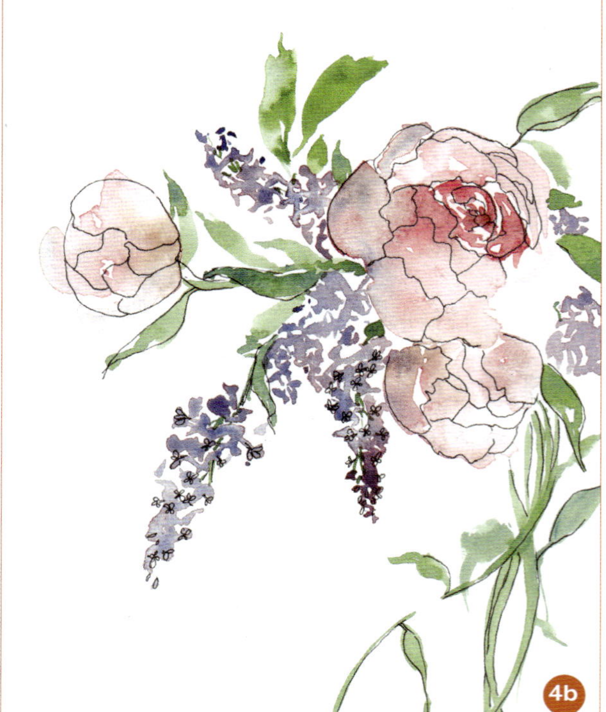

Step 3: After you are done with your Vinyasa, come back to paint some stems and leaves. Take a good look at your thumbnail before loading your brush with sap green and a bit of French ultramarine. Since you already did your yoga (good for you!), you can get a cup of tea while you wait for the greens to dry.

Step 4: I know by now it looks a little messy, but loose watercolor always does that. You can clean up the shapes now with your fineliner. So, grab your 01 fineliner and get started on drawing. Remember you already did the peonies (page 95) and the lilacs (page 83), so you just need to do it once again. Don't add too much ink to the lilacs, stems and leaves since they are just supporting actors. We want the most focus on the star peony.

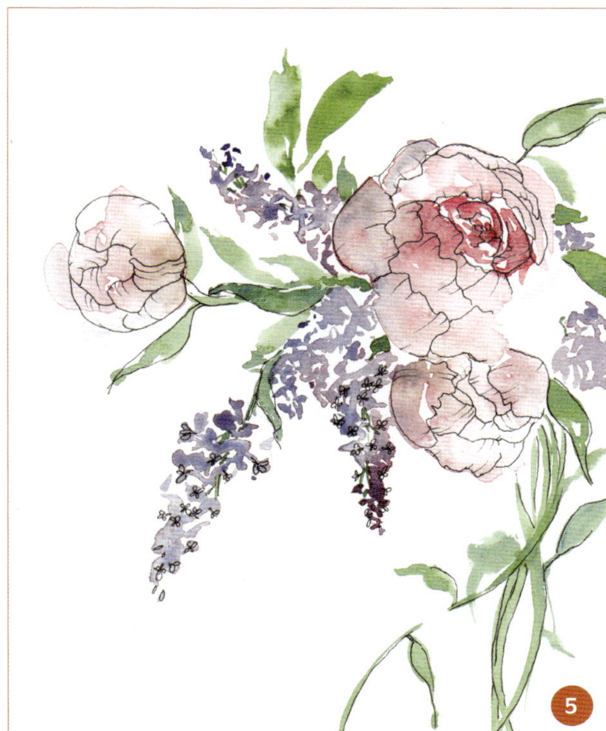

Step 5: When you are happy with your lines, add a few details to the peonies with the 005 fineliner.

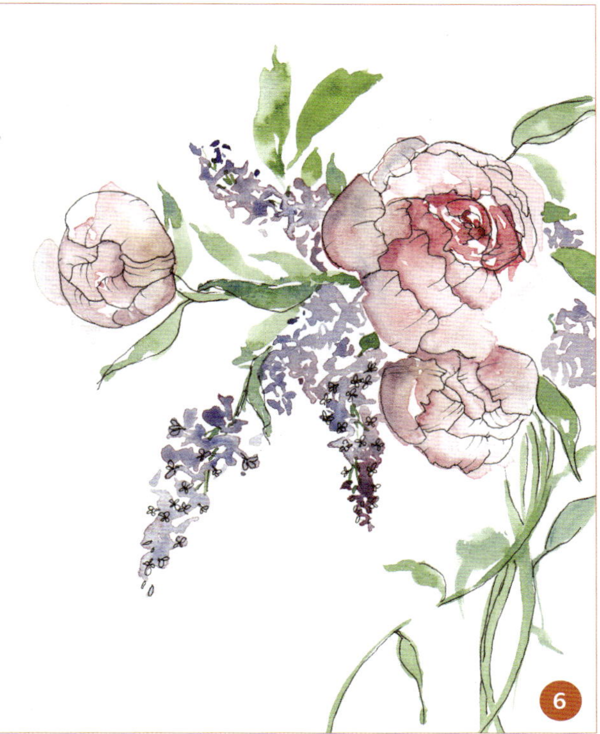

Step 6: And finally, you can add a bit of soft painted shadows between the petals in quinacridone rose to shape them better. See page 25 if you forgot how to do this.

And you are there! You did your yoga and finished a painting of peonies and lilacs. That is so impressive! Congrats!

a field of poppies

When drawing compositions, you don't have to stick to just bouquets and small posies. Flowers can be placed in so many ways, like wreaths, garlands, branches and fields. In this step-by-step guide, I want to show you another way of drawing poppies—and this time, not just a few, but an entire field of them. Because, as you already know, I love poppies.

Materials

Pencil and eraser

Paper: Canson Montval 300gsm (140lb) cold press

Watercolor brush: size 7

Water and cloth

Palette

Fineliners: sizes 005, 01 and 02

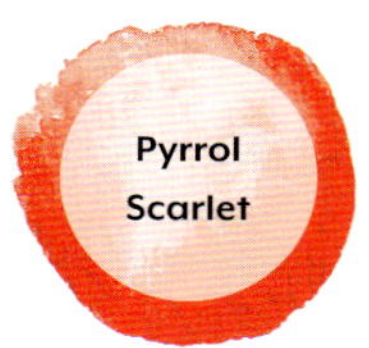

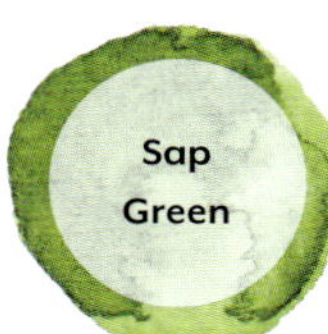

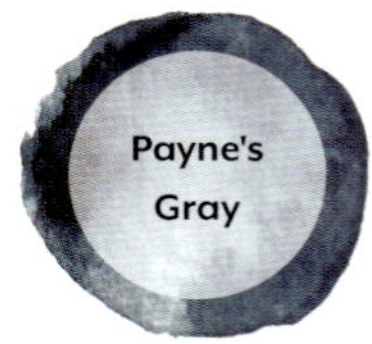

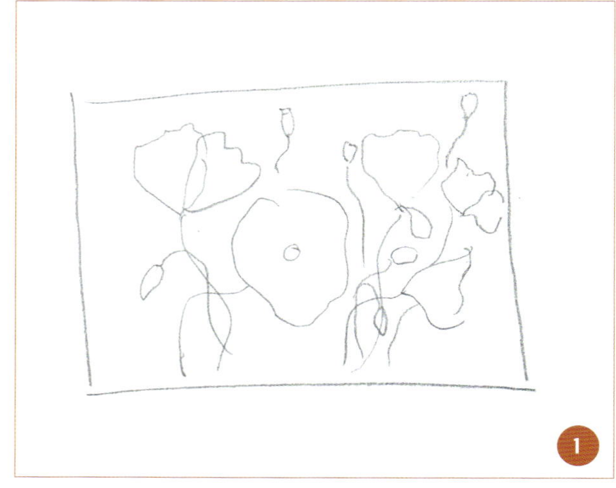

Colors

Step 1: As always, start out by drawing a thumbnail or two. The beauty about the poppies is their dancing stems, so you want to make sure to highlight that by making plenty of room for stems. Also, think about showing the entire flower, from green buds to the seedpods that already lost all their red petals.

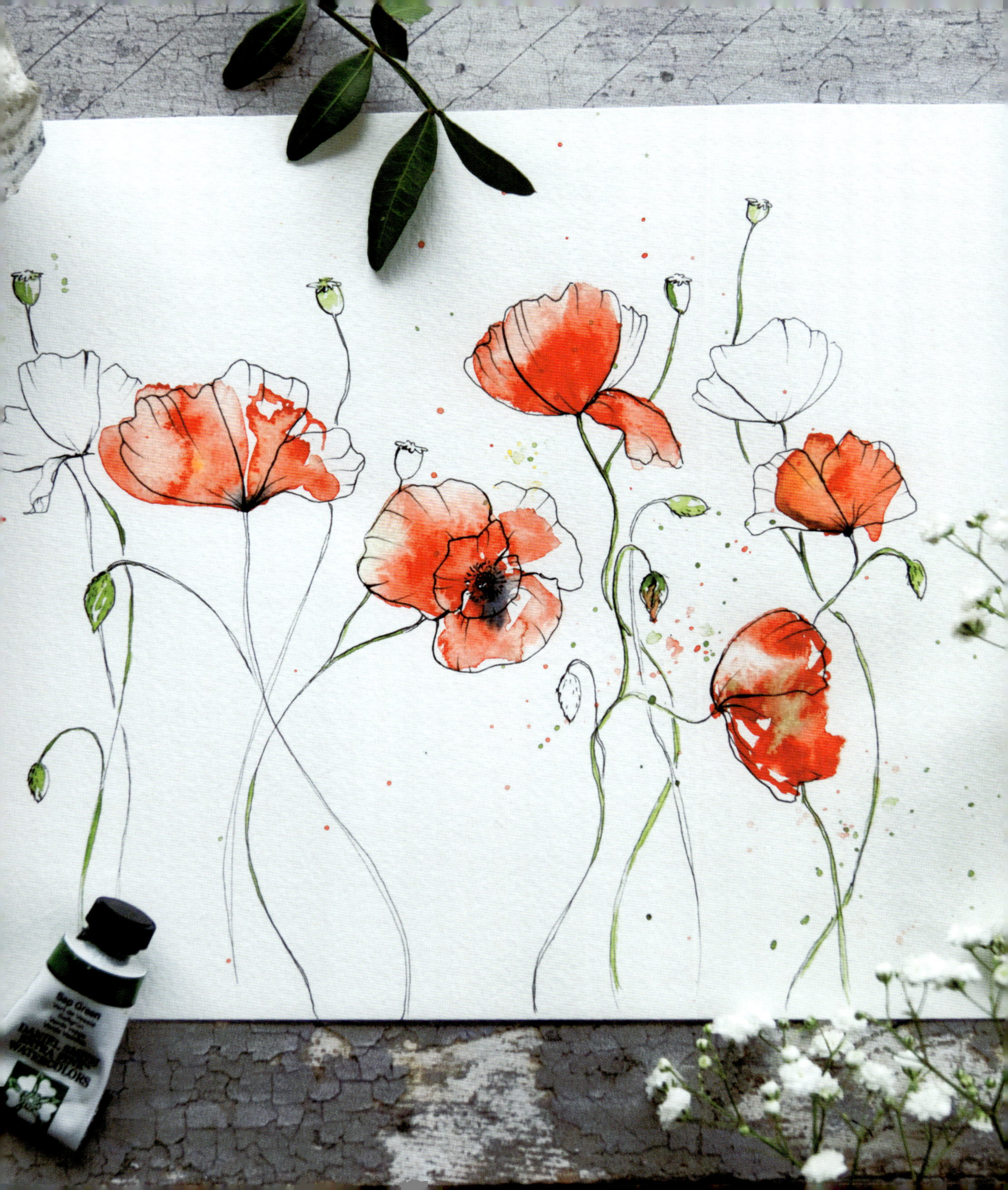

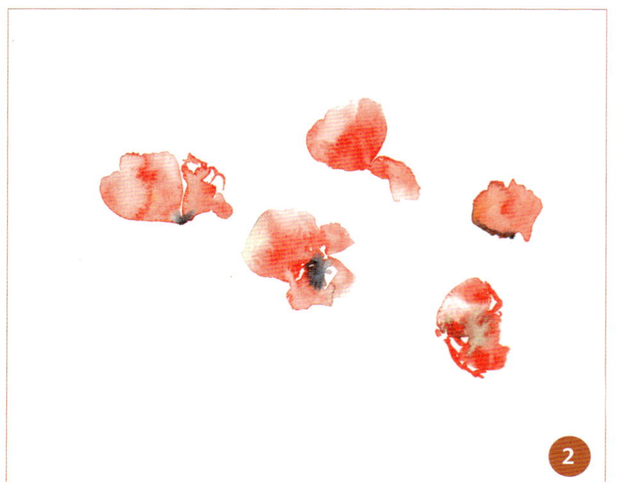

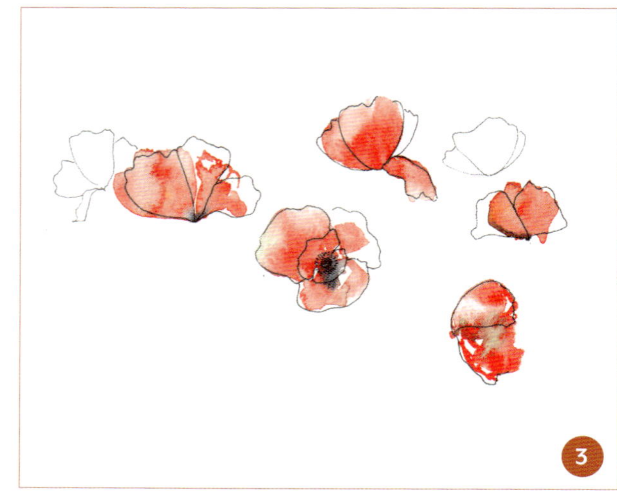

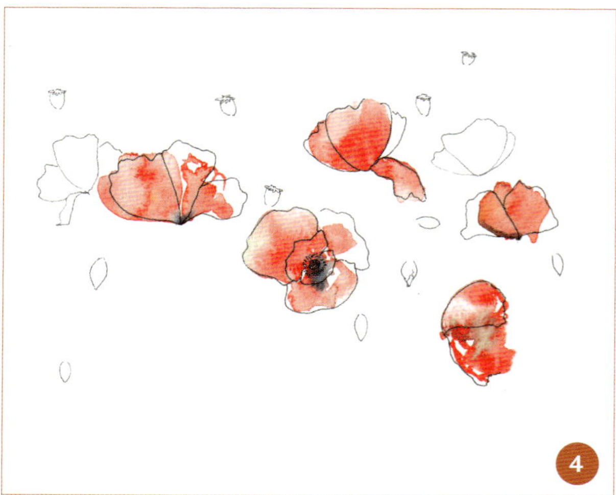

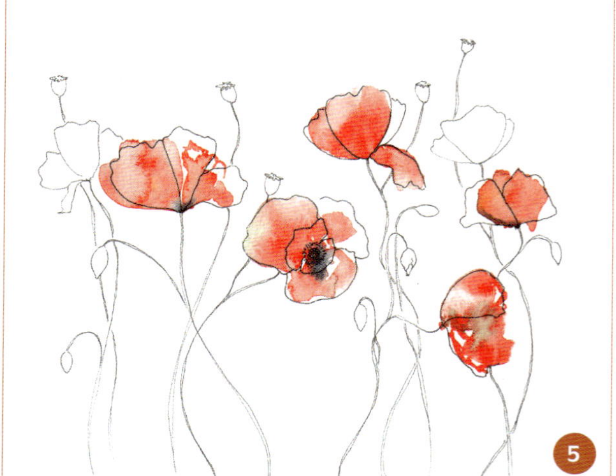

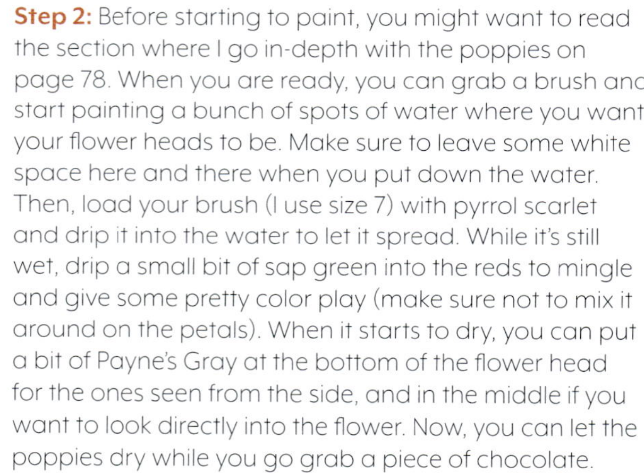

Step 2: Before starting to paint, you might want to read the section where I go in-depth with the poppies on page 78. When you are ready, you can grab a brush and start painting a bunch of spots of water where you want your flower heads to be. Make sure to leave some white space here and there when you put down the water. Then, load your brush (I use size 7) with pyrrol scarlet and drip it into the water to let it spread. While it's still wet, drip a small bit of sap green into the reds to mingle and give some pretty color play (make sure not to mix it around on the petals). When it starts to dry, you can put a bit of Payne's Gray at the bottom of the flower head for the ones seen from the side, and in the middle if you want to look directly into the flower. Now, you can let the poppies dry while you go grab a piece of chocolate.

Step 3: Let's get some shapes in this drawing. Get your 01 fineliner and draw some simple petal shapes. Allow some to follow the paint you already put down, but also draw some flowers with no color at all. Take a look at pictures of poppies to get inspired to draw different shapes.

Step 4: Now it's time to get some buds and wilted seedpods. Draw them in here. The young flower buds mostly hang down from the weight and the seedpods are reaching for the sky.

Step 5: You don't have to put away your fineliner, because now you can draw the dancing stems in. It's okay if you want to draw them first in pencil. Keep the lines flowy, curved and overlapping. Drawing these is

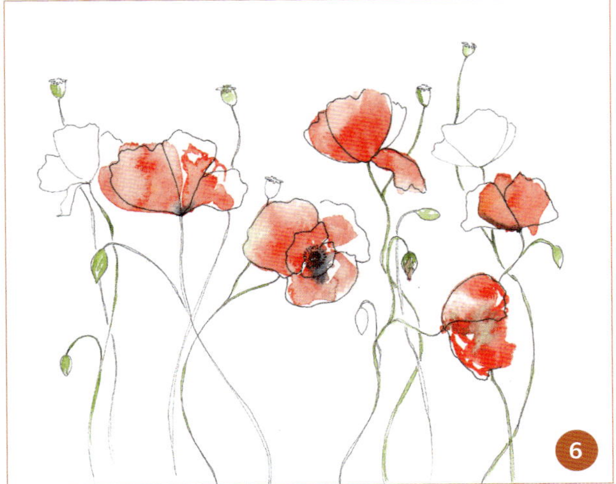

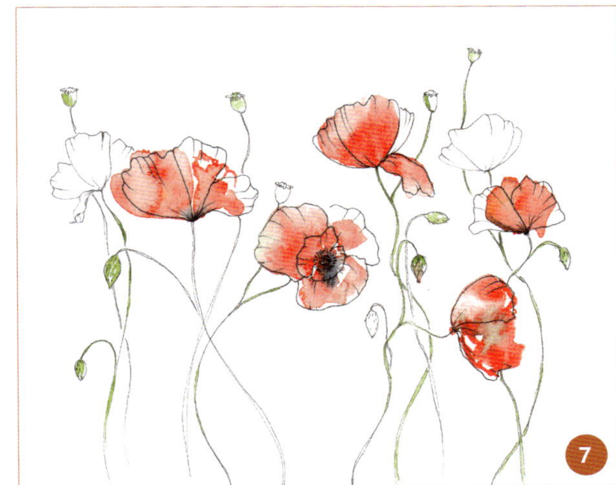

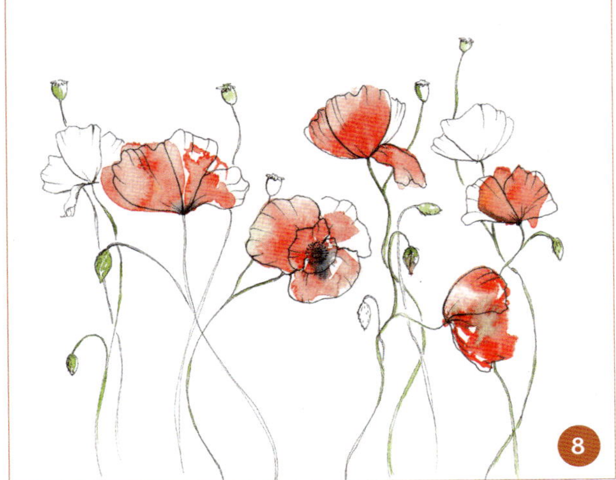

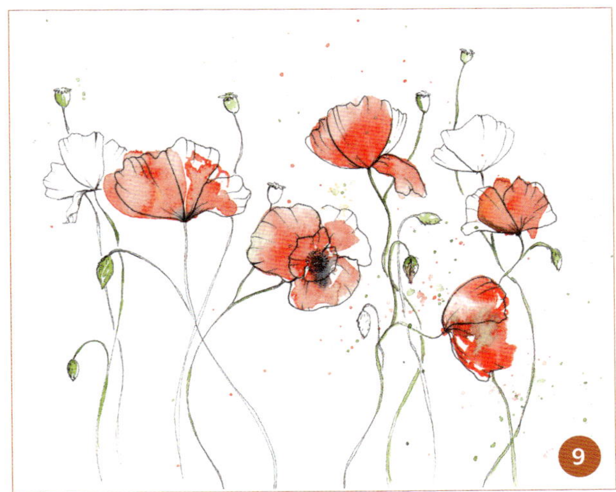

all about confidence. Try to draw them in one quick line instead of slowly working the way from flower to ground.

Step 6: Get your paints back on the table and load your brush with sap green this time. Quickly paint the different green parts while leaving white space. Finally, put a bit of red on the tip of your brush and add some to the bottom of one of the buds. Then, you have a bud that soon will join the floral party.

Step 7: While you wait for the greens to dry, you can put in a few detail lines on the petals with the 005 fineliner.

Step 8: Then, grab your 02 fineliner to strengthen a few of the lines. Here, I mostly drew on the left side and the bottom of the petals to give an impression of the sun shining from the upper right.

Step 9: Finish the drawing off with a great paint splatter in green and red. Fields are filled with pollen, insects and dust, and paint splatters are a super easy way to show that.

You are so great! You just painted an entire field of poppies! That also means that there is only one more tutorial left—it's a good one.

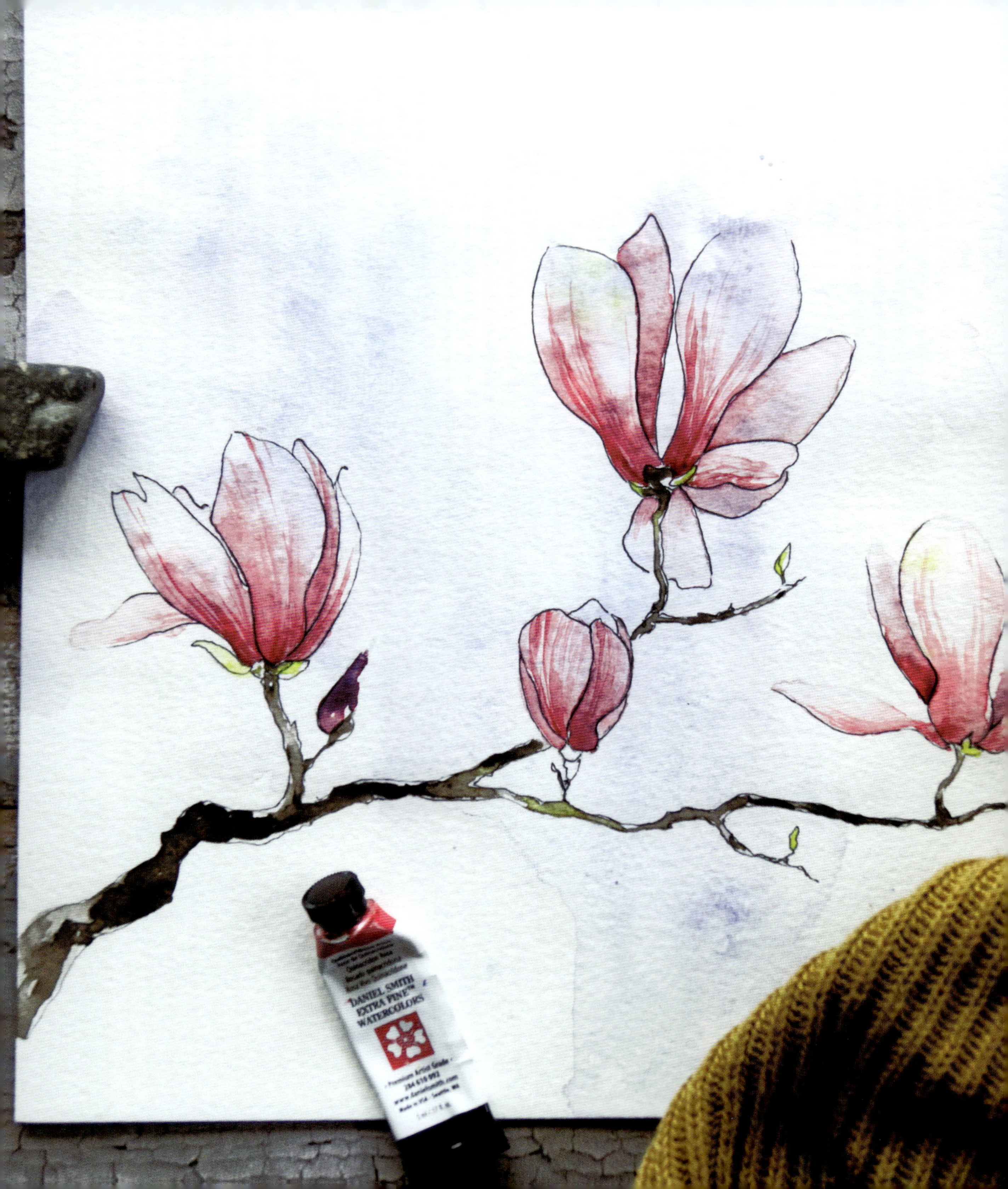
DANIEL SMITH
EXTRA FINE™
WATERCOLORS
Premium Artist Grade

a branch of spring magnolias

I don't know what it is, but there is something so beautiful about elegant blooms on a rough, barky branch. The contrast makes it even better than when the flower is held high on a stem (in my opinion). So, that's why I chose this composition as the final project in the book. Also, I introduce you to a new technique here on these last few pages. I am going to show you how to do a watercolor wash first that actually shines through the flowers to create an overall mood. This technique can be really fun to play with, but also a bit tricky because you risk losing your white space. But we are here to learn and experiment, so let's just jump in.

Materials

Pencil and eraser

Paper: Canson Montval 300gsm (140lb) cold press

Watercolor brushes: sizes 4 and 9

Water and cloth

Palette

Fineliner: size 01

Colors

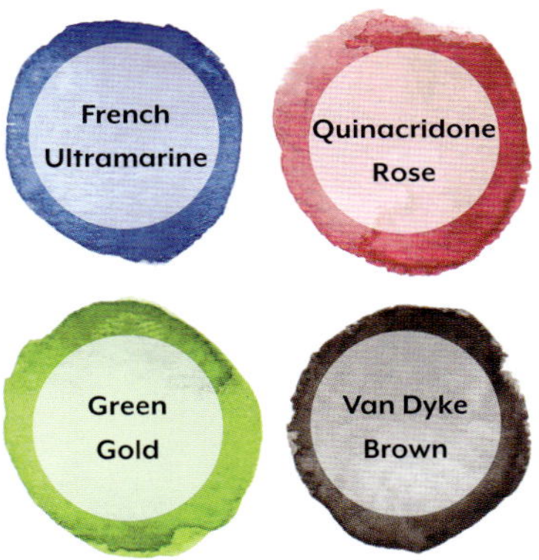

Mixes

The background is an uneven mix of quinacridone rose and French ultramarine. Make sure to mix a lot so you have enough for the entire background.

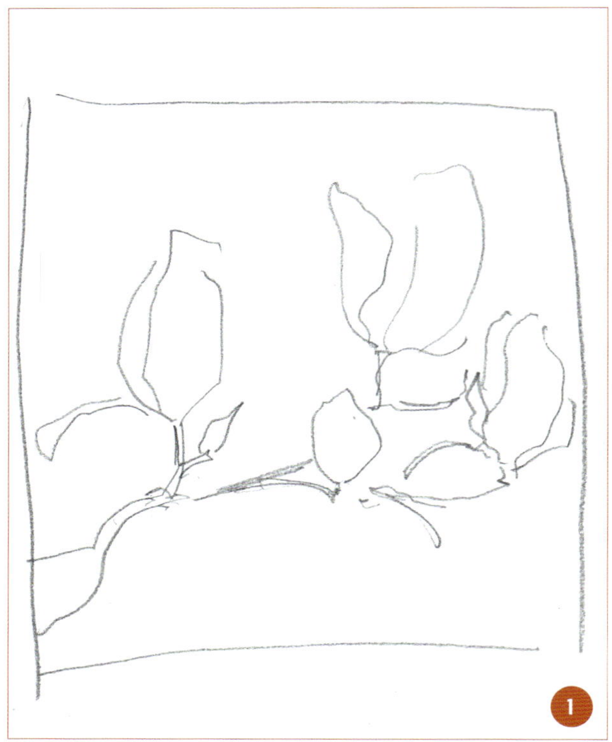

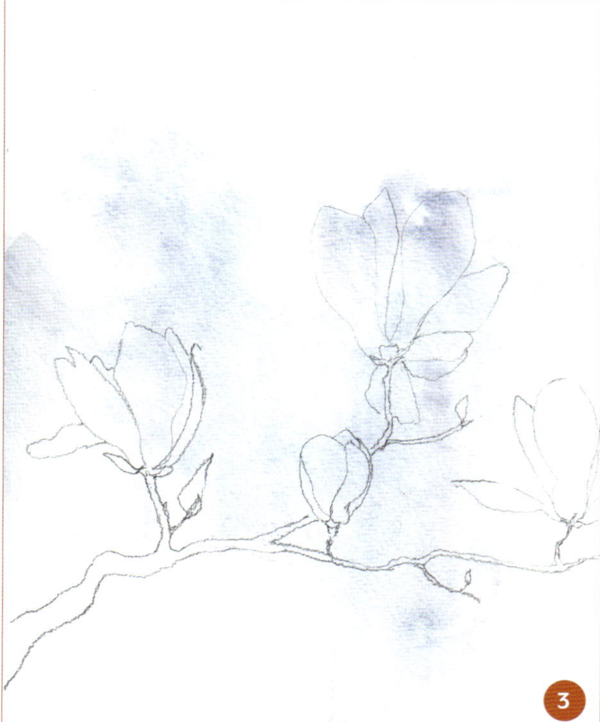

Step 1: When you draw your thumbnails, think about the number of blooms (uneven is always good) and think about adding a bud or two. Also consider where you want your branch to run. Before doing our sketch on paper, we are going to do a background. For more on the magnolia's shape, see page 61.

Step 2: Wet a good amount of your paper with clean water. With your size 9 brush, drip in the mix of French ultramarine and quinacridone rose you prepared. In some areas, it will be bluer and some will be more rose, and that is perfect. I tilted my paper to let it run a little while drying, but you can also just place it flat on the table. It will take a good amount of time to dry, so maybe leave it for now and come back tomorrow.

Step 3: It's finally dry! Now, you can start sketching with your pencil. As you can see, I chose to draw three big blooms that all look different from each other, as well as two smaller buds. If you are in doubt about drawing a magnolia, think of it almost like a tulip—tall petals hugging each other. The only difference is that the magnolia is a bit narrower at the bottom and the petals often turn in different directions. Attach them to the branch with a small twig and add some small leaves below the flowers.

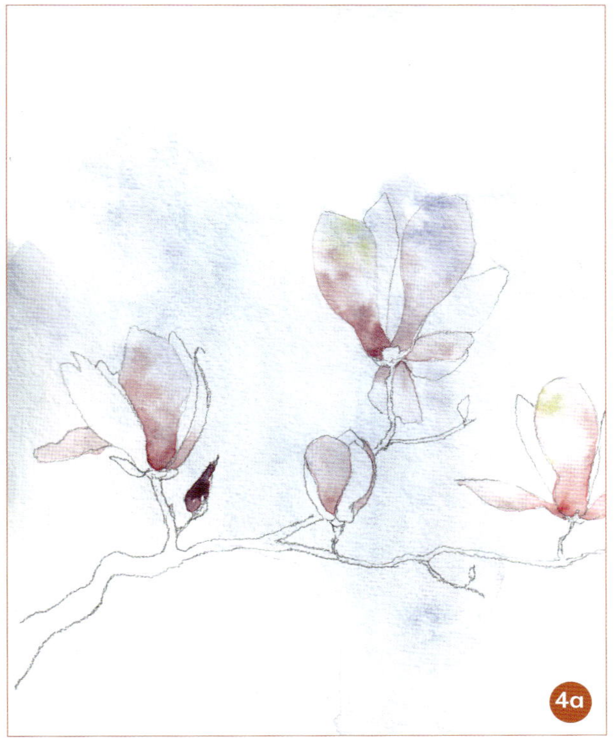

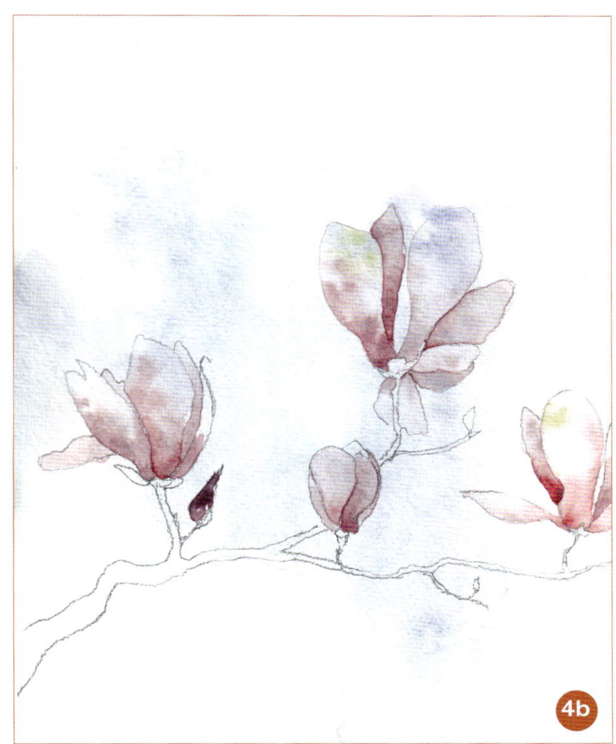

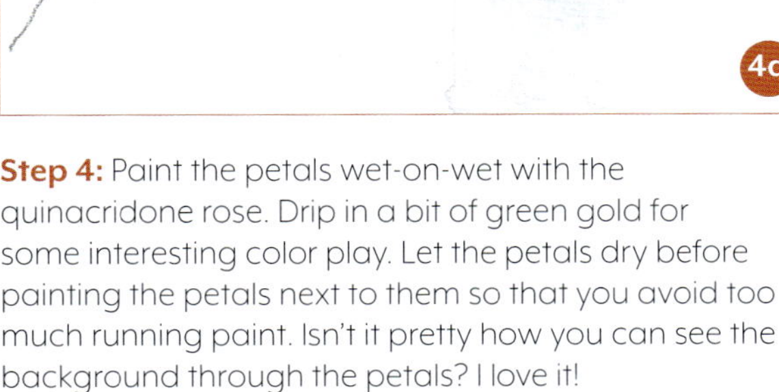

Step 4: Paint the petals wet-on-wet with the quinacridone rose. Drip in a bit of green gold for some interesting color play. Let the petals dry before painting the petals next to them so that you avoid too much running paint. Isn't it pretty how you can see the background through the petals? I love it!

Step 5: While the petals dry, you can get out your 01 fineliner. Draw the outlines following the pencil lines. Notice that I didn't outline all the way to the top on some of the petals. That's because it makes them blend a bit with the background, which is magical. You can now get your eraser and remove the pencil lines. You might not be able to remove all of them because you painted over them. Think of them as part of the charm. But if you don't like that, just outline before painting and you are all good.

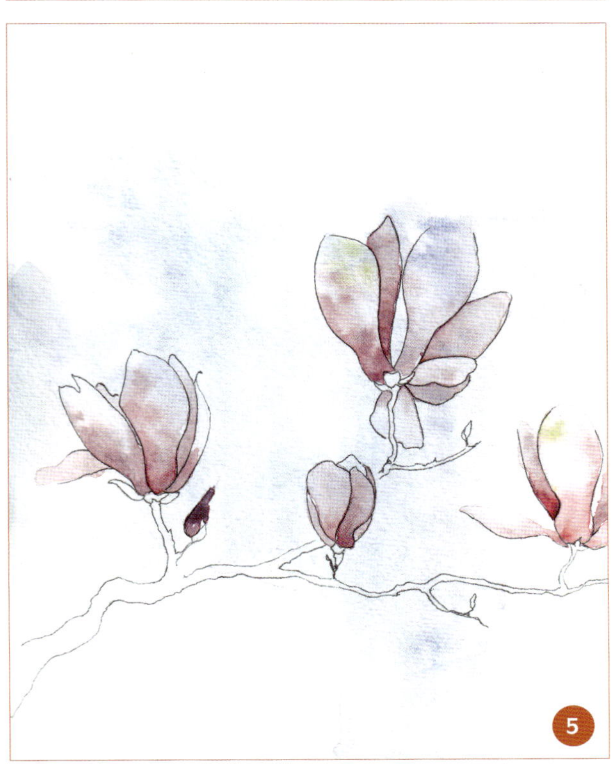

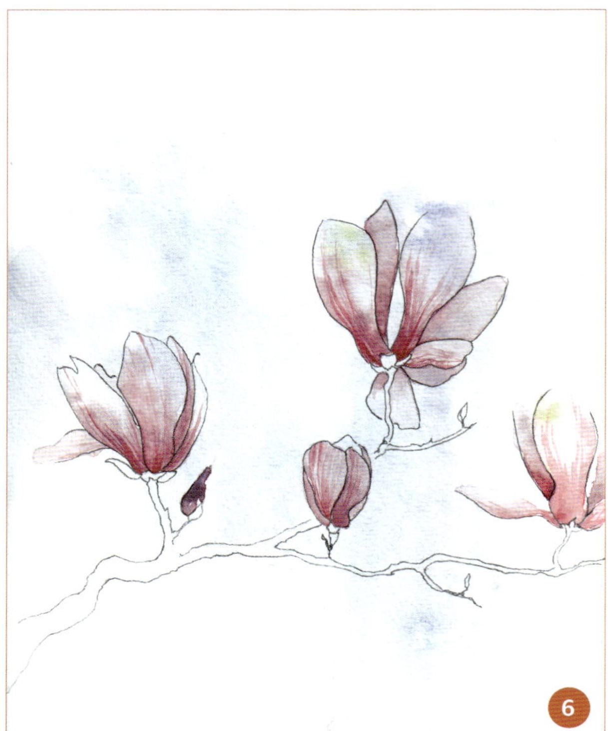

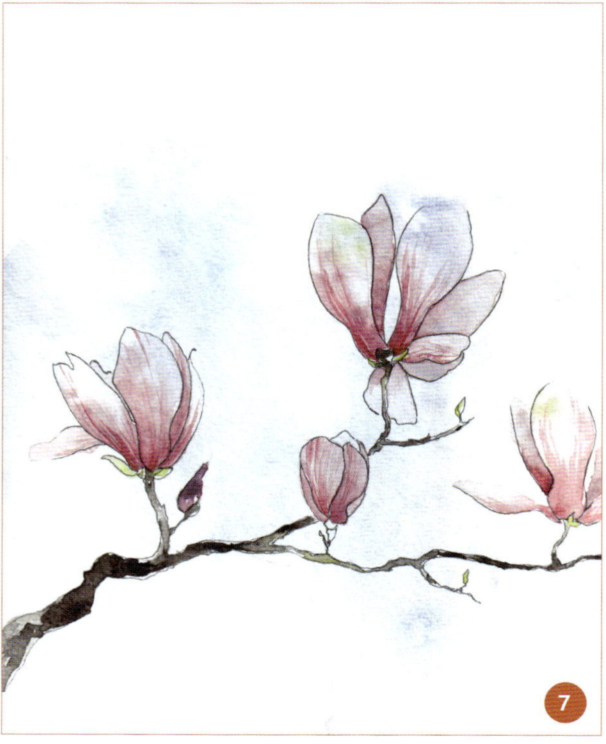

Step 6: Load your size 4 brush with a pretty thick quinacridone rose. Now, with the tip, paint the beautiful stripes on the magnolia petals. Let the lines follow the shape of the petals and, if you are in doubt about the technique, you can always go back to page 64 to see how we did it there. If the lines get a tad too heavy, just soften them with a damp brush.

Step 7: We are already at the final step—can you believe it? First, load your brush with some green gold and paint the small green leaves wet-on-dry. Then, dip your brush in the Van Dyke brown and roughly paint in the stem. Make sure to leave white space to give it texture. While it's still wet, drip in a thicker load of Van Dyke brown in places and also a bit of the green—and that is actually it!

While you wait for it to dry, I want to say a big old congratulations: you painted the final project in the book, and I am so happy for you! Please treat yourself by putting them all next to each other and sharing them with everybody you know. This is so impressive. More importantly, look at how you've grown and maybe also notice if there are some projects you want to redo.

part IV: where to go from here

Hopefully by now, you are super excited about drawing and painting flowers in watercolor and ink. Maybe you are even feeling a few things, like pride in what you created or inspired to try new techniques, and maybe you even find it easier to sit down and focus in your creative space for a while—because creating art regularly will do just that. There are many ways to continue your education and here are a few suggestions:

YouTube: There are a ton of free tutorials from a lot of teachers out there, myself included. This is a great next step if you want to take this style even further.

Online Courses: Many watercolor teachers offer online courses. They are usually a lot more in-depth than the YouTube tutorials and often, you even get feedback from the teacher.

Local Workshops: If you are lucky, there will be teachers in your area. They might not teach this very niche topic, but perhaps they teach watercolor, drawing or something else that can expand your creativity.

These are all great steps. But there is another way to go if you are feeling courageous. Just take your sketchbook and take a look at page 106 about finding inspiration. Pick one and go out and start sketching on your own. This is the best way to learn.

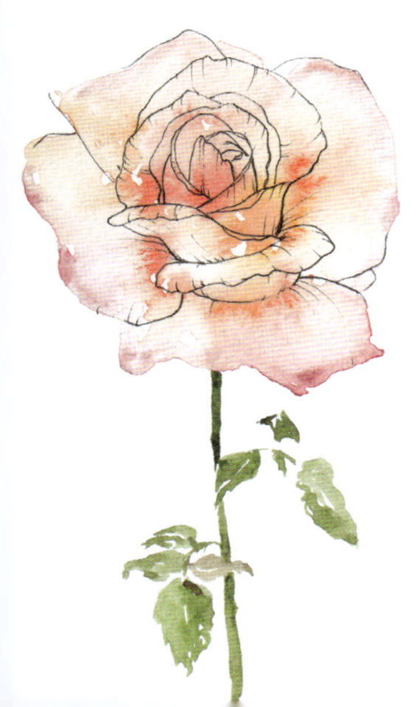

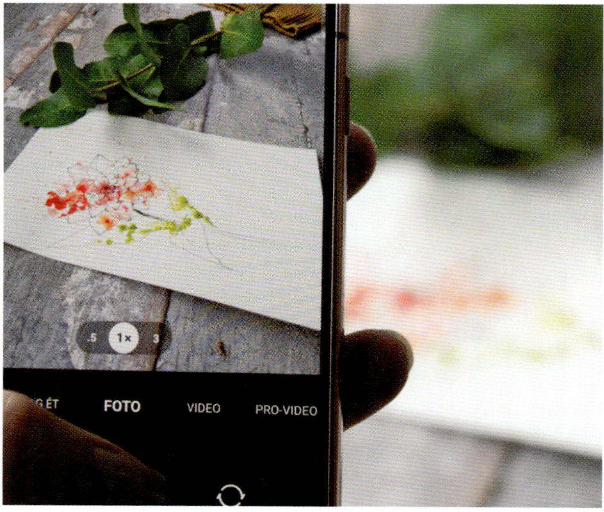

share your work

Sharing your work can seem super scary and you might not want to in the beginning. But I have to tell you that sharing is the best thing that could ever have happened to my own work. Early on, I shared my drawings on Facebook groups dedicated to watercolor and ink and on Instagram. And I've got to tell you, the support and community on social media actually helped me turn watercolor into a lifestyle instead of just a temporary fling.

Find Fellow Artists

Just painting watercolors at home at the kitchen table can get a little lonely. Maybe you are lucky to have your kids next to you painting, or maybe even friends that you can share the experience with. But most people do it just for themselves. This might be perfect for you, but if you want to join a community, it's totally possible. I recommend starting on Instagram, which is, after all, about aesthetics. Make a quick search on hashtags like #lineandwash, #watercolorandink and #lineandwashflowers and, if you want to continue the list, take a look at which hashtags everybody else is using. Start using the hashtags, following inspiring accounts and start commenting. Soon you might even make lasting friendships there.

A lot of artists create monthly challenges with prompts every day to follow. You can search for #drawingchallenge, #watercolorchallenge or something similar to find them. It's super fun to see what everybody creates and it's the fast lane to creating connections on the platform.

Only See Yourself in the Mirror

Before diving all-in on social media, you have to know about a very common trap. When joining a place with so many artists, it can seem overwhelming as a beginner. You can even feel defeated or not good enough. I know this is so much easier said than done, but please try not to compare yourself to them. It's all about practice and everybody is on different creative journeys. That's why the very most important thing to remember is that you have no idea how long they've been there. For all we know, they could have been painting for their entire life. If you really have to compare yourself with anything, then compare yourself to you. See the first thing you posted and the tenth post. Then, you will see how far you moved already just by practicing.

make art a habit

If you are feeling the energy boost creating gives you, this might be the perfect time to make a new habit. You don't have to wait for new year resolutions to do something good for yourself.

Creating art on a regular basis will give you a lot of the same benefits as meditation: inner peace, increased focus and a deeper sense of YOU. As a bonus, it also gives you beautiful art to hang on your walls or give as super thoughtful gifts. I tell you, it's the best feeling to receive a gift list for Christmas from your sister and to have her list art from you at the top! It's so cool and the biggest compliment.

To get all these perks, all you need to do is set up a regular practice. I know this sounds boring, but it's actually just to frame your painting process so it's easier for you to sit down when you have time.

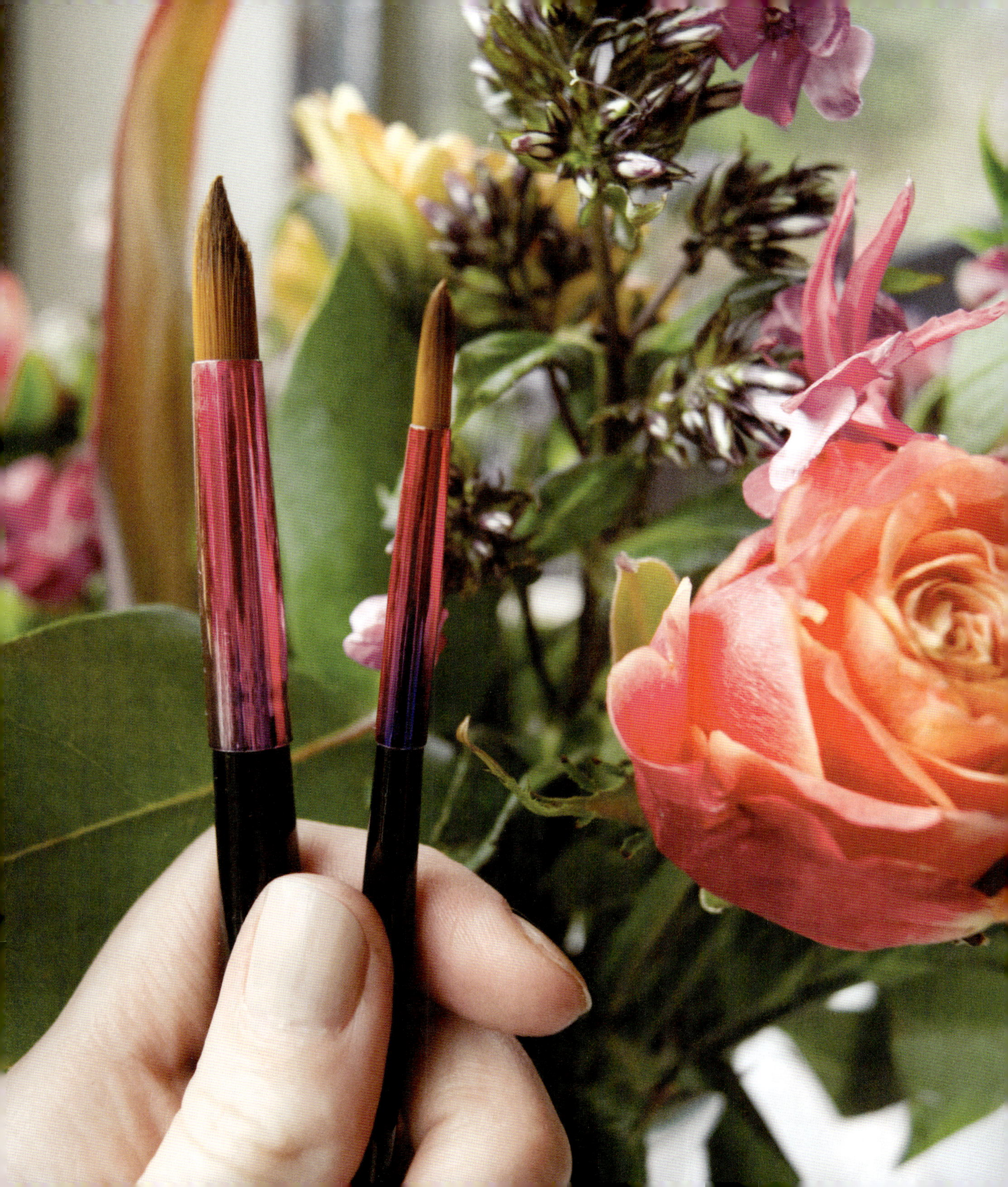

here are five tips for facilitating your art habit

1. Put all the supplies you will need in a box. This will make it super easy to get it all out when the kids are finally playing.
2. Put that box in a place where you can see it most of the time. This will make it present to you so that you don't forget when scrolling Facebook seems like the best idea.
3. Take a look at what you do on a daily basis. Where can you find fifteen minutes? Is it cutting down on Netflix? Scrolling social media? Or maybe just getting up fifteen minutes earlier in the morning?
4. Make sure to find a reference before sitting down. You can choose a plant in your house, keep a folder of references on your computer or take and store photos on your phone. Just make sure it's ready to sketch when you sit down.
5. Don't be hard on yourself. We are all humans and have busy lives. So don't beat yourself up if you miss a day. Five days a week is so much better than none, and by the way so are four, three and two days. When you miss a day, just make sure to evaluate the circumstances. Is it because it's not easy enough? Do you need to make more time? Or do you need a new subject to paint to get your creative juices flowing?

here are three tips for finding inspiration

So, you were able to finally sit down with twenty minutes to yourself, only to spend them scrolling Instagram because you don't know how or what to paint.

There is a ton of inspiration out there and here, I list three ways to find a nice thing for you to sketch:

1. Get out into the garden, sit down with your sketchbook and actually sketch from life. To me, this is the most fulfilling for several reasons. You can sketch the plant from all the angles you like while feeling the wind and hearing the birds' chirps. What's not to like?

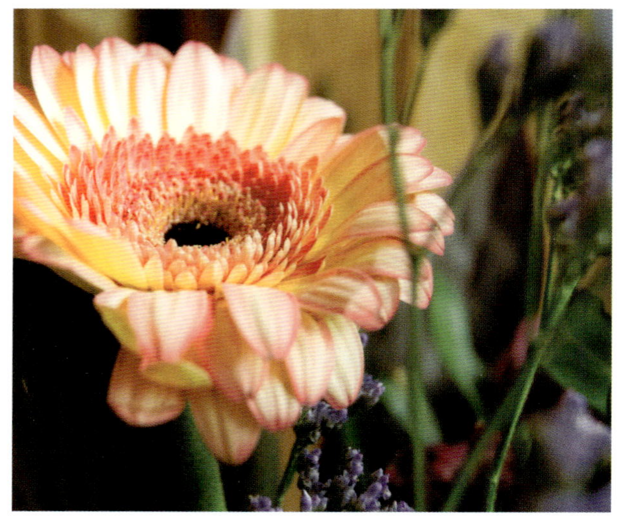

2. Get out your camera or phone and snap some pretty pictures when you are in your own or a public garden, the forest, the jungle, the moon—wherever you see something pretty you want to paint.
3. Paint from a stock photo. There are a lot of free photos you can interpret online. Just make sure that it's actually okay to use the photo and check for a commercial right as well. You might end up loving your sketch so much that you want to sell it, and then it would be a shame if it were illegal, right?

don't be a copycat

It's perfectly okay (and normal!) to be inspired by other artists. Inspiration is great, but copying is not cool—at all. Therefore, find inspiration in other people's techniques, subjects and colors, but take that inspiration and make it your own. Find references that speak to you, observe colors and shapes and go from there instead of blindly copying.

That being said, of course you can follow tutorials painting what the teacher does. Just make sure to not sell it off as your own. After all, the creative idea happened in another artist's brain.

acknowledgments

As you know by now, flowers are used to say something important. And I think there is something really important left to say, and that is a great big thank-you, because this book would not have happened if it was just me drawing on the couch.

First, I want to send a chrysanthemum to my sweet and supportive editor, Aïcha, for trusting me all the way through this project. And alongside her is the incredible team at Page Street. They all deserve a big, lush bouquet of bright blooms for their great work—I couldn't have done it without you.

Then, I want to send happy daisies to my sweet kids who always encourage me to get more flowers when we are in the supermarket, even if it means they have to sit and hold so many that they almost disappear in the trolley. I want to send a hydrangea to my parents for making my childhood home filled with flowers and beauty, and if you want a small fun fact here, the rose I used in the step-by-step tutorial on page 86 is actually directly from their garden.

I also want to send a big bunch of lilacs to all my incredible followers and students around the globe. You get lilacs because they inspire you to let your inner child go, be carefree and experiment—just like I hope you will do after reading this book.

And finally, a real red rose for my loving and supportive husband, who always stands by me when I come up with new, crazy ideas (and believe me, that is true love because there are a LOT of them).

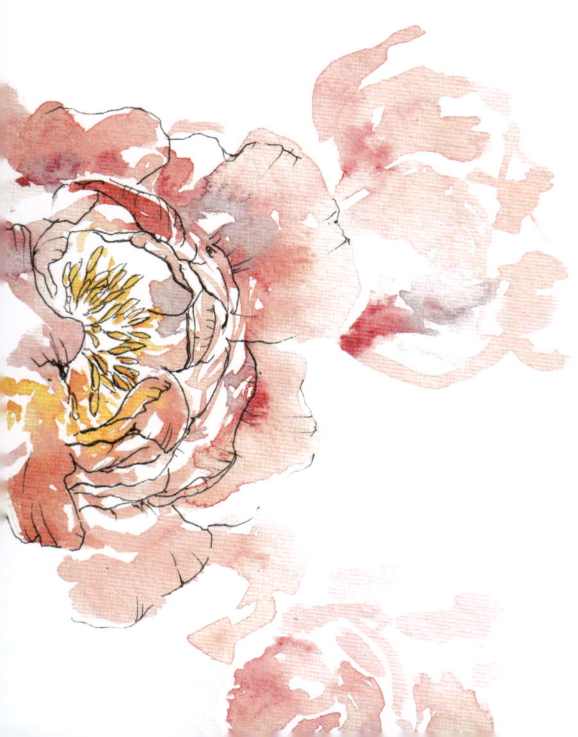

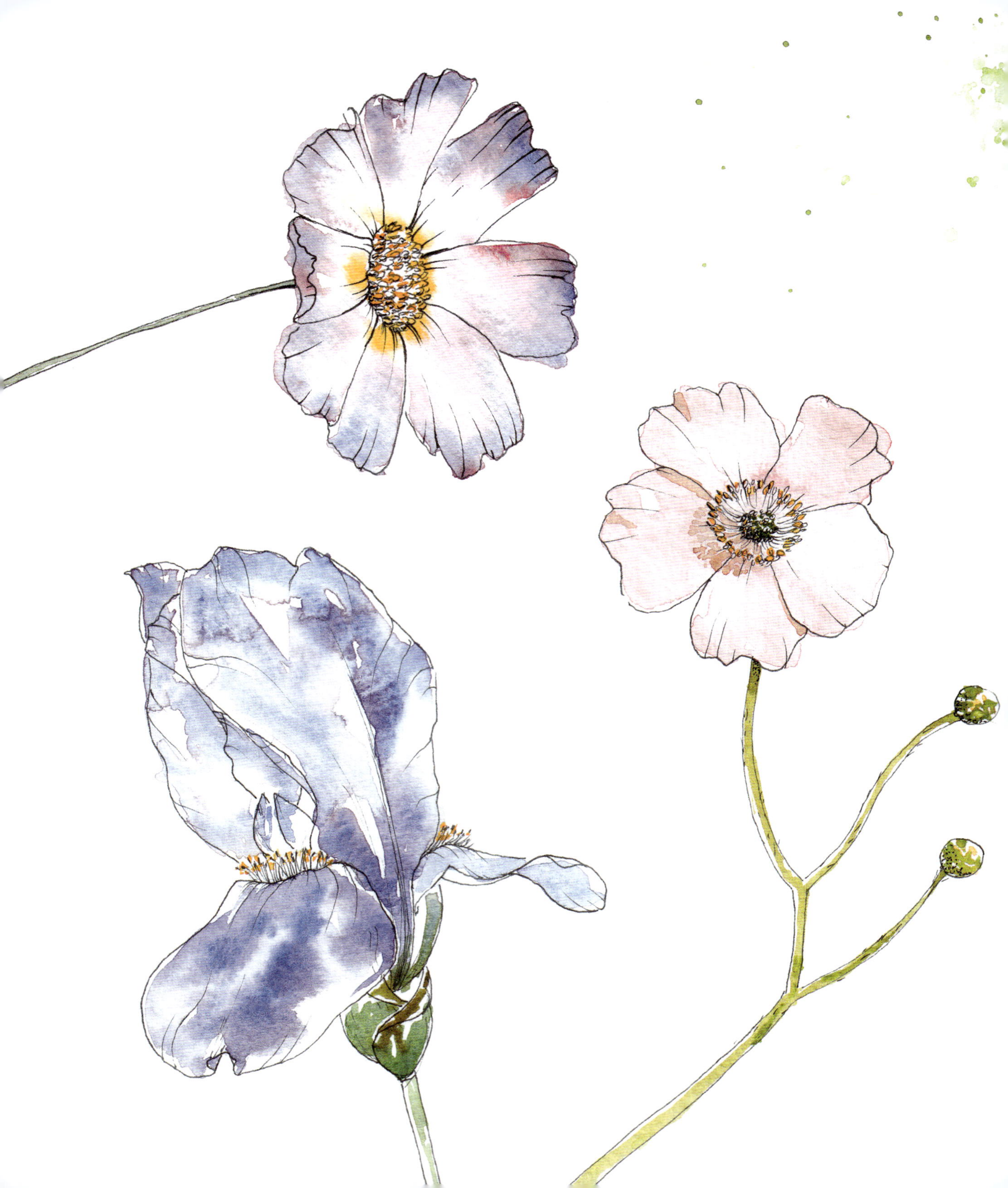

meet camilla

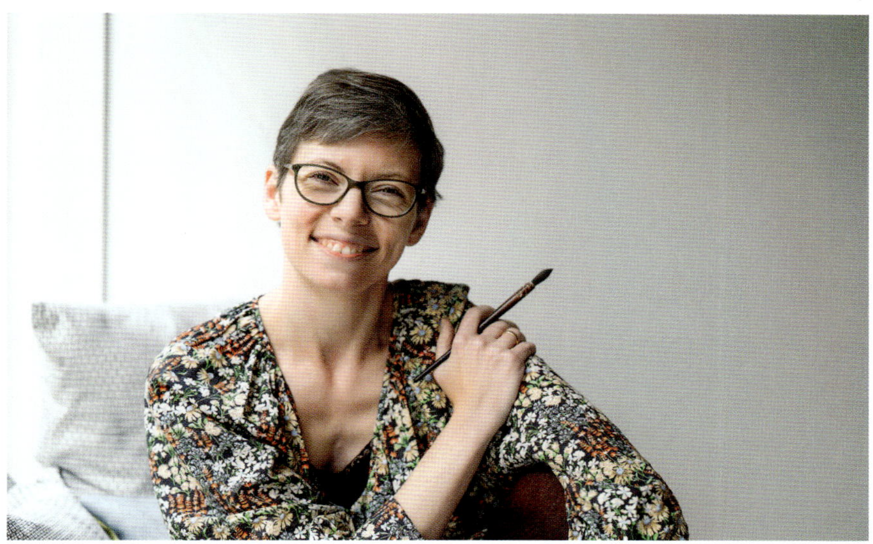

Camilla is the artist juggling brushes and fineliners in this book. She lives in Denmark out in the country surrounded by nature, flowers and with an occasional cow in the backyard. She shares her life with her husband, two chubby cats, three chicks and two sweet, little troublemakers. And in spite of always having toys to pick up or clothes to wash, she almost always finds twenty minutes a day for sketching. After all, who needs clean clothes when you can draw a pretty flower? She has been teaching watercolor to thousands of students all over the globe, and she hangs out on Instagram as @camilla_damsbo_art. You can check out her courses and read even more on her website, www.camilladamsboart.com.

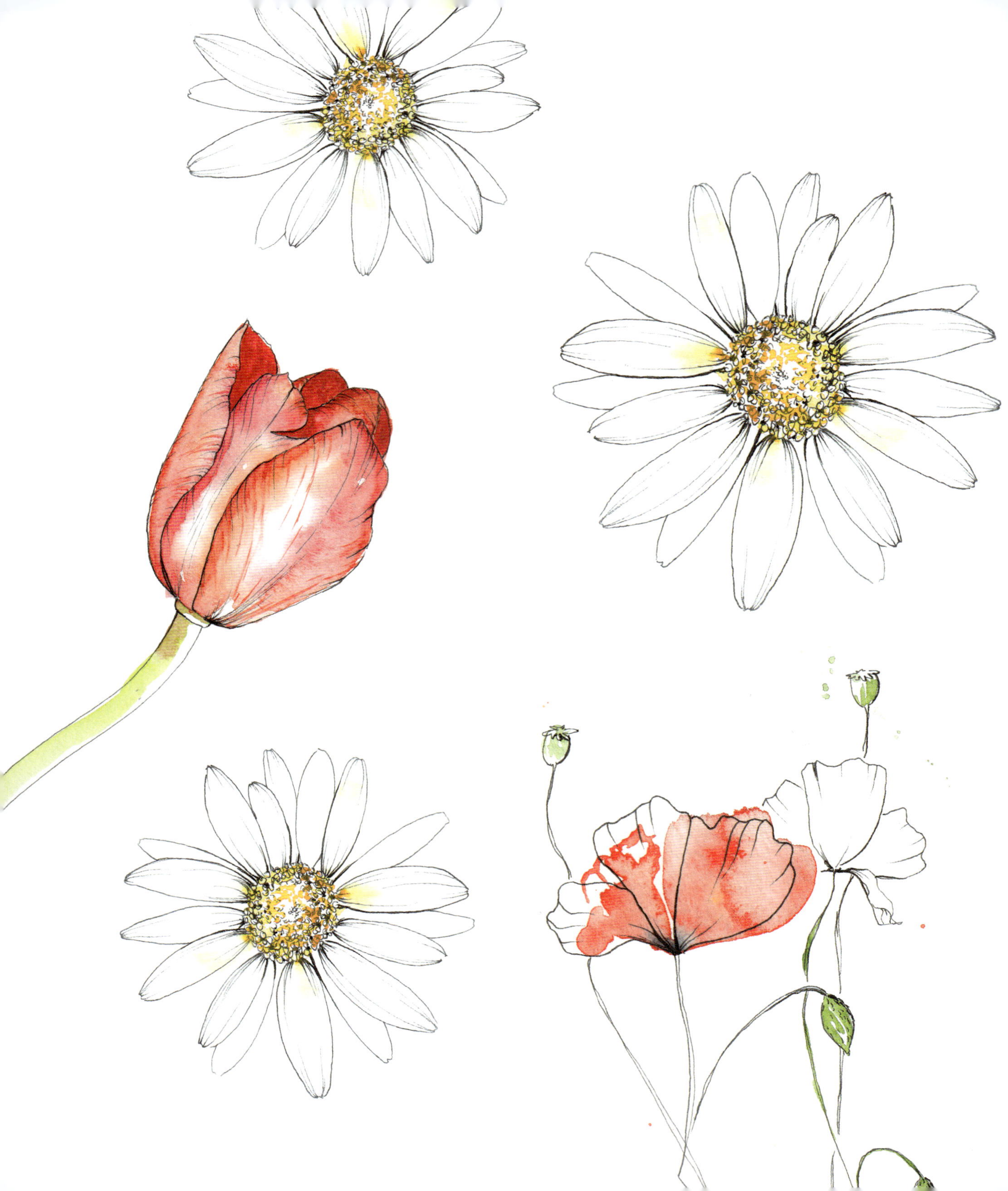

index

A

additional resources, 133

anemone, 55–60

art, as habit, 134–36

B

bouquet of peonies and lilacs, 119–23

branch of spring magnolias, 129–32

brushes, 12

C

colors

- alternative, 13
- choosing, 15–16
- mixing, 15–16

comparison, 134

compositions, 105–32

- bouquet of peonies and lilacs, 119–23
- branch of spring magnolias, 129–32
- dancing bouquet of cosmos and daisies, 114–18
- experimenting and honing personal style, 106
- field of poppies, 124–27
- flower placement, 106
- red and white tulips in a glass vase, 109–13

copying, 136

cosmo, 45–48, 114–18

D

dahlia, 75–77

daisy, 29–31, 114–18

dancing bouquet of cosmos and daisies, 114–18

drybrushing, 21

E

eraser, 14

experimenting, 106

F

fellow artists, finding, 134

field of poppies, 124–27

fineliners, 12, 16, 17, 19

flowers, sketching, 22–25

foreshortening, 23

fundamentals, 11–25

basic inking techniques, 18–19

basic watercolor techniques, 20–22

choosing colors, 15–16

planning for success, 16–17

sketching flowers, 22–25

supplies, 11–25

G

gerbera, 40–43

H

habit, art as, 134–36

hibiscus, 99–103

hydrangea, 91–94

I

inking techniques, basic, 18–19

iris, 37–39

L

layering, 21

leaves, sketching, 24

light and shadow, sketching, 25

lilac, 83–85, 119–23

line variation, 19

M

magnolia, 61–64, 129–32

P

paint, 13

alternative colors, 13

choosing colors, 15–16

mixing, 22

paper, 14

pencil and eraser, 14

peony, 95–98, 119–23

perfectionism, 18

personal style, 106

plumeria, 33–35

poppy, 78–81, 124–27

R

red and white tulips in a glass vase, 109–13

resources, additional, 133

rose, 86–90

S

shading, 19

shadow, sketching, 25

sharing your work, 134

single flowers, 27–103

- anemone, 55–60
- cosmo, 45–48
- dahlia, 75–77
- daisy, 29–31
- gerbera, 40–43
- hibiscus, 99–103
- hydrangea, 91–94
- iris, 37–39
- lilac, 83–85
- magnolia, 61–64
- peony, 95–98
- plumeria, 33–35
- poppy, 78–81
- rose, 86–90
- snowdrop, 70–73
- sunflower, 65–69
- tulip, 49–54

sketching flowers, 22–25

snowdrop, 70–73

stems, sketching, 24

style, honing personal, 106

success, planning for, 16–17

sunflower, 65–69

supplies, 12–14

- brushes, 12
- fineliners, 12
- paint, 13
- paper, 14
- pencil and eraser, 14

T

tracing board, 17

tulip, 49–54, 109–13

W

watercolor techniques, basic, 20–22

wet-on-dry, 20–21

wet-on-wet, 21

white space, 22